BEST MEN
OF THE
BAR

BEST MEN • OF THE • BAR

THE EARLY YEARS OF THE
AMERICAN BAR ASSOCIATION
1878–1928

JOHN AUSTIN MATZKO

INTRODUCTION BY KELLEN R. FUNK

TALBOT
PUBLISHING
Clark, New Jersey

ISBN 978-1-61619-587-8

TALBOT PUBLISHING

AN IMPRINT OF

THE LAWBOOK EXCHANGE, LTD.

33 Terminal Avenue
Clark, New Jersey 07066-1321

Please see our website for a selection of our other publications and fine facsimile reprints of classic works of legal history:
www.lawbookexchange.com

Library of Congress Cataloging-in-Publication Data

Names: Matzko, John Austin, author.
Title: Best men of the bar : the early years of the American Bar Association, 1878-1928 / by John Austin Matzko.
Description: Clark, NJ : Talbot Publishing An Imprint of The Lawbook Exchange, 2019. | Includes bibliographical references and index.
Identifiers: LCCN 2019020018| ISBN 9781616195878 (hardcover : alk. paper) | ISBN 1616195878 (hardcover : alk. paper)
Subjects: LCSH: American Bar Association--History.
Classification: LCC KF326 .M38 2019 | DDC 340.06/073--dc23
LC record available at https://lccn.loc.gov/2019020018

Printed in the United States of America on acid-free paper

To the memory of
Rachel Grace Smith Matzko
(1943 – 2009)

Table of Contents

Preface

During the late twentieth century, historians and sociologists proposed that American professionalism had arisen from the greed and xenophobia of elites whose monopolistic impulses spurred them to exclude outsiders from their chosen domains. It was a hypothesis that developed, in part, as a reaction to an earlier, and by then unfashionable, theory that the rise of professions in turn-of-the-century America had facilitated the ascent of able and morally worthy women, immigrants, and other marginalized Americans from the economic and social periphery to the center of national life.[1]

An old joke has it that a certain child psychologist began his career with three theories and no children and ended with three children and no theories. In this book, my burden has not been to theorize about professionalism but to examine one of the "children," the "best men of the bar" who created and sustained the early American Bar Association. Comparatively few bar association histories have been written, and most of these are anecdotal pieces commissioned for anniversaries.

Though I am an academic, I have a healthy skepticism about the sorts of stories academics like to tell. In his fine retrospective sociology, *American Lawyers,* Richard Abel

---

1. Rebeca Roiphe, "A History of Professionalism: Julius Henry Cohen and the Professions as a Route to Citizenship," 40 *Fordham Urban Law Journal* 33-36 (2012).

declares his preference for "quantitative data over qualitative accounts," data that can transmute "complex reality to something that can be counted."[2] In this book I have rather aimed in the opposite direction, intending to write a narrative history of the early years of the American Bar Association, using as my literary model George Martin's graceful *Causes and Conflicts: The Centennial History of the Association of the Bar of the City of New York, 1870-1970.*[3] Narrative history has its own weaknesses, but at least the final product is arguably more nuanced and almost always more fun to read.

Anyone familiar with Peter Novick's *That Noble Dream* will appreciate the difficulty of claiming objectivity for one's scholarly work, but at least I can say that I researched this book with few preconceptions and discarded along the way some of those I started with.[4] I am not a lawyer, and I have no connection with the American Bar Association. (My middle name is a tribute to my only non-immigrant grandparent, not to the legal positivist.) In part, I concluded this study in 1928 because the American Bar Association holds almost none of its records before that date, and I was able to write authoritatively without having to ask the ABA for permission to look at anything.

Though I advance no grand theory about professionalism, this book does have a thesis: that the early American Bar

---

2. Richard L. Abel, *American Lawyers* (New York: Oxford University Press, 1989), 13.

3. George Martin, *Causes and Conflicts: The Centennial History of the Association of the Bar of the City of New York, 1870-1970* (Boston: Houghton Mifflin, 1970).

4. Peter Novick, *That Noble Dream: The 'Objectivity Question' and the American Historical Profession* (Cambridge: Cambridge University Press, 1988).

Association developed within the reform tradition of the late nineteenth century rather than as a reaction to that tradition; that though a chief goal of the Association was to emulate the success of organized medicine in professional gatekeeping, the ABA did not oppose political or social change so long as that change could plausibly be overseen by the judiciary; and that only during the second decade of the twentieth century, when it became clear that the legal profession was incapable of guiding contemporary trends, did the Association begin to develop into a conservative pressure group.

This book was first a 1984 dissertation, "The Early Years of the American Bar Association, 1878-1928," (https://doi.org/10.18130/V3G914) written at the University of Virginia under the direction of William Henry Harbaugh (1920-2005). He and my second reader, Charles W. McCurdy were generous in their encouragement. My late wife, Rachel Smith Matzko (1943-2009) proofread all the dissertation chapters, discovered a host of syntactical errors, and tried to cure me of beginning sentences with untethered demonstrative pronouns. While researching this topic in pre-internet days, with archival resources scattered over the country, I made many requests by mail and received kind responses from a host of patient, and now nameless, librarians to whom I remain grateful. I have retained earlier citations to paper sources even though most modern readers will have access to many of the cited works online.

Introduction

Kellen R. Funk*

Like another prominent New York City lawyer before him, Henry Nicoll always seemed to be "in the room where it happened"[1] during formative moments of the New York bar. Scion of the patroon Van Rensselaer family, Nicoll served briefly in Congress and was a delegate to the New York constitutional convention of 1846, a historic assembly that overhauled the New York court system and established the commissions that would reform and modernize American legal practice. Towards the end of his life, Nicoll became a founding member of the Association of the Bar of the City of New York, the first modern American bar association and a model for the American Bar Association founded a few years later. In the ABCNY's first opening address, Nicoll struck a tone of urgency. "Without some link which should connect and bind the more worthy of the profession together," he declared, the American bar would have to "accept its destiny and be eventually destroyed." He urged the city bar—and other bar associations to follow—to organize in order "to create a spirit of professional brotherhood, to create in the members of our profession a regard for the profession."[2]

---

* Associate Professor of Law, Columbia Law School.

[1] Lin-Manuel Miranda, *Hamilton: An American Musical* (2015).

[2] Remarks of Henry Nicoll, 1 *Association of the Bar of the City of New York Report* 8 (1870).

Twenty-five years earlier at the constitutional convention, Nicoll's invocation of the profession of law had been quite different. Despite his Whiggish upbringing, Nicoll had allied with the radical Barnburner faction of New York's Jacksonian Democrats. In that setting, Nicoll had hurled the term "professional gentleman" as an epithet to describe someone beholden to dry and dusty forms, someone whose imagination was too constrained by traditional practices to see that law and equity, counsellors and lawyers, fees and costs were all mere words that "sacrifice [reality] for the sake of form." For the younger Nicoll, professionalism stood in the way of law reform, reform whose "only and paramount object" was "to redress a wrong or enforce a right . . . in the simplest manner."[3]

The older Nicoll recanted his earlier views. He blamed "that Constitution"—whose judiciary article he had significantly influenced—for delivering "almost a death blow to the legal profession." Its chief defect, Nicoll explained to the ABCNY, was its opening of the legal profession to all comers. The 1846 constitution abolished a myriad of apprenticeship periods and examinations as requisite for admission to the bar and replaced them with the simple provision that any male citizen, twenty-one years old, of good character and possessing "the requisite qualifications of learning" could be admitted to practice. The state's newly elective judiciary, Nicoll groused, was all too willing to find those requisite qualifications in "the merest tyro," so that all "honorable distinctions which formerly existed in the profession were

---

[3] William G. Bishop & William H. Attree, eds., *Report of the Debates and Proceedings of the Convention for the Revision of the Constitution of the State of New York* 600-01 (1846) (Remarks of Henry Nicoll).

abolished." Nicoll lamented that the bar "had been reduced to a mere collection of individuals without class or rank—a dull dreary level of enforced equality," though he recognized that "it may sound strange in a democratic community to talk in this way."[4]

* * *

What does it mean to claim the law as one's profession, and what is a legal profession *for*? This book traces some of the ambivalences of America's elite lawyers in the formative age of modern professional consciousness by relating a history of the early years of the American Bar Association, the institutional expression of that consciousness. Founded by seventy-five mostly East Coast lawyers in Saratoga Springs in 1878, by 1928 the ABA had 26,000 members, some 2,000 of whom attended its annual meeting. What is striking about these numbers is not their dramatic growth but rather their relative paucity. In 1910, the American Medical Association boasted over 70,000 members, about half the physicians in the United States; and the AMA maintained a kind of control over medical education and credentialing that the bar could only dream of (and dream it did—see Chapter 6 below).

By the 1920s bar association leaders were well aware that the organization was struggling to outgrow its origins as a gentlemen's social club, closed to all but the Henry Nicolls of succeeding generations. They continually wrestled with the question of what professionalization was for: Was it to control (if only to stifle) law reform, as the younger Nicoll maintained? Was it to establish honors and class distinctions

---

[4] Remarks of Henry Nicoll, 1 *Association of the Bar of the City of New York Report* 8-9 (1870).

among practitioners? Was it both, or something else entirely? After-dinner speeches anxiously wrangling over these questions has become a mainstay of American intellectual and political history. Richard Hofstadter's foundational work, *The Age of Reform,* made these addresses the centerpiece of his thesis that Progressive Era lawyers faced a "crisis of self-respect." Their "ambiguous situation" arose from a conflict between their traditions of "independent professionalism and the realities of modern commercial practice." Despite maintaining supposedly independent law firms, the leaders of the bar enjoyed—and loathed—a "profitable subservience" to corporations that revealed just how greatly the late-nineteenth-century bar had become a "captive profession."[5]

Hofstadter offered his conclusions tentatively, "until we know more about the history of [the legal] profession," but sixty years later elements of his analysis remain standard components in the historiography of the legal profession. Throughout the nineteenth century, lawyers, citing Tocqueville's *Democracy in America,* prided themselves in being the aristocracy of the new nation, a profession that not only advised parties in their narrow disputes but also mediated between the upper and lower classes of society. By the 1890s, however, the profession that had once opened social mobility to all comers was now divided into wealthy servants of corporations and lowly (usually immigrant) "scramblers." Lawyers who sought to preserve moral independence from clients fled to law schools, the home of the profession's displaced conscience, while newly erected bar associations "represented the unsympathetic efforts of the richer lawyers

---

[5] Richard Hofstadter, *The Age of Reform* 156-58 (1955).

with corporate connections to improve the reputation of the profession as a whole at the expense of their weaker colleagues."[6] *The Best Men of the Bar* answers Hofstadter's call to tell us more about the legal profession. While building on Hofstadter's work to place the legal profession in the broader context of the age of reform, it also challenges the centrality of corporate lawyering in Hofstadter's account and subsequent works that relied on it.

The Best Men of the Bar began as a dissertation defended in 1984. At the time, graduate education in legal history was only just emerging, and the reliable dissertation-to-monograph pipelines we enjoy today had not yet been established. Despite the central importance of the ABA to the turn-of-the-century class stratification of the bar, the accreditation of legal education, the emergence of the "canons" of legal ethics, and the settlement of the codification controversy with model laws and restatements, no institutional history of the ABA appeared in the intervening years. Literatures have arisen devoted to the entrance of women and African Americans to legal practice in the late nineteenth century, while the internal dynamics of the elite (mostly male and white) bar during the New Deal has received sustained attention.[7] But as

---

[6] Hofstadter, *The Age of Reform*, 157-58. With the remaking of Harvard Law School by Christopher Columbus Langdell in the 1890s, law professors were hired straight out of law school, before getting the chance to dirty their hands in the actual practice of law. See John H. Langbein et al., *History of the Common Law: The Development of Anglo-American Legal Institutions* 963 (2009).

[7] For sterling examples of each, see Jill Norgren, *Rebels at the Bar: The Fascinating, Forgotten Stories of America's First Women Lawyers* (2013); Kenneth W. Mack, *Representing the Race: The Creation of the Civil Rights*

of yet, the elite of the bar to which women, minorities, and New Deal progressives were reacting has been relatively neglected. While it is regrettable that a thirty-year-old work still has much to tell us about the institutional bar, it is a joy to see that work finally in print, ready to instigate a long overdue conversation.

Indeed, *The Best Men of the Bar* presciently offered a number of arguments that today puts the work right at home in contemporary historiography of America's legal profession, particularly in its focus on the control of legal education (see Chapter 6) and the interconnections between codification and access to the profession (see Chapter 9). In other ways, the book opens new horizons for scholarly exploration. Historians of science and medicine may benefit from the comparative study of professions offered here.[8] The primary sources on which the work draws are also replete with religious rhetoric and ministerial analogies, a kind of intellectual interdependence between law and religion that scholars generally have not recognized outside the antebellum era.[9]

The central argument of the book is one that both anticipates recent literature yet also extends it by disrupting our conventional attempts to describe the elite bar of the Gilded

---

Lawyer (2014); Daniel R. Ernst, *Tocqueville's Nightmare: The Administrative State Emerges in America, 1900-1940* (2014).

[8] For useful surveys of the organized historical and scientific professions in the United States (both oriented around the theme of objectivity), see Peter Novick, *That Noble Dream: The 'Objectivity Question' and the American Historical Profession* (1988); Lorraine Daston & Peter Galison, *Objectivity* (2007).

[9] For a recent examination of legal "competency" in the context of early American evangelical revivalism, see Susanna L. Blumenthal, *Law and the Modern Mind: Consciousness and Responsibility in American Legal Culture* (2016).

Age and Progressive Era in the United States. One need only survey the subtitles to see that innumerable studies of legal history take the 1870s through the 1920s and beyond as a whole.[10] In general these accounts portray an unchanging organized profession across this period, one whose elite members were more or less uniformly devoted to a "Classical Legal Orthodoxy" that mistrusted democratic politics and uniformly opposed social reform. In these accounts the ABA has been the avatar of conservative retrenchment. While recent studies have challenged the notion of a monolithic legal orthodoxy, *Best Men of the Bar* clarifies the story by dividing the ABA's early history into two periods: one that drew on and was shaped by the age of reform, and a later period of reaction and retrenchment.

In the remainder of this introduction I will survey the major historiographical debates about the turn-of-the-century American legal profession to illustrate the power of this argument. One of the recurring themes of the works surveyed below is the slightly embarrassed admission that the Gilded Age bar in many ways countered the trend towards conservatism that developed later in the Progressive Era.

* * *

---

[10] See Morton J. Horwitz, *The Transformation of American Law, 1870-1960: The Crisis of Legal Orthodoxy* (1991); Barbara Young Welke, *Recasting American Liberty: Gender, Race, Law, and the Railroad Revolution, 1865-1920* (2001); Edward A. Purcell, *Litigation and Inequality: Federal Diversity Jurisdiction in Industrial America, 1870-1958* (1992). Cf. Charles W. McCurdy, "American Law and the Marketing Structure of the Large Corporation, 1875-1890," 38 *Journal of Economic History* 631 (1978).

The decade after the Civil War was a time of intense transformation in American society and law. Barely a generation after the founding, a national state had emerged that raised money, conscripted soldiers, prosecuted war, and redefined and redistributed property rights in unprecedented ways and on staggering scales. New texts were added to the Constitution, all employing the traditional language of America's court-centered legality: due process, privileges and immunities, equal protection of the law. Both citizenship and the franchise became matters of national definition and regulatory authority.

Sweeping as these changes were, recent literature emphasizes another development of post-bellum America that may have been even more significant for the legal profession: the rise of large railroad corporations. The 9,000 miles of track laid by 1850 already far outdistanced European railroads. During the last quarter of the century, track mileage grew dramatically: 53,000 miles in 1870; 87,000 miles in 1880; 163,000 miles in 1890.[11] During the 1880s, the most highly capitalized industrial corporations—of which there were very few—were valued at just over $10 million. The top ten railroad corporations, however, boasted values exceeding $100 million with the largest, the Pennsylvania Railroad, well over $200 million.[12] While various segments of the American bar may have puzzled over the implications of Reconstruction for national public authority and private orderings, nearly every lawyer had some interaction with the railroads that had

---

[11] Welke, *Recasting American Liberty*, 7-15.

[12] Horwitz, *Transformation of American Law*, 95; see generally Richard White, *Railroaded: The Transcontinentals and the Making of Modern America* (2011)

threaded through cities and across the land. By the turn of the century, for instance, 10% of all streetcar operating expenses went to hire legal counsel and pay damage awards for accidental injuries—the second-largest budget item after wages.[13]

A national marketing strategy relying on the rails, Charles McCurdy demonstrates, was until the 1870s and 1880s severely hampered by states using a variety of legal strategies to favor local producers. "State and local officials prescribed marketing practices, enacted discriminatory schemes of mercantile licensing and taxation, proscribed the entry of unfavored articles of commerce, and devised inspection laws to improve the competitive position of their citizens relative to producers in other states." Rather than lobby the various state legislatures in a probably futile effort to change these laws, sewing manufacturers and meatpacking corporations resorted to the federal courts to strike down these laws. These corporations "instructed their local marketing agents to invite arrest and conviction," and then "hired counsel who succeeded in persuading the Court that existing canons of constitutional construction had to be modified to accord with the changing structure of business enterprise." A national market of states that formed a "free trade unit" was thus created only by persistent legal effort that required two things: "skillful counsel" that could be retained to work exclusively on this litigation year-round and "litigants with sufficient resources to finance scores of lawsuits."[14]

The foundational effort to integrate a history of the legal profession into the broader history of these social transformations is Morton Horwitz's *Transformation of American Law,*

---

[13] Welke, *Recasting American Liberty*, 29.

[14] McCurdy, "American Law and Marketing Structure," 632-35, 648.

the second volume of which appeared shortly after *Best Men of the Bar* had been completed. Although Horwitz seeks "to challenge what continues to be the dominant form of legal historiography of the Gilded Age," his basic interpretation strongly echoes Hofstadter's thesis that the progressive movement had really been a conservative detour from the main tradition of American reform.[15] Viewing elite lawyers as professionals suffering the anxieties of social displacement, Hofstadter argued that "lawyers on a moral holiday" supplied "the cast of Progressive thought and the recruitment of Progressive leaders."[16] Horwitz, in turn, agrees that the crisis of Gilded Age lawyers was a crisis of two conservatisms: "An old conservativism, rooted in an increasingly nostalgic vision of the naturalness and necessity of a decentralized, competitive market system, struggled with a new conservatism that proclaimed the inevitability and efficiency of large organizations that derived from economies of scale."[17]

Horwitz contends that uniting the two conservative sides of the elite bar was an absolute commitment against state-sponsored redistribution of property, the fundamental tenet of what Horwitz calls "Classical Legal Thought." Horwitz sets out a detailed intellectual history of jurisprudence covering many areas of public regulation and private law to show how "heightening social conflict produced by immigration, urbanization, and industrialization" spurred "orthodox legal thinkers and judges . . . to create an autonomous legal culture

---

[15] Horwitz, *Transformation of American Law*, 7.
[16] Hofstadter, *Age of Reform*, 156-63.
[17] Horwitz, *Transformation of American Law*, 66.

as part of their 'search for order.'"[18] Mobilized by the intellectual leaders of the bar, Classical Legal Thought clung to a rhetoric of science to shield legal reasoning from the reach of popular politics and its redistributive possibilities. A major part of this scientific effort was the hardening division between public and private spheres of law to shield the latter category—which gradually annexed the law of corporations—from state interference. The ultimate ideals of this venture, not fully expressed until the turn of the century, was a natural-entity theory of the corporation (treating corporations as legal persons) and freedom of contract according to individual will, so that only voluntary contracts could allocate property in society.[19]

The flaw in this vision, Horwitz contends, was the captive profession. The quest for general scientific principles of law may have divorced jurisprudence from politics, but it increasingly divorced it from social reality as well. A general, classless legal science began to seem less credible as lawyers such as S.C.T. Dodd and William Nelson Cromwell systematically dismantled through the federal courts state regulations on their corporate clients. "The integrity of private law—and of the power of common law judges," Horwitz contends, "rested on the assertion that judges were not policymakers." But as increasing numbers of judges—themselves former railroad counsel—promoted business growth through their decisions, "the judicial function began to be overwhelmed by the overtly instrumental use of private law to advance utilitarian objec-

---

[18] The allusion is to Robert H. Wiebe, *The Search for Order: 1877-1920* (1967). Horwitz, *Transformation of American Law*, 10.

[19] Horwitz, *Transformation of American Law: Crisis of Legal Orthodoxy*, chs. 3 and 4.

tives."[20] Classical Legal Thought thus sowed the seeds of its own destruction, a destruction that occurred when the Legal Realists of the 1920s adamantly insisted on restoring political critique to legal reasoning.

Yet a close look at the evidence shows that these arguments about the Gilded Age rest largely on statements and pronouncements made the 1890s or later. Horwitz's system of Classical Legal Thought did not find its full expression until after the turn of the century, and he concedes "it was not the Supreme Court of the Gilded Age" that magnified corporate power or adhered strictly to a logic of free contract.[21] While a standard interpretation has it that rights for freedmen ultimately became rights for corporations, McCurdy's analysis shows that lawyers created the national market in the 1880s, not through the Fourteenth Amendment but through the Commerce Clause, a standard fixture of antebellum jurisprudence.[22] Edward Purcell's account of postbellum federal litigation likewise finds that federal decisions in the 1870s were actually quite pragmatic and sympathetic towards the struggle of individuals against corporate power. It was not until the 1890s that courts regularly undermined plaintiffs' efforts to stay in state courts and increasingly found corporations protected by the Fourteenth Amendment.[23] These concessions raise a question about what really propelled the legal profession during the Gilded Age towards a crisis in the following decades.

---

[20] Horwitz, *Transformation of American Law*, 80-83, 112.

[21] Horwitz, *Transformation of American Law*, 79.

[22] McCurdy, "American Law and Marketing Structure," 642.

[23] Purcell, *Litigation and Inequality*, 82.

Recent work has challenged Horwitz's account by showing how elite common law lawyers, particularly Horwitz's main target James Coolidge Carter, were often political progressives who supported redistributive legislation such as the progressive income tax.[24] Kunal Parker argues that nineteenth-century jurists conceived of a common law that was able to work with and to shape democracy by making history and organic growth over time foundational legal concepts. Parker concludes that the elite champions of the common law, particularly thinkers like Carter, did not form a reactionary force that stood in the way of democracy or a democratic economy.[25] Similarly, Lewis Grossman's work argues that Carter and figures like him are best understood as legal "Mugwumps"—the faction of northeastern elites who bolted the Republican Party in 1884 over disagreements about civil service reform. Such reform, Grossman argues, was the lifeblood of Mugwumpery, and the leaders of the movement unhesitatingly linked their arguments to a waning Jacksonian democracy, even when such commitments entailed the need for legislation. On this account, the distrust of legislation among the elite bar stemmed not from a reaction against distributive democracy but an apprehension that legislators were more easily corrupted or hoodwinked into counterproductive "reforms" than was the better educated and cautious judiciary.[26] My own work accords with these

---

[24] See, for instance, David M. Rabban, *Law's History: American Legal Thought and the Transatlantic Turn to History* 322-77 (2013).

[25] Kunal M. Parker, *Common Law, History, and Democracy in America, 1790-1900: Legal Thought before Modernism* 230-41 (2011).

[26] Lewis A. Grossman, "James Coolidge Carter and Mugwump Jurisprudence," 20 *Law & History Review* 577 (2002).

arguments and shows that the elite lawyers who most fit Horwitz's description of political and economic "orthodoxy"—those most committed to a laissez-faire political economy with full private rights secured to corporations—were the arch-codifiers David Dudley Field and his brother, the Supreme Court Justice Stephen J. Field.[27] As it turns out, opposition to the legislature did not mean opposition to social democracy, nor was support for legislation at odds with a full commitment to an anti-populist laissez-faire regime.

Though written well before these recent accounts, *The Best Men of the Bar* offers a fairly complete synthesis of them in the institutional setting of the early ABA. Chapter 4 in particular draws the strands of elite legal ideologies together to conclude that "the few scholars who have studied the *ABA Reports* of this period have exaggerated its support for laissez-faire economics." In turn, the themes that could pass for a more-or-less common vision of the Gilded Age legal elite sound strikingly like Grossman's account of legal Mugwumpery (but without the clumsy label!). The turn to a more militant political conservativism arises only with, and largely in reaction to, the Great War and the Russian Revolution. The question such an account invites is whether the common vision of the legal elite was transformed wholly by outside forces, or whether certain factors internal to the logic of legal practice also spurred the reaction.

* * *

---

[27] Kellen Funk, *The Lawyers' Code* (forthcoming); see also See Philip J. Bergan, "David Dudley Field: A Lawyer's Life" and Charles W. McCurdy, "Stephen J. Field and the American Judicial Tradition" in *The Fields and the Law: Essays* (1986).

Despite a growing literature on law and society in the "Age of American Enterprise," scholars since Hofstadter have conducted very few close studies of the elite commercial legal profession. Introducing one early set of essays, editor Gerard Gawalt declared the post-bellum era a time "when law replaced religion as the controlling element in American society" and lawyers "became the new high priests of an increasingly legalistic, industrial society."[28] The data from the studies produced a more complicated picture, however. Wayne Hobson's study of large law firms, for instance, concluded that "grinding hard work, long hours, and the lack of any aim higher than money and prestige" created feelings of "cynicism and alienation" in the bar's leading figures.[29]

The rise of large corporate law firms remains a complex and still little-understood phenomenon of the post-bellum era. During the nineteenth century, the basic organization remained the partnership; rarely if ever did a firm employ more than three lawyers. During the Gilded Age, several firms broke from this tradition and hired more lawyers, but the largest firm at the end of the era employed only ten.[30] These modest changes in growth obscure more significant changes in work culture. "During this time," Hobson notes, "the counselor replaced the advocate at the head of the profession, as the skills of rhetoric and courtroom advocacy

---

[28] Gerard Gawalt, "Introduction" in *The New High Priests: Lawyers in Post Civil War America* (Gerard Gawalt, ed., 1984), xvii.

[29] Wayne K. Hobson, "Symbol of the New Profession: Emergence of the Large Law Firm, 1870-1915," in *New High Priests*, 21.

[30] Hobson, "Emergence of the Large Law Firm," 7. Not until the 1930s would firms grow to seventy lawyers; the first firm to employ a hundred lawyers did so in the 1950s. Lanbgein et al., *History of the Common Law*, 1037.

came to seem less important than technical competence and the skills of the negotiator and facilitator."[31] As more corporate clients began to favor dealmaking and out-of-court settlements, the most sought-after attorneys confined themselves increasingly to office work. By and large, however, lawyers managed their own offices—in-house counsel remained a rarity through the Gilded Age, and lawyers prided themselves in remaining institutionally independent from their clients.[32]

These generalizations apply most forcefully to New York City, "which accounted for more than half of all large firms until 1898."[33] The city was also the home of the first modern bar association, organized in 1873 after a period of intense litigation between New York lawyers representing the dueling attempts of Jay Gould and Cornelius Vanderbilt to control the Erie Railroad.[34] Lawyers in the Upper and Deep South, however, apparently resisted efforts to follow New York's patterns of organization, into either bar associations or increasingly larger firms.[35] Until the end of the era, Philadelphia firms remained under the control of old leading families, though a degree from Harvard could open the doors of firms in Boston and New York to upwardly mobile strivers.[36]

---

[31] Hobson, "Emergence of the Large Law Firm," 3.

[32] See Hofstadter, *Age of Reform*, 161.

[33] Hobson, "Emergence of the Large Law Firm," 10.

[34] See George Martin, *Causes and Conflicts: The Centennial History of the Association of the Bar of the City of New York, 1870-1970* (1997).

[35] W. Hamilton Bryson & E. Lee Shepard, "The Virginia Bar, 1870-1900" and Michael de L. Landon, "Another False Start: Mississippi's Second State Bar Association, 1886-1892," in *New High Priests*.

[36] Hobson, "Emergence of the Large Law Firm,"14-15.

Whatever the regional variations in organization and personnel, the transition from trial advocacy to office work appears to have obtained everywhere the railroads hired counsel (which was, increasingly, everywhere). Such a transition was the most salient marker of the new divided bar, bifurcated between the more affluent railroad lawyers and the "scrambling bar" who lacked the advantage of a consistent clientele. "Having forsaken the courthouse for the law office," John Matzko noted in an early synthesis of his work on the ABA, "the most affluent lawyers were unlikely even to know the members of the lower caste 'police-court lawyers,'" an ignorance that was reflected when elite office lawyers organized bar associations primarily for their own benefit.[37] There were a couple of exceptions to this office/scrambling distinction: During the 1870s, African Americans and women for the first time entered the legal profession. Their numbers were small—in 1890 the black bar of Texas numbered only twelve—and courtroom practice was rarely open to them. Most African American and women lawyers thus employed their skills in office work.[38]

Gawalt's collection of studies is perhaps best known for introducing the seminal work of Robert W. Gordon on the unfolding crisis of the bar at the end of the Gilded Age. Throughout the era, Gordon argues, lawyers clung tenaciously to a republican ideology that expected one "to mediate between the universal vision of legal order and the

---

[37] John A. Matzko, "'The Best Men of the Bar': The Founding of the American Bar Association," in *New High Priests*, 78.

[38] Maxwell Bloomfield, "From Deference to Confrontation: The Early Black Lawyers of Galveston, Texas, 1895-1920," in *New High Priests*, 152; Langbein et al., *History of the Common Law*, 1078-83.

concrete desires of his clients." The problem was not so much that lawyers increasingly worked in offices or for corporate clients, but that those clients regularly hired them to combat republican restrictions on corporate power and liberal critiques of corporate growth. By thinking of their profession in republican terms while simultaneously carrying out a legal attack on republican ideals, lawyers "helped bring on the crisis of legitimacy that they now proposed their services to relieve."[39]

To that end, Gordon maintains, lawyers banded together in bar associations, not so much, as Hofstadter had it, to control the lower echelons of the bar, but "as a cure for their own condition."[40] The Association of the Bar of the City of New York, after all, was organized primarily to reign in the elite lawyers of the Erie Railroad, and, later in the decade, to scrutinize the efforts of David Dudley Field as he defended William "Boss" Tweed in court. These projects never addressed the central problem, which, Gordon concludes, was "the poverty of modern liberalism." Through all their Gilded Age reform efforts, lawyers nevertheless remained committed "to the classical opposition of public and private spheres of action, to the notion that private practice is one thing, and public power is another," even though corporate lawyers would have known better than anyone "how all

---

[39] Robert W. Gordon, "'The Ideal and the Actual in the Law': Fantasies and Practices of New York City Lawyers, 1870-1910," in *New High Priests*, 58, 60-61.

[40] Gordon, "The Ideal and the Actual in the Law," 56-57.

'private' action is 'publicly' constituted, and has 'public' consequences."[41]

Gordon has since produced a full literature on the instabilities and contradictions of legal professionalism in the United States.[42] Of particular relevance here is the debate Gordon has carried on with Norman Spaulding, who argued that lawyers' Gilded Age rhetoric of decline was little different from professional rhetoric in any other era. "Morally activist civic republicanism," Spaulding concludes, "operated as an ideal—a deeply contested, often self-serving, and, on the facts of law practice from the time, somewhat abnormal and unnatural ideal." Alongside Gordon's republicanism, Spaulding finds a longstanding "conception of lawyering defined by commitment to zealous, client-centered service and profound skepticism about the lawyer's capacity to act as a moral judge of his clients' ends" that dated back well before the antebellum era. If anything, Spaulding argues, the withdrawal of elite lawyers from courtrooms into offices would have blunted

---

[41] Gordon, "The Ideal and the Actual in the Law," 56-57, 67. Cf. Horwitz, *Transformation of American Law: Crisis of Legal Orthodoxy*, 51, noting that "ordinary lawyers could no longer find in their own experiences of the world a clear distinction between public and private realms."

[42] Robert W. Gordon, "Legal Thought and Legal Practice in the Age of American Enterprise, 1870-1920," in *Professional Ideologies in America*, ed. G. Geison (1983); Robert W. Gordon, "The Independence of Lawyers," 68 *Boston University Law Review* 1 (1988); Robert W. Gordon, "The Citizen Lawyer: A Brief Informal History of a Myth with Some Basis in Reality," 50 *William & Mary Law Review* 1169 (2009).

lawyers' slavishness to their clients, removing the pressures of courtroom performance to distort their mediation.[43]

In response, Gordon agrees that Spaulding has identified historical roots to an apolitical, zealous advocate ideal, where, "like the invisible hand of the market, which aggregates selfish interests into a virtuous equilibrium, the procedures of the legal system bring clients' private interests into harmony with public goals and values."[44] Gordon nevertheless contends that institutional changes during the Gilded Age altered the framework of this lawyerly debate and created a crisis that was not just rhetorical. "As late as the 1870s, even the lawyers who appeared most often for railroad clients in court appeared almost as often for individuals suing the railroads," Gordon observes. But during that decade, railroads began contracting only with lawyers who would agree never to oppose railroad interests. Publicly minded lawyers accordingly had to abandon practice for the railroads entirely, heading off to law schools or the purely public sector of government work. The private and public functions of lawyering then, could be performed by lawyers dedicated only to one or the other. Thus the lawyers' self-constructed conceptual world of free contract documented by Horwitz came home to them in the form of exclusive railroad agreements that they were essentially powerless to dispute.

Like Hofstadter's study, Sven Beckert's *Monied Metropolis* shows how professional changes to lawyering could be integrated into a broader historical narrative. Although

---

[43] Normal W. Spaulding, "The Myth of Civic Republicanism: Interrogating the Ideology of Antebellum Legal Ethics," 71 *Fordham Law Review* 1397-99 (2003).

[44] Gordon, "Citizen Lawyer," 1170.

Beckert excludes professional lawyers from "the center of New York's bourgeoisie" as a contrast to Europe, he nevertheless notes their status among the city's elite and documents the ways lawyers "bridged the worlds of business and the state as did no other sector of the city's economic elite, translating the railroads' economic might into unrivaled political influence."[45] Beckert also shows how Horwitz's Classical Legal Thought was by no means all that "classical." Ideology among the city's bourgeoisie shifted over time, and it was only towards the end of the Gilded Age that the New York elite "made the defense of the prerogatives of property the centerpiece of their shared beliefs," unaccompanied by any other trappings of an old republican ideology.[46]

Keeping Beckert's study of the wider economic and cultural world in mind, one possible synthesis of this literature would unite the narratives of Horwitz, Spaulding, and Gordon. Lawyers by tradition held to an ideal of mediating between rich and poor, but following the temptation to join the ranks of New York's bourgeois class, lawyers increasingly became servants to, rather than mediators of, the wealthy classes. Where liberal ideology of public and private spheres had once helped to protect all individuals from a coercive state, it increasingly became a tool to shield the property of private corporations from public interference. And whereas elite lawyers formerly mediated all manner of disputes and social conflicts, by the end of the Gilded Age they mediated only between corporate interests, helping to negotiate deals between large banks and large manufacturers. Far from being

---

[45] Sven Beckert, *The Monied Metropolis: New York City and the Consolidation of the American Bourgeoisie, 1850-1896* at 7-8, 149 (2001).
[46] Beckert, 7-8, 149, 179.

the "high priests" of American society, American society replaced them, and "new sorts of brokers" took their place.[47] An increasingly prominent band of social reformers continued to hire the services of lawyers, but were not themselves lawyers.[48]

The detailed institutional study that follows helps to remind us, however, that corporate lawyering was by no means the dominant mode of lawyering at the end of the nineteenth century, even among the elite bar. Corporate firms remained small, and corporate counsel could be easily outvoted by the many prominent lawyers who served in state and municipal government and were often at odds with their corporate brethren. Indeed, by accounting for the early years of the organized national bar, *The Best Men of the Bar* shows that if elite lawyers had cause to lament their displaced social and political influence, it was because even the small elite bar's social politics were so rarely aligned. Class consciousness did not easily translate to perceptible class interests. Government lawyers opposed corporate counsel. State bars jealously guarded their power. Those with particular agendas in legal education or codification drifted in and out of formal alignment with the ABA. By the end of its first fifty years, the ABA could hardly boast about its influence on American law, much less on American life: a model statute adopted by a handful of states, a few reports cited beyond its own publications, numerous spin-off organizations for whose work the ABA itself could claim little credit.

---

[47] See Daniel T. Rodgers, *Atlantic Crossings: Social Politics in a Progressive Age* (1998), 4, 24.

[48] See, for instance, Sarah Deutsch, *Women and the City: Gender, Space, and Power in Boston, 1870-1940* (2000), 128, 149-50.

Indeed, the ABA's work on codification is a particularly striking example of the organization's ineffectiveness. Despite the fact that promotion of "uniformity of legislation" was the single substantive legal commitment of its founding charter (see Chapter 1), the ABA could never quite agree on which bodies of law ought to made uniform or what the uniform legislation should say. Even when under the guidance of its president-codifier David Dudley Field the association agreed to press Congress for a uniform procedure code, its lobbying efforts remained unsuccessful for more than thirty years until Congress finally enacted the Rules Enabling Act in 1934 and the Supreme Court appointed a civil rules advisory committee the following year.[49] Although the conventional story of the American bar has been told as a retreat into apolitical technocracy, plenty of lawyers at the time recognized the political stakes of even a procedure code and contested the uniform legislation on political grounds. Populist Senator Thomas Walsh framed his opposition by saying that he was "for the one hundred [lawyers] who stay at home as against the one [corporate lawyer] who goes abroad."[50] The account that follows is filled with such instances—not retreats from politics, but an engagement in politics by an elite bar that was

---

[49] Stephen B. Burbank, "The Rules Enabling Act of 1934," 130 *University of Pennsylvania Law Review* 1015 (1982).

[50] Thomas J. Walsh, *Reform of Federal Procedure: Address Delivered at the Meeting of the Tri-State Bar Association at Texarkana* (April 23, 1926), 2. s. See also Stephen N. Subrin, "Federal Rules, Local Rules, and State Rules: Uniformity, Divergence, and Emerging Procedural Patterns," 137 *University of Pennsylvania Law Review* 1999 (1989). For an overview arguing for the "modernity" of a populism that both criticized centralization and corporatism but also emulated them for an effective politics, see Charles Postel, *The Populist Vision* (2007).

nevertheless so diverse in interests that its politics often nullified itself. As Henry Nicoll had discovered, the politics of professionalization were difficult to predict.

* * *

The well-worn aphorism that all history is at bottom merely autobiography is grossly overstated, but not entirely false. The author of this book is a dear friend and mentor, my undergraduate advisor who introduced me to the field of legal history. Though not a practicing lawyer, he is every bit a consummate professional—in every virtuous sense of the word. Jack Matzko has poured thousands of hours into teaching undergraduates first how to think, and then how to write. (Indeed, he surely winced at the breezier passages of this introduction!) Undoubtedly heavy course loads contributed to waylaying the progress of the original dissertation to book manuscript. It is thrilling to see the work complete and a deserving scholar properly recognized. Knowing this about Jack, I offer readers a final advisement: "The Best Men of the Bar" is not, I think, an ironic title, or at least not fully ironic. Despite the straightforward chronicle of fifty years of bumbling lawyers striving mightily, and only just succeeding, to make their organization not entirely inconsequential, there is a certain charity of tone and even a sense of admiration throughout the work for those who found it worthwhile to take the time and tidy up their corner of the kingdom. That is where I see Jack most in this work; and the work itself is one part of his own tidying.

May 2019

BEST MEN
• OF THE •
BAR

Chapter 1

The Founding

On August 21, 1878, fewer than a hundred lawyers gathered in the narrow courtroom behind the Saratoga Springs town hall to organize the American Bar Association. Those who had lent their names and respectability to the affair risked some embarrassment. A majority of those who had signed the call for the meeting were not even there.

During an era when state and local bar associations were at best feeble, organizing a national association may have struck many American lawyers as premature. During most of the nineteenth century, bar associations had withered as standards for admission to the legal profession had declined. Such professional discipline that did exist was enforced largely through peer pressure and a marketplace that encouraged "a scrambling bar of shrewd entrepreneurs."[1] This "scrambling bar" was hardly conducive to the growth of bar associations. Many of those that did remain existed solely to support a law library. Others—perhaps the majority—were chiefly social. The only surviving publications for some are banquet menus.[2]

---

1. Lawrence M. Friedman, *A History of American Law* (New York: Simon and Schuster, 2005), 237.

2. Roscoe Pound, *The Lawyer from Antiquity to Modern Times* (St. Paul:

Nevertheless, following the Civil War, renewed interest in bar associations arose as a consequence of professional and societal change. Between 1850 and 1870, the number of urban lawyers grew faster than the cities they lived in, and the elite of the bar were unable to maintain even informal oversight of their profession. Elite lawyers who had abandoned the courthouse for the law office often did not even know lower caste practitioners.

Consequently, bar associations formed after the Civil War tended to restrict membership to the "decent part" of the profession, "primarily well-to-do business lawyers, predominantly of old American stock."[3] If the elite could no longer control admission to the profession, they could at least restrict the membership of bar associations and thereby distance themselves from men who—in the hyperbole of one New York bar leader—were "seen in almost all our courts, slovenly in dress, uncouth in manners and habits, ignorant even of the English language, jostling and crowding and vulgarizing the profession."[4]

During the late nineteenth century, elite lawyers were conscious of having lost some of their former influence in

---

West Publishing Company, 1953), 246; Philip J. Wickser, "Bar Associations," 15 *Cornell Law Quarterly* 390 @ 401 (1930); Albert P. Blaustein, "New York Bar Associations Prior to 1870," *American Journal of Legal History* 12 (1968), 50; Samuel Haber, *The Quest for Authority and Honor in the American Professions, 1750-1900* (Chicago: University of Chicago Press, 1991), 129.

3. Friedman, *History of American Law*, 495; Wickser, "Bar Associations," 396; James Bryce, "The Legal Profession in America," *McMillan's Magazine*, 25 (January 1872), 214; Adolph H. Grundman, "The Early History of the Colorado Bar Association: 1898-1938," 14 *Colorado Lawyer* 7 (1985).

4. Samuel Hand, "Annual Address of the President," 3 *New York State Bar Association Proceedings* 67 @ 71 (1880).

American political life.[5] At least during the 1840s, the myth of the office seeking the man was conceivable; by the 1870s, it was not. In 1871, the *American Law Review* complained that a "great democratic flood" had filled "the bench with political partisans, the minor legal offices with political hacks, and the bar with an indiscriminate herd of camp followers."[6] Although elite lawyers continued to quote Tocqueville's declaration that the American aristocracy could be found among the bench and bar, the sentiment had a dull ring by the 1870s.[7] As James Bryce wrote in the following decade, lawyers might be wealthy enough, but not nearly so wealthy as the capitalists. The millionaire, said Bryce, was a "much more frequent and potent personage" than he had been during the antebellum period, and "he outshines everybody in the country."[8] Likewise, the rise of science-based professions like medicine, engineering, and chemistry, further eroded the prestige of lawyers. In 1875, law school dean William G. Hammond (1829-1894)—an engineer as well as a lawyer—wrote that the bar had "lost its privileged position."[9]

---

5. James Bryce, *The American Commonwealth* (London: Macmillan and Co., 1888), 2: 490; Audra L. Prewitt, "American Lawyers and Social Ferment," Ph.D. dissertation, Northwestern University, 1973, 16-17.

6. "Summary of Events," 5 *American Law Review* 556 (1871).

7. Alexis de Tocqueville, *Democracy in America* (1835) [Reeve-Bowen translation, ed. Phillips Bradley], 355.

8. Bryce, *American Commonwealth,* 2: 490. Richard Hofstadter, *The Age of Reform: From Bryan to F. D. R.* (New York: Alfred A. Knopf, 1955), 155-163, discussing a slightly later period, emphasized what he called a "status revolution" that encouraged some lawyers to adopt reformist views.

9. W. G. Hammond, "The Legal Profession—Its Past, Its Present, and Its Duty," [speech delivered before the Iowa State University Law Department] 11 *Albany Law Journal* 113 @ 114 (1875); Joseph Katz, "The Legal Profession, 1890-1915," unpublished M.A. thesis, Columbia University,

Selective bar associations might simultaneously increase the lawyers' income, put the legal profession on a more scientific basis, and influence all levels of government.[10] In the late nineteenth century, Americans had been peculiarly aggressive in creating voluntary associations, an activity further stimulated by improved communication and transportation and an increase in leisure time.[11] The more affluent the lawyer, the greater the likelihood he would have the time and money to participate in social activities that exuded an aura of serious purpose. What better way for the elite to separate themselves from the scrambling bar than by holding elegant banquets? "If it were for nothing more than to be in the fashion and to protect their class interest," wrote the editor of the *Albany Law Journal*, "it would be proper for lawyers to formally unite."[12]

All of these predisposing factors were evident in the formation of the Association of the Bar of the City of New York (ABCNY) in 1870. Usually credited to a conflict between elite lawyers and the Tweed Ring, the ABCNY was actually organized as much for professional, as civic, reasons.[13] In 1868, capitalists vying for control of the Erie

---

1954, 18-21.

10. "Professional Organization," 6 *Albany Law Journal* 233 (1873); Walter B. Hill, "Bar Associations," 5 *Georgia Bar Association Reports* 51 @ 75 (1888).

11. Arthur Schlesinger, "Biography of a Nation of Joiners," *American Historical Review* 50 (1944), 16-18; Haber, *The Quest for Authority,* 158-59; Howard Mumford Jones, *The Age of Energy: Varieties of American Experience, 1865-1915* (New York: Viking Press, 1970), 166-170; Bryce, *American Commonwealth,* 2: 239-240.

12. 13 *Alb. Law J.* 423 (June 17, 1876).

13. James Willard Hurst, *The Growth of American Law: The Lawmakers* (Boston: Little, Brown and Company, 1950), 286; James Grafton Rogers, "The American Bar Association in Retrospect," in *Law: A Century of*

Railroad managed to array the leaders of the New York bar against one another, and when judges, as well as lawyers and legislators, proved for sale, the legal system nearly collapsed. Shortly after an attempt was made to decide railroad ownership by recourse to a pitched battle on the Erie tracks outside Binghamton, a call for the organization of the New York City bar began to circulate.

Speeches delivered at the organizational meeting suggest that the new association was intended to restore "the honor, integrity, and fame of the profession," a goal Henry Nicoll (1812-1879) believed, could be achieved by gathering together "all that is intelligent, all that is honest, all that is honorable in this Profession."[14] (The latter was pretty nearly defined by an entrance fee of $50 and annual dues of $40—easily $1000 each in 21st century terms). "We have become simply a multitude of individuals, engaged in the same business," said one of the founders. "And the objects and the methods of those engaged in that business are very much dictated by those who employ them.... Power is the thing we are first to aim at. The use of it we are to determine afterwards."[15]

The ABCNY did not move immediately against either Boss Tweed or the robber barons, erstwhile employers of most of its members. Instead, it purchased a brownstone and installed rare books, a full-time librarian, busts of eminent lawyers, and a punch bowl filled with a beverage "brewed

---

Progress (New York: New York University, 1937), 1: 173; Everett P. Wheeler, *Sixty Years of American Life* (New York: E. P. Dutton & Company, 1917), 323-24.

14. Speeches of William M. Evarts and Henry Nicoll, 1 *Association of the Bar of the City of New York Report* 8, 28 (1870), quoted in George Martin, *Causes and Conflicts: The Centennial History of the Association of the Bar of the City of New York* (Boston: Houghton, Mifflin Company, 1970), 33-34.

15. "Lawyers in Council," 1 *Alb. Law J.* 219 (March 19, 1870).

according to a special recipe furnished by the nearby Century Club." When the Association did get around to prosecuting Tweed in 1873, David Dudley Field (1805-1894), its most unconventional member, defended the boss.[16]

Other bar associations organized during the period were even less vigorous. At best, they endorsed politically inoffensive procedural reforms or court reorganization schemes. At worst, they adopted fee scales and excoriated the "shysters" who undercut them. Most associations continued the social tradition of the antebellum societies. One convened only at funerals. "Not much life in our organization," the secretary confessed.[17]

Only in a metaphorical sense, then, could a national bar association have been viewed as a capstone of state and local organizations. In 1878, there were probably no more than seven city, and eight state, bar associations in the whole country; and had the organization of a national association awaited the formation of bar associations in a majority of states, the American Bar Association would not have been organized until after the turn of the twentieth century.[18]

---

16. George Martin, *Causes and Conflicts*, 3-86; 5 *American Law Review* 556 (1871); Haber, *Quest for Authority*, 208-210. "It was not so much his defense of Fisk and Tweed in the courts that angered association members, but rather their belief that he had knowingly made use of corrupt judges to get advantageous rulings." (209)
17. Walter B. Hill, "Bar Associations," 5 *Georgia Bar Association Reports* 65 (1888); Friedman, *A History of American Law*, 541-42. Wickser, "Bar Associations," 417-18, lists bar associations and their dates of organization, but the data is not entirely accurate.
18. Wickser, "Bar Associations," 396, 417; Robert Wiebe, *The Search for Order* (New York: Hill and Wang, 1967), 117.

Nevertheless, as early as 1870, the idea of a national lawyers' organization was mooted by two influential legal periodicals, the *Albany Law Journal* and the *Chicago Legal News.*[19] An attempt to organize was actually made in 1876, though with such negligible results that the founders of the American Bar Association may not even have known about it.

This attempt at organization began among leaders of the "United States Law Association," a lawyer referral service of 2500 members who collected debts on commission.[20] State legislatures had discriminated against out-of-state creditors in favor of resident debtors, and bill-collecting lawyers were unable to take their cases to the Supreme Court because of long delays and prohibitive costs.

In May 1876, the Law Association announced a call for a "Congress of Lawyers" to be convened in Philadelphia on June 20. The effort turned into a comedy of errors. Invitations were mistakenly printed with a July, rather than a June date, and fewer than sixty lawyers appeared for the meeting. Half of these then wandered off to view the nearly completed Centennial Exhibition. When the organizers presented their

---

19. 3 *Chicago Legal News* 68 (November 26, 1870); 13 *Alb. Law J.* 171 (March 11,1875);16 *Alb. Law J.* 268 (October 13, 1877); Gustave Koerner to Simeon Baldwin, August 3, 1878, printed in Simeon Baldwin, "The Founding of the American Bar Association," 3 *American Bar Association Journal* 658 @ 680 (1917).

20. The United State Law Association was an unrelated successor to the American Legal Association (1849-1854), the first national referral service. Maxwell Bloomfield, *American Lawyers in a Changing Society, 1776-1876* (Cambridge: Harvard University Press, 1976), 154-155. Information regarding the "Congress of Lawyers" has been gleaned from the *Albany Law Journal* and the *Philadelphia Inquirer, Public Ledger,* and *Press* of June 21-22, 1876; 13 *Alb. Law J.* 375 (May 27, 1876).

plans to the remaining handful, their ideas were immediately labeled "impracticable" and "impossible."[21] The Law Association had assembled the wrong sort of lawyers. Elite lawyers rarely collected debts on commission; and in the late nineteenth century, it was the elites who had both the necessary resources and the broader interests necessary to create a national association.

Even so, the establishment of the American Bar Association might have been delayed longer had it not been for the catalyst of Simeon E. Baldwin (1840-1927), the youngest and most precocious of nine children born to a prominent New Haven family.[22] Because poor eyesight prevented service in the Civil War, Baldwin continued his study of law at Yale and Harvard before returning to his father's law office. Shrewdly specializing in corporate practice, Baldwin gained the New York and New England Railroad as a client, and shortly emerged as one of the most notable members of the Connect-

21. 13 *Alb. Law J.* 375 (May 27, 1876); *Philadelphia Inquirer* (June 22, 1876), 2.

22. The only scholarly biography of Baldwin is Frederick H. Jackson, *Simeon Eben Baldwin* (New York: King's Crown Press, 1955). See also Frederick H. Jackson, "Simeon E. Baldwin: Father of the American Bar Association," 39 *ABAJ* 686 (1953); James Grafton Rogers, *American Bar Leaders: Biographies of the Presidents of the American Bar Association, 1878-1928* (Chicago: American Bar Association, 1932), 61-65. Charles C. Goetsch, *Essays on Simeon E. Baldwin* (West Hartford, Conn.: Connecticut School of Law Press, 1981) makes excellent use of the Baldwin diaries and correspondence, but unfortunately the diaries contain little of importance relating to the American Bar Association. One of Baldwin's great-grandfathers was Roger Sherman, signer of the Declaration of Independence. His grandfather had been an influential Federalist and founder of an antislavery society, and his father, who had served Connecticut both as a senator and governor, argued the *Amistad* case in association with John Quincy Adams.

icut bar. In time Baldwin became Chief Justice of the Connecticut Supreme Court; still later, governor of the state.

From his youth Baldwin had been an organizer and joiner. Probably no one else in American history has held the presidencies of so many professional societies. Between 1890 and 1910 he was president of the American Bar Association, the American Historical Association, the American Social Science Association, the International Law Association, the American Political Science Association, and the Association of American Law Schools.[23]

Yet despite his organizational proclivities, Baldwin was neither cozy nor clubby. Outside his immediate family, he projected an air of aloof formality. His capacity for work was enormous, a reflection both of his patrician upbringing and of personal tragedy. After 1872, following the death of his eldest daughter and the descent of his wife into total insanity, Baldwin submerged himself in work. "Melancholy is a foe to be expelled at any cost," he said, "and preoccupation is often the only thing that avails to shut it out."[24]

To a large extent Baldwin's consuming energy was directed toward the concerns of Gilded Age reform. Baldwin

---

23. Vice-president of a number of other organizations, notably the American Association for the Advancement of Science, Baldwin was a member of such diverse groups as the YMCA (president, 1884-1886), the New Haven Colony Historical Society (president, 1884-1896), the Board of Park Commissioners of New Haven, the American Economic Association, the New England Tariff Reform League, the Union International de Droit Pénal, the General Hospital Society of Connecticut, the Conference of Congregational Churches of Connecticut (moderator, 1881), and the Sons of the American Revolution.

24. Frederick C. Hicks, *Yale Law School: 1895-1915: Twenty Years of Hendrie Hall* (New Haven: Yale University Press, 1938), 84.

was one of "The Best Men," men of "breeding and intelligence, of taste and substance," who, if they believed office-holding to be their birthright, at least counted public office a public trust rather than a public trough. These Gilded Age reformers—of whom an uncommon number were urban journalists and lawyers—were loosely unified around a distaste for the contemporary political morality, viewing themselves as political independents whose goals, they believed, could be made acceptable to both parties.[25]

During his long life, Baldwin touched all the bases of Gilded Age reform. He waged a continuing, though unsuccessful, struggle to rid Connecticut of its grossly malapportioned electoral districts. He urged Senator George Edmunds of Vermont to run for the Republican presidential nomination in 1880 against that *bête noir* of reformers, James G. Blaine. He mobilized support for the establishment of a civil service system in state government, and he organized Connecticut's Civil Service Reform Association. When the Republican Party nominated Blaine in 1884, Baldwin bolted, organizing and serving as president of the Connecticut Independent Republicans.

Many of Baldwin's reform interests were law related. While still in his twenties, Baldwin prepared a digest of Connecticut law, and he gained an instant reputation when it became a standard reference work. By the end of the nine-

---

25. John G. Sproat, "*The Best Men*": *Liberal Reformers in the Gilded Age* (New York: Oxford University Press, 1968), 4-10. See also Gerald W. McFarland, "Partisan of Non-Partisanship: Dorman B. Eaton and the Genteel Reform Tradition," *Journal of American History*, 54 (March 1968), 806-822; Morton Keller, *Affairs of State: Public Life in Late Nineteenth Century America* (Cambridge: Harvard University Press, 1977), 276-79, 550-52.

teenth century, Baldwin had also joined penologists in advocating an odd assortment of reforms directed against the penitentiary system: probation, parole, indeterminate sentences, the reintroduction of the whipping post, and castration for rape. Baldwin was also among the first Americans to advocate outlawing heroic measures to prolong the lives of the terminally ill.[26]

Much of Baldwin's energy was devoted to improving legal education. As a professor at Yale Law School from 1869 to 1912—including the two years when he was governor of Connecticut—Baldwin successfully advocated lengthening the law school course from two to three years. He also introduced the first graduate law program in the United States.[27]

In September 1877, Baldwin presented his educational reforms to the American Social Science Association (1865-1909), the only national organization that provided a forum for discussion of legal topics. The ASSA had been founded by a group of philanthropists and social Don Quixotes whose urge for reform had led them—as it would their Progressive successors—to a quest for scientific knowledge. Believing in absolute truth, in natural laws that governed human conduct, and in man's ability to discover these laws by collecting empirical data, society members claimed that social science might become "the science of the age" and produce "an earthly

---

26. Jackson, *Baldwin*, 82ff., 139-40, 134. Although most Mugwumps eventually returned to the Republican fold post-Blaine, Baldwin became a Democrat.

27. Jackson, 94-95, 125-132, 106, 136, 214. Baldwin was unenthusiastic about the major contemporary innovation in legal education, the casebook method instigated by Christopher Columbus Langdell at Harvard. Simeon E. Baldwin, "Education for the Bar in the United States," *American Political Science Review*, 9 (August 1915), 437-448.

paradise—an enchanted ground."[28] Eventually, the utopianism of the ASSA began to seem impracticable when compared with more hardheaded notions of reform; and the Association collapsed—though not before it had served as the matrix from which emerged the American Economic Association, the American Political Science Association, the American Historical Association, and the American Bar Association.

During an informal conversation at the 1877 ASSA meeting, someone casually suggested the creation of a national association of lawyers, and the thirty-eight-year old Baldwin immediately threw his organizational skills behind the proposal. A former college classmate encouraged him, suggesting such an organization would stimulate legal reform.[29]

At the annual meeting of the Connecticut State Bar Association in January 1878, Baldwin moved that a committee of three be appointed to consider the propriety of organizing a national association of lawyers. More active and businesslike than most of its counterparts, the Connecticut Association approved the motion and appointed Baldwin, Governor Richard D. Hubbard (1818-1884), and William Hamersley (1838-1920) as committee members. A favorable assessment by the committee was assured because both the governor and

---

28. Carroll Wright, "The Growth and Purpose of Bureaus of Statistics," *Journal of Social Science*, 25 (1888), 2-3; Daniel Coit Gilman, "Opening Address"(1880), quoted in Mary O. Furner, *Advocacy and Objectivity: Crisis in the Professionalization of Social Science* (Lexington: University Press of Kentucky, 1975), 21.

29. Baldwin credited the suggestion to Louisiana attorney Felix P. Poché. Simeon E. Baldwin, "The Founding of the American Bar Association," 658; Baldwin diary, July 12, 1916; Anthony Higgins to Simeon E. Baldwin, October 15, 1877, Baldwin Family Papers, Yale University.

Hamersley, a friend of Baldwin's and a founder of the state association, were sympathetic to legal reform.[30]

Baldwin then traded on the reputation of the governor to gain endorsements for the proposed association from thirteen prominent attorneys: Hubbard himself, Judge Charles Devens (1820-1891) of Massachusetts, Charles O'Conor (1804-1884) of New York, Secretary of State William M. Evarts (1818-1901) of New York, S. Teackle Wallis (1816-1894) of Maryland, former Senator Charles R. Buckalew (1821-1899) of Pennsylvania, Alexander R. Lawton (1818-1896) of Georgia, Carleton Hunt (1836-1921) of Louisiana, former Senator John B. Henderson (1826-1913) of Missouri, former Senator Lyman Trumbull (1813-1896) of Illinois, Governor George Hoadly (1826-1902) of Ohio, Judge Thomas M. Cooley (1824-1898) of Michigan, and Senator Stanley Matthews (1824-1889) of Ohio.[31]

---

30. Jackson, *Baldwin,* 80; Baldwin, "The Founding of the American Bar Association," 659; "William Hamersley," *National Cyclopaedia of American Biography* [*NCAB*], 19: 371; "Richard Dudley Hubbard," *NCAB,* 10: 342; Victor M. Gordon, ed., "A History of the First One Hundred Years of the Connecticut Bar Association, 1875-1975," 49 *Connecticut Bar Journal* 201 (1975), 201-226.

31. Baldwin, "The Founding of the American Bar Association,"659. Although Baldwin did the lion's share of the work, Hubbard and Hamersley were not complete ciphers, each writing to leading lawyers with whom they were acquainted. Hamersley to Baldwin, June 1, 1878, Baldwin Papers. There are discrepancies in Baldwin's reminiscences about the names and the numbers of lawyers to whom requests for signatures were sent.

The young Melvil Dewey (1851-1931) founded the American Library Association in 1876 using the same strategy as Baldwin: gaining endorsements from the most influential librarians in the country for his proposed organization. Wayne A. Wiegand, *The Politics of an Emerging Profession:*

When Devens, O'Conor, Wallis, Buckalew, Henderson, and Cooley either did not respond or declined to allow their names to be used, Baldwin invited "a few others" to endorse the organizational effort. These included Senator Benjamin Bristow (1832-1896) of Kentucky, Henry Hitchcock (1829-1902) of Missouri, Richard McMurtrie (1819-1894) of Pennsylvania, John K. Porter (1819-1892) of New York, Charles Train (1817-1885) of Massachusetts, J. Randolph Tucker (1823-1879) of Virginia, and Edward J. Phelps (1822-1900) of Vermont. Today, few of these men would be familiar even to American historians, but in their day, they were prominent figures. At the turn of the 21st century, thirteen remained of sufficient historical prominence to warrant a sketch in *American National Biography.*[32]

A composite portrait reveals striking similarities in background and political viewpoint. Nine of the twenty were Democrats, and eight were Republicans, but nearly all had a history of political independence. Charles Devens and Stanley Matthews had defended the Fugitive Slave Laws to their political detriment before becoming colonels in the Union army. Carleton Hunt, who held strong Union sympathies, fought for the Confederacy. After the war the twenty, almost to a man, opposed the Radicals. O'Conor, Tucker, and Hoadly represented Jefferson Davis or his estate; Trumbull and

---

The American Library Association, 1876-1917 (New York: Greenwood Press, 1986), 4-13.

32. The following have biographical entries in John A. Garraty and Mark C. Carnes, eds., *American National Biography* (New York: Oxford University Press, 1999), 24 volumes: Bristow, Buckalew, Cooley, Devens, Evarts, Henderson, Hoadly, Hunt, Matthews, O'Conor, Trumbull, Tucker, and Wallis. Three more—Hitchcock, Lawton, and Phelps—have sketches in the older *Dictionary of American Biography* (1928-1936).

Henderson were two of the seven Republicans who saved Andrew Johnson from conviction at his impeachment trial. Some of the twenty switched from one party to another, an oddity in Gilded Age politics. Henderson and Cooley moved from Democrat to Republican, Matthews from Democrat to Republican to Liberal Republican, and Hoadly and Trumbull from Democrat to Republican to Liberal Republican to Democrat.

Only a few of these twenty men had learned their law privately in the manner of Abraham Lincoln. Fourteen had attended college, and a majority had attended law school or had served an apprenticeship in another lawyer's office, or both. Of the six who did not sign the call, four had not attended college.

In 1878, the average age of the twenty was fifty-seven. Most had served in some state or federal office. All were prosperous and did a substantial amount of corporation work, although none were corporation lawyers in the modern sense of that term.

Their most striking similarity was as liberal reformers. O'Conor and Evarts were the chief prosecutors of Boss Tweed; Wallis was president of the Civil Service Reform Association of Maryland; Buckalew reformed the penal code of Pennsylvania; Hunt became city attorney of New Orleans under a reform administration; Bristow and Henderson investigated and prosecuted the Whiskey Ring; Cooley later became Chairman of the Interstate Commerce Commission under Grover Cleveland; Train, as a congressman, served as manager of impeachment proceedings against a corrupt judge; and even McMurtrie, an apolitical black-letter lawyer who had helped return an escaped slave to the South, nevertheless concerned himself with hospital reform and had managed to extract a considerable amount of federal taxes from the firm of investment banker Jay Cooke. Conspicuously absent from the call was the name of that brilliant individualist of the New York bar, David Dudley Field, whose defense of Boss Tweed had further alienated him from professional colleagues already offended by his egotism.[33]

Only four of the fourteen who signed the call—Bristow, Hitchcock, Phelps, and Hunt—attended the organizational meeting. The remainder (saving Randolph Tucker and Alexander Lawton) played no significant role in Association affairs. Nevertheless, their places were taken by a similar, though slightly younger, group which included Baldwin himself, Luke Poland (1815-1887) of Vermont, James Broadhead (1819-1898) of Missouri, George G. Wright (1820-1896) of Iowa, John H. B. Latrobe (1803-1891) of Maryland, Thomas Jenkins Semmes (1824-1899) of Louisiana, William Allen Butler (1825-1902) of New York, and Francis Rawle (1846-1930) of Pennsylvania.[34]

---

33. Wayne K. Hobson, *The American Legal Profession and the Organizational Society, 1890-1930* (New York: Garland Publishing, 1986), 221; "Richard C. McMurtrie," 42 *American Law Register* 845-85 (1894). John K. Porter, who had defended President Grant's corrupt private secretary Orville E. Babcock, was a bit of an exception, but he did serve as the first president of the New York State Bar Association and had been included at the request of O'Conor, who suggested that his former legal apprentice replace him on the call. Charles O'Conor to Richard Hubbard, May 14, 1878, in Baldwin, "The Founding of the American Bar Association," 663-664.

For excellent discussions of Field's running battle with the Association of the Bar of the City of New York, see George Martin, *Causes and Conflicts*, 55-60, 88-103, and Samuel Haber, *The Quest for Authority and Honor in the American Professions, 1750-1900* (Chicago: University of Chicago Press, 1991), 209-210.

34. All members of the "Saratoga clique," identified as such by James

This "Saratoga clique," which was to direct the Association for at least its first decade, was also reform-minded. Broadhead had acted as special counsel for the government in the Whiskey Ring scandal, and Poland was noted for his congressional investigations of the Crédit Mobilier, the Ku Klux Klan, and the carpetbag government of Arkansas. The only significant difference between the men asked to sign the call and the members of the "Saratoga clique" was the more vigorous interest of the latter in reforming legal education.

After Baldwin had acquired the approval of fourteen bar leaders, he printed a call for organization that had already been circulating for several months in manuscript. Baldwin represented himself as a sort of secretary who would report the views of the recipients to the August meeting.[35] In trying to determine which elite lawyers might be interested in the project, Baldwin was forced to rely on personal acquaintance and word of mouth. A third of those invited lived in Connecticut or the neighboring states of New York and Massachusetts.[36]

Grafton Rogers, received biographical sketches in the *Dictionary of American Biography*. Poland, Broadhead, and Latrobe also have entries in *American National Biography*. Lawton, Hunt, Hitchcock, and Tucker were either members of the ASSA or had attended the 1877 meeting of the Judicial Department at which Baldwin had spoken. James Grafton Rogers, "The American Bar Association in Retrospect," 176-178. Rogers' informal sources probably overestimated the importance of the clique in the early years of the Association.

35. "Call for a Meeting to Form an American Bar Association," 1 *American Bar Association Reports* [*ABA Rep*] 4 (1878).

36. Francis Rawle, "How the Association Was Organized," 14 *American Bar Association Journal* [*ABAJ*] 375 (1928); Baldwin, "Founding of the American Bar Association," 671-672. Baldwin kept a large notebook, no longer extant, containing the names of the 607 men to whom the call was sent.

Baldwin chose Saratoga Springs as the meeting site because wealthy lawyers often vacationed at this era's most fashionable spa. Saratoga was central to the East, from which the ABA was to draw most of its members, and its racetrack and cool temperatures appealed to Southerners. As the only resort of its day with three large hotels, Saratoga had already established a reputation for accommodating professional organizations.[37]

About 80% of those who received Baldwin's call ignored it, sixty-four men expressed approval but replied that they could not attend, and fifty-four said they would come.[38] Those who responded favorably to Baldwin's call seemed to have had reasonably congruent notions about what a national bar association should accomplish. The reforms they considered necessary for the good of the profession were included in the four purposes adopted by the Saratoga assembly as Article I of the Association's constitution: "to advance the science of jurisprudence, promote the administration of justice and uniformity of legislation throughout the Union, uphold the honor of the profession of the law, and encourage cordial intercourse among members of the American bar."[39]

In an era of rising prestige for scientific professions, the belief that a national bar association ought "to advance the science of jurisprudence" was meant literally. In his reply to

---

37. George Waller, *Saratoga: Saga of an Impious Era* (New York: Bonanza Books, 1965), 75; Rawle, "How the Association Was Organized," 375. On Gilded Age Saratoga, see R. F. Dearborn, *Saratoga and How to See It* (Albany: Weed, Parson's & Co., 1873); Hugh Bradley, *Such Was Saratoga* (New York: Doubleday, Doran and Company, Inc., 1940), and Gerald Carson, *A Good Day at Saratoga* (Chicago: American Bar Association, 1978).
38. Rawle, "How the Association was Organized," 375.
39. 1 *ABA Rep* 16 (1878).

Baldwin, Judge Gustave Koerner (1809-1896) anticipated that the meetings of the new association would become "scientific conferences of Jurists [that would] assist in laying practical measures of reform before the National and State legislatures."[40]

The promotion of "uniformity of legislation throughout the Union" was perhaps the greatest concern of Baldwin's correspondents and one that could not be effectively addressed by local or state associations. Burgeoning national corporations and expanding interstate trade made the diversity of commercial law annoyingly inefficient for lawyers. Even at the first meeting, a Committee on Commercial Law was authorized to examine laws concerning negotiable paper, "looking toward further uniformity in the law on that subject."[41]

To "uphold the honor of the profession" was a euphemism for raising standards of legal education and admission to the bar. Many of Baldwin's correspondents feared that the new organization might founder unless its membership could be restricted to those of "high standing in the profession." Only gentlemen, it was believed, could carry forward "such true reforms as [were] in harmony with the progressive spirit of the age." At the organizational meeting both Baldwin and Henry Smith (1829-1884) of Albany, former speaker of New York State Assembly, "argued forcibly" that the new association should admit no unworthy members.[42]

---

40. Gustave Koerner to Baldwin, August 3, 1878, in Baldwin, "The Founding of the American Bar Association," 680.

41. Gustave Koerner to Baldwin, August 3, 1878, and Senator Charles Jones to Baldwin, August 10, 1878, in Baldwin, "The Founding," 680, 682.

42. Judge E. W. Stanley to Baldwin, July 24, 1878, and Chief Judge William C. Ruger to Baldwin, August 1, 1878, in Baldwin, "The Found-

Baldwin perhaps hoped to de-emphasize the final objective of the ABA, establishing "cordial intercourse among members of the bar." Baldwin listed it last both in the constitution and the preliminary circular, although in the call itself "comparison of views and friendly intercourse" appeared first. But even sociability had a serious side, as for instance, the restoration of harmony among northern and southern lawyers following the Civil War and Reconstruction.[43]

The convention could hardly have been better timed to expedite the "road to reunion." The organizational meeting followed the Compromise of 1877, which ended Reconstruction, and it took place during a Southern yellow fever epidemic that stimulated organized relief efforts in the North and subsequent expressions of gratitude from the South.[44] Elite lawyers, who were often pragmatic in their politics and who represented the interests of national economic development, moved in the vanguard of Americans who wanted to overcome the bitter sectionalism that followed the Civil War.[45]

---

ing," 677, 679; Green Durbin to Baldwin, July 23, 1878, 688; *New York Tribune*, August 22, 1878, 1. "Upholding the honor of the profession" was of great importance to Baldwin. "Why," he queried his diary, "am I with my scholarly tastes and capabilities groveling among ants, . . . when my mind might find more congenial occupation in other fields? But is there any aim higher than that of raising the standard of your profession?" (Baldwin diary, February 8, 1874, Baldwin Papers.)

43. Gustave Koerner to Baldwin, August 3, 1878, in Baldwin, "The Founding," 680; Rogers, "The American Bar Association," 180. Koerner wrote that a national bar association would have "a most powerful tendency to weaken mutual prejudices, to produce harmonious and fraternal feelings amongst an influential and leading class of men, and would be a means of cementing our Union, so lately disrupted."

44. Paul H. Buck, *The Road to Reunion, 1865-1900* (Boston: Little, Brown and Company, 1937), 140-41.

45. "Current Topics," 18 *Alb. Law J.* 141 (August 24, 1878); Jacob Weart,

Only hours after its appointment, a committee to report a constitution for the Association returned with a completed draft. Baldwin had actually written it during his summer vacation. It was adopted by the Association with only minor alterations.[46]

The unanimous election of James O. Broadhead as the first president of the Association symbolized both the strengths and the weaknesses of the new organization. Broadhead was the epitome of the "best men of the bar." A native of Charlottesville, Virginia, he had attended the University of Virginia for a single session before moving to Missouri, where he later became a lecturer at St. Louis Law School (later, Washington University). Broadhead was "a rather old-fashioned country practitioner . . . careless about details, sometimes slipshod in his work," who, nevertheless, successfully represented railroad interests before the United States Supreme Court. A strong Union man during the Civil War, he was in great part responsible for preventing the fall of Missouri to the Confederacy. Then after the war, he became a Democrat and took a former Confederate officer as a law partner. Broadhead acquired a reputation as a reformer from his fierce prosecutions of the Whiskey Ring, a notorious Collector of Internal Revenue in St. Louis, and the venal Chief Clerk of the Treasury Department. Not a theorist or

---

"The American Bar Association: Its History for the First Sixteen Years of its Existence and its Impress Upon the Thought of the Nation," 27 *New Jersey Law Journal* 338 (1904).

During the second meeting, Edward J. Phelps declaimed, "We come together from all parts of our country—our common country—from the scenes of desolation and sorrow on all hands, that God alone can estimate .... Let it all pass. We come to bury the armed Caesar, not to praise him." Edward J. Phelps, "Chief Justice Marshall," 2 *ABA Rep* 173 @ 191 (1879).

46. Baldwin, "The Founding," 691-693; 33 *ABA Rep* 54 (1908).

even very versatile in the law, Broadhead was renowned for his integrity. One contemporary called him "the most independent figure in the history of Missouri." Another said he was "a lion—when he was awake."[47]

Perhaps Senator Charles Jones (1834-1897) of Florida best summarized the motives of the ABA founders when, in his reply to the call, he urged that elite lawyers ought to "study the laws, not alone for profit" but to provide "a calm conservative power which can expose fallacies, point out abuses, and suggest reforms without violence or shock to our government."[48] Reflecting that optimism, Baldwin confided to his diary that the American Bar Association had been "born nicely [with] full weight and good prospects."[49]

---

47. Rogers, *American Bar Leaders,* 1-8; "James O. Broadhead: A Subject for Reappraisal," *Missouri Historical Society Bulletin,* 27 (January 1971), 125-128.

48. Charles Jones to Baldwin, August 10, 1878, in Baldwin, "The Founding," 681-82. Jones himself played no role in the Association because he soon descended into madness. Judy Nicholas Etemadi, "'A Love-Mad Man': Senator Charles W. Jones of Florida," *Florida Historical Quarterly* 56:2 (October 1977), 123-137.

49. Simeon Baldwin diary, August 31, 1878, Baldwin Family Papers.

Chapter 2

Struggles for Survival
1878-1891

Though Association leaders were conservative reformers at heart, during its first dozen years the ABA endorsed professional change only if it had no other choice. Contemporaries noted and ridiculed its timidity. Still, the leadership believed caution was a priority as the association struggled to survive. One member recalled that during the early years, he never met with the chairman of the Executive Committee "without a discussion as to whether the Association could live."[1]

The position of the American Bar Association was, in many ways, analogous to other professional societies founded during the late 1870s and early 1880s, such as the American Chemical Society (1876) and the American Historical Association (1884). All three organizations were organized in New York by men under forty; the ABA and AHA even shared a common parent in the American Social Science

---

1. Jacob Weart, "The American Bar Association: Its History for the First Sixteen Years of Its Existence..." 27 *New Jersey Law Journal* 292 @ 295 (1904); Francis Rawle to Simeon Baldwin, August 6, 1879, and May 26, 1884, Baldwin Papers.

Association.[2] A few influential members in all three groups made the key decisions, and all three surmounted a challenge from a professional competitor.

The American Bar Association had some good luck, but its early leaders also deserve credit for reducing the odds of failure. Their prudence stimulated a steady growth members, so that by 1891, the American Bar Association, if not truly a professional organization, at least passed for one in public regard.

Its official governing body was the Executive Committee.[3] Originally consisting of the Secretary, the

---

2. Kenneth M. Reese, "American Chemical Society: The First100 Years," *Chemical & Engineering News*, 54 (April 6, 1976), 22-31; David D. Van Tassel, "From Learned Society to Professional Organization: The American Historical Association, 1884-1900," *American Historical Review*, 89 (1984), 929-956.

3. With only minor changes, Simeon Baldwin's simple constitution served the Association until 1936. It provided for a General Council consisting of one member from each state and territory, chosen by members present at the annual meeting. The General Council was the nominating committee for Association officers and, as such, became the focus of attention for prospective Association presidents. Local Councils composed of a vice-president and at least two other members from each state or territory made nominations for membership. The vice-presidents and Local Council members were usually chosen more for their reputation back home than for their prominence in Association affairs. For instance, John Norton Pomeroy learned of his selection as a vice-president by reading about it in a newspaper. The Association soon learned not to rely on the vice-presidents for any serious work. Edson R. Sunderland, *A History of the American Bar Association and its Work* (Chicago: American Bar Association, 1953), 18; James Grafton Rogers, *American Bar Leaders: Biographies of the Presidents of the American Bar Association, 1878-1928* (Chicago: American Bar Association, 1932), 223; Francis Rawle to Simeon Baldwin, January 10, 1880 & October 17, 1890, Baldwin Papers; Nathan

Treasurer, and three other members, the Executive Committee expanded seven times before 1936 until it became a committee of fifteen. Only one treasurer and two secretaries served the Association before 1902, and the elected members of the Executive Committee tended to have long tenures. Thus, the Executive Committee served as a stabilizing—and sometimes stultifying—influence in Association affairs. Between annual meetings the Committee discussed the next program and approved expenses. When, in 1884, a member had the temerity to ask for a report, the chairman coolly replied that the "various processes and modes by which we arrive at certain ends would not be interesting to hear."[4]

Supplementing the Executive Committee was an inner circle of intimates, the "Saratoga clique."[5] Irving Browne, the acerbic editor of the *Albany Law Journal*, called them a "mutual admiration ring" that managed Association affairs "as childishly as possible."[6] (The American Historical Association had a

---

William MacChesney, 41 *ABA Rep* 631-32 (1916); F. Dumont Smith, 52 *ABA Rep* 76 (1927). John Norton Pomeroy to Baldwin, November 30, 1879, Baldwin Papers. When, in 1883, the Committee on Judicial Administration requested "summaries of the judicial systems in the respective states" from all the vice-presidents, it received one reply in 1884 and three more in 1885—at which point the Committee gave up.

4. Sunderland, 19-21; 4 *ABA Rep* 10 (1881); Edward O. Hinkley to Simeon Baldwin, January 8 and 10, 1880, Francis Rawle to Simeon Baldwin, April 12, 1893, Baldwin Papers; 10 *ABA Rep* 12-13 (1887); Luke P. Poland, 7 *ABA Rep* 7-8 (1884).

5. Rogers, *American Bar Leaders*, ix.

6. 20 *Albany Law Journal* 176 (1879); 22 *Alb. Law J.* 162 (1880). Irving Browne (1835-1899) was the H. L. Mencken of the contemporary legal press, "the son of two persons of strongly contrasting personality...a Universalist clergyman of austere character, and...a lady of attractive personality and social charm." In 1879 Browne became editor of the *Albany Law Journal* and quickly brought it "to a foremost place among the

similar circle known as the Nucleus Club, which "met annually at a gay champagne dinner where fundamental policy decisions were made—or so, at least, many members believed.")[7]

To those outside the inner circle, the most prominent member of the early ABA seemed to be Luke Poland, Chairman of the Executive Committee from 1878 until his death shortly before the tenth annual meeting. A tall, flinty Vermonter given to fashions from the age of Daniel Webster, Poland communicated industry, honesty, and the spirit of Horatio Alger. Except for his fidelity to the Republican Party (to the extent of swallowing hard and supporting Blaine in 1884), he was typical of the gentlemen reformers who had organized the Association. As a senator he sponsored national bankruptcy legislation and a revision of the federal statute law. His independence and opposition to the Radicals earned him the admiration of congressional moderates and cost him a federal judgeship. Poland's age and dry humor made him a Benjamin Franklin-like figure at the Saratoga meetings.[8]

Edward O. Hinkley (1824-1896) proved a happy choice as secretary. Although a minor figure at the bar, Hinkley had held a few public offices in Baltimore and, like other founding

---

legal periodicals of his day." Browne brought his skeptical eye to bear on the new American Bar Association, and his irreverent treatments of the second through the tenth ABA meetings are delightfully readable. In 1893 Browne resigned his editorial position and joined the faculty of the Buffalo Law School. *Dictionary of American Biography*, 3: 165-166; George Kirchwey, "Irving Browne," 49 *Alb. Law J.* 212-14 (1899).

7. Ray Allen Billington, "Tempest in Clio's Teapot: The American Historical Association Rebellion of 1915," *American Historical Review* 78 (1973), 348.

8. James Fairbanks Colby, "Luke Potter Poland," *DAB*, 8: 33-34; "Luke P. Poland," 10 *ABA Rep* 431 (1887); Weart, "The American Bar Association," 294-95; 30 *Alb. Law J.* 161 (1884); 19 *American Law Review* 777 (1888).

members of the ABA, was an active spokesman for good government and civil service reform. Hinkley was courteous, diligent, deferential, a man who reveled in routine.[9]

Even more significant to the success of the Association was Francis Rawle, who served as treasurer and as a *de facto* executive secretary. Rawle had been born into a distinguished Philadelphia legal family and had graduated from Phillips Exeter, Harvard, and Harvard Law School. An oarsman at Harvard, he kept his tall frame "in trim to the last with systematic exercises." Rawle held the post of treasurer for twenty-four years. Even after his term of office as president in 1902–03, Rawle remained influential in Association affairs for another quarter century, outliving all the other charter members.[10]

In temperament the polar opposite of Hinkley, Rawle was stiff, censorious, and a worrier over trifles; but he nonetheless proved an excellent administrator. Rawle assumed the two biggest jobs of the early Association: planning the banquet and editing the annual *Report.* He seems to have had a fine sense of discernment about such then-important matters as the arrangement of banquet toasts.[11] Misspellings and

9. "Edward Otis Hinkley," 19 *ABA Rep* 653 (1896); 30 *Alb. Law J.* 161 (August 30, 1884) and 36 *Alb. Law J.* 161 (August 27, 1887); Hinkley to Rawle, August 27, 1881; Rawle to Baldwin, May 26, 1884, April 13, 1893, and May 4, 1894, Baldwin Papers.

10. Rogers, *American Bar Leaders*, 121-125; Rogers, "The American Bar Association in Retrospect," 176-177; "Francis Rawle," *DAB*, 15: 400-401; "Rawle, Francis," Roger K. Newman, ed., *The Yale Biographical Dictionary of American Law* (New Haven: University Press, 2009), 447.

11. Rawle to Baldwin, August 6, 1879, May 26, 1884, July 11, 1888, October 17, 1890, April 12, 1893, May 4,1894, Baldwin Papers; Edward Hinkley to Henry St. George Tucker, May 2, 1905, Tucker Papers; "The

typographical errors in the *Report* are extremely rare, though Rawle was not above excising remarks he thought "meaningless and badly expressed" or discussions he believed too heated to properly represent the dignity of the American Bar Association.[12]

At Saratoga the annual meetings—always held in August for the first twenty-five years—were composed of three parts: the delivery of speeches and papers, the reports of committees and, when time allowed, general discussion. By constitutional provision, the president was required to open the meeting with an address summarizing "the most noteworthy changes in statute law" during the previous year. It was a chore to collect and deliver this dreary catalog, but because such a compilation was unavailable elsewhere, both presidents and their audiences persevered for thirty-five years.[13]

The annual meeting also featured three to five other speeches. Speakers were chosen by the Executive Committee, often at the suggestion of some member of the inner circle with attention paid to geographical balance. In the Association's infancy, speakers of the proper quality were difficult to enlist for an unpaid duty during a vacation month. Rawle and Hinkley frequently composed a list of possible

---

American Bar Association," 20 *Alb. Law J.* 176 (August 30, 1879); Weart, "The American Bar Association," 294; Rogers, *American Bar Leaders*, 123.

12. Rawle to Baldwin, December 22, 1879, September 6, 1883, January 17, 1888, Baldwin Papers. As an example of Rawle's ruthless editing, compare Irving Browne's lively account of the ABA debate over possible solutions to the backlog of cases on the Supreme Court docket with the bland version given in the *Report*. 26 *Alb. Law J.* 141 @ 142 (August 19, 1882); 5 *ABA Rep* (1882).

13. "The American Bar Association," 18 *American Law Review* 871 (1884); *New York Times*, August 29, 1889, 5; *Detroit Evening News*, August 27, 1895, 6.

speakers and then wrote invitations until they received the proper number of acceptances.[14]

Unsurprisingly, speeches varied dramatically in quality. But then neither Baldwin nor the other founders believed that speechmaking would accomplish the true objective of the organization. Rather they hoped that standing committees would prepare detailed reports on which the Association might eventually act.

Unfortunately, the standing committee system was never effective. Presidents tended to appoint prominent figures to committee positions with little regard as to whether they would report—or even appear—at the next meeting. Even conscientious committeemen had difficulty conferring because, for balance, members were often geographically separated. Frequently two or three committee members would reach agreement on a report by mail or in hasty conference before the meeting. Some committees rarely made any report; membership on the Grievance Committee was purely honorific.[15] The Association program was usually too

---

14. By-Law I, 5 *ABA Rep* 116 (1882); Rawle to Baldwin, January 17, 1888. Luke Poland to Baldwin, May 24, 1882; Rawle to Baldwin, May 26, 1884, October 17, 1890, April 12, 1893; Henry Hitchcock to Baldwin, February 18, 1884; Lyman Trumbull to Baldwin, December 31, 1890; Rawle to Baldwin, May 26, 1884; Edward Hinkley to Baldwin, June 14, 1884; Rawle to Baldwin, April 12, 1893, Baldwin Papers. Rawle was regularly put out with both the speakers and their choice of topics. Rawle to Baldwin, July 11, 1888, Baldwin Papers. For their effort, speakers received two hundred copies of their speech. 3 *ABA Rep* 9 (1880).

15. Sunderland, *American Bar Association*, 21-22; Simeon Baldwin, 33 *ABA Rep* 54 (1908); Baldwin to Rawle, January 20, 1888; 22 *Alb. Law J.* 162 @ 163 (August 28, 1880); Henry Hitchcock to Baldwin, April 12, 1886, July 15, 1886, & September 23, 1889; William Allen Butler to Baldwin, August 4, 1879, January 18, 1882, January 31, 1882, and September 7, 1885; Rawle to

crowded to permit proper discussion of committee reports in any case, and the holiday atmosphere that enveloped Saratoga at the height of the social season was hardly conducive to the consideration of controversial questions.

Still, good fellowship and shared professional gossip was put to serious use. Prospective judges or district attorneys solicited recommendations from professional friends in other parts of the country in order to demonstrate that they had some reputation outside their own communities.[16] Social activities also helped smooth over ever-present political differences that threatened professional unity.[17]

Even if the ABA had curtailed its social activities and abandoned the elite resort of Saratoga, annual meetings would still have given short shrift to committee reports. The prevailing attitude was that decisions committing the Association ought to be reached deliberately and that making

---

Baldwin, June 13, 1882; Baldwin to members of the ABA Committee on Jurisprudence and Law Reform, December 20, 1886, Baldwin Papers. Twenty years later the politics of choosing convention speakers, committee members, and the next meeting site remained very much the same. Henry St. George Tucker Papers, October 1904 - July 1905.

16. Rawle to Baldwin, May 5, 1887, Baldwin Papers, in regard to the recommendation of Walter George Smith to be a U.S. District Attorney. Baldwin to President Benjamin Harrison, October 27, 1890, March 5, 1891; The White House to Baldwin, March 23, 1891; Baldwin to R. S. Taylor, March 28, 1891; Horace Lurton to Baldwin, March 23, 1891; George G. Mercer to Baldwin, January 18, 1894, January 20, 1894; Frederick Wadhams to H. St. G. Tucker, November 27, 1912, Tucker Papers; Hampton Carson to President Grover Cleveland, January 22, 1894, Baldwin Papers; Frances Casey Meldrim, "How the 7th Army Corps Happened to Encamp in Savannah," Meldrim Family Papers, Box 3.

17. Hobson, *The American Legal Profession and the Organizational Society*, 225ff; J. H. Kennard to Baldwin, October 10, 1884, Baldwin Papers; 14 *American Law Review* 446 (1880); 40 *ABA Rep* 6 (1915).

no decision was preferable to making a controversial one. Considering its brief history and limited membership, the Association could ill afford divisive squabbles, especially about matters about which it could, in any case, do nothing but express an opinion. Still, some Association leaders appreciated the irony that an organization founded to reform the legal profession took pains not to disturb the status quo.[18]

As a rule, motions exciting any controversy were immediately tabled, postponed, or referred back to committee. For instance, at the second annual meeting in 1879, Carleton Hunt, dean of the law department of the University of Louisiana (Tulane), presented as the report of the Committee of Legal Education, a detailed proposal advocating stiff law school requirements necessary for admission to the bar. When his motions were tabled, Hunt returned the following year with revisions that he predicted would receive "unanimous approval." Instead, the Association again tabled three of Hunt's four resolutions and settled for a watered-down version of the fourth which, in effect, allowed that law was worthy of study. Sunderland's official history notes dryly that "for some reason [the] tremendous burst of committee activity suddenly died, and nothing further was done in the field of legal education for 9 years."[19]

---

18. John L. T. Sneed, 5 *ABA Rep* 89 (1882); 12 *ABA Rep* 27 (1889); John W. Stevenson, "Address of the President," 8 *ABA Rep* 149 @ 199 (1885); 2 *ABA Rep* 19 (1879); 4 *ABA Rep* 51-52 (1881); 5 *ABA Rep* 32 (1882); Cortlandt Parker, "Address of the President," 7 *ABA Rep* 147 @ 201 (1884); 10 *ABA Rep* 21 (1887).

19. 20 *Alb. Law J.* 176 @ 177 (August 30, 1879). For instance, a fairly non-controversial resolution recommending a national bankruptcy law was referred to committee in 1886, reported on favorably in 1887, but not approved by the Association until 1889—and then without recommending

Two proposals to reform criminal law suggested by Simeon Baldwin met an identical fate. Edward Hinkley did no better with a proposal that the Association establish a standing committee on constitutional law. Irving Browne sneered that the Association had decided there was no need for such a committee, "or to speak more accurately, no conclusion was reached, which is more in accordance with the habit and traditions of the association."[20] Because Hunt, Baldwin, and Hinkley were all members of the Association's inner circle, the rough handling given to their proposals clearly reflects the Association's reluctance to endorse reformist schemes.

Strangely, the Association received heightened reputation from two controversies in which inertia was either not an alternative or could be ranged on either side of the question. The first of these controversies centered on a long-standing professional disagreement about whether the traditional judge-made law of English-speaking nations ought to be replaced by a Napoleonic-style code. In 1884, the chief American proponent of codification, David Dudley Field, joined the ABA and immediately proposed a select committee to investigate remedies for "delay and uncertainly in judicial

---

of any of the specific bills proposed by the committee. 9 *ABA Rep* 79 (1886); 10 *ABA Rep* 344-358 (1887); 12 *ABA Rep* 29, 35 (1889); 20 *Alb. Law J.* 176 @ 177 (August 30, 1879); 2 *ABA Rep* 209-236 (1879); 3 *ABA Rep* 15 (1880); 3 *ABA Rep* 13-37 (1880); 4 *ABA Rep* 30, 237-301 (1881); Sunderland, 73.

20. 8 *ABA Rep* 22 (1885); 10 *ABA Rep* 55-78 (1887); "American Bar Association," 21 *American Law Review* 1001 (1887); 34 *Alb. Law J.* 161 (August 28, 1886); 4 *ABA Rep* 10-24 (1881); 24 *Alb. Law J.* 161 (August 27, 1881); 20 *Alb. Law J.* 176 @ 177 (August 30, 1879) and 30 *Alb. Law J.* 161 (August 30, 1884); *New York Times,* August 19, 1887, 4; 28 *Alb. Law J.* 161 (September 1, 1883).

administration." Appointed chairman of the committee in accordance with parliamentary tradition, Field appeared the following year with fourteen recommendations for the reform of the judicial system. Thirteen were innocuous. The fourteenth proposed that the "the law itself should be reduced, so far as possible, to the form of a statute"—the word "statute" being substituted for "code" in deference to the sensibilities of lawyers who choked at the mention of Field's Code of Civil Procedure, which had been enacted by the state of New York in 1848. Anti-code members managed to postpone debate until the following year on the ground that codification was the most important matter ever brought before the Association. ("When, in Heaven's name, was anything else of importance ever brought before it?" jeered Browne.)[21]

The postponed debate lasted a day and a half, with Field performing in his usual abrasive manner.[22] In the end, a compromise was proposed: "The law itself should be reduced, so far as its substantive principles are settled, to the form of a statute." The Association passed this proposal 58 to 41, although no one could say for sure what it meant.

---

21. The best introduction to the codification controversy is Lawrence M. Friedman, *A History of American Law*, 3rd ed. (New York: Simon and Schuster, 2005), 293-98, and George Martin, *Causes and Conflicts* (Boston: Houghton Mifflin Company, 1970), 142-157; see *8 ABA Rep* 323-449 (1885); 9 *ABA Rep* 325-358 (1886); 19 *American Law Review* 777 @ 780 (1885). Many years later Elihu Root recalled New York lawyers "in consultation with the author, describe the book as 'your damned code, Mr. Field.'" Elihu Root, "The Layman's Criticism of the Lawyer," 30 *ABA Rep* 386 @ 399 (1914). 32 *Alb. Law J.* 161 (August 29, 1885).

22. John Hinkley, "Reminiscences of the American Bar Association," 21 *ABAJ* 452 @ 455 (1935); 9 *ABA Rep* 11-74 (1886); *New York Times*, August 21, 1886, 2.

Newspapers and legal journals gave the palm to Field and the codifiers, but as Hinkley's son wrote, "[N]o one did any more codifying or less codifying than before the controversy."[23]

Choosing sides in the codification debate was more a matter of a member's geography than his ideology. Lawyers from the South and West, who typically practiced under codes, supported Field, while those who lived in the Northeast defended common-law pleading. Although Association leaders were probably annoyed at Field's co-option of their agenda, they were not in agreement about codification.

The same geographical, rather than ideological, divisions marked a debate about possible solutions to the crippling backlog of cases on the contemporary Supreme Court docket. On this question inertia was not an viable choice. To make any claim to professional responsibility, the Association had to recommend a solution.

By 1880 the number of pending cases on the United States Supreme Court docket had reached 1,212, a staggering burden that resulted partly from the growth of commercial and patent legislation and partly as a by-product of Reconstruction. For political reasons, Congress had simplified the procedure for removing cases from state to federal courts; and corporations, which preferred the appointed judiciary of the federal system, soon swamped

23. Hinkley, 455; 34 *Alb. Law J.* 161 @ 162 (August 28, 1886); *New York Times,* August 21, 1886, 41; Austen G. Fox, 9 *ABA Rep* 59 (1886). By the time Max Radin wrote a short history of the Association in 1939, even that quasi-endorsement of codification had become non-history. Max Radin, "The Achievements of the American Bar Association," 25 *ABAJ* 1007 (1939). Likewise, when James D. Andrews referred to the controversy in 1906, he asserted that the "battle fell against Mr. Field." 29 *ABA Rep* 58 (1906).

them. In 1881, the American Bar Association established a nine-member special committee of politically prominent members to suggest a course of action. That committee then split five to four. The minority, all from the Northeast (and therefore within a reasonable distance of the Supreme Court), endorsed dividing the Court into three divisions, the justices assembling *en banc* to consider only constitutional or other very important questions. The committee majority adopted the plan of Illinois senator (and former Justice) David Davis (1815-1886), which established intermediate circuit courts of appeal.[24] After an emotional debate (most of which Rawle struck from the *Report*), the majority's report prevailed by twelve votes.[25]

Of course the endorsement of the ABA did not enact the Davis bill. The party holding power in one branch of Congress was loath to deliver to a President of the opposite party the vast patronage involved in appointing so many new judges. But eventually the situation grew so critical that the Supreme Court justices themselves felt compelled to speak out.[26]

Finally, when Republicans regained control of both houses of Congress in 1888, the ABA's special committee successfully urged President Benjamin Harrison to address

---

24. Felix Frankfurter and James Landis, *The Business of the Supreme Court: A Study in the Federal Judicial System* (New York: The Macmillan Company, 1927), 72-73, 80-81, 83, fn. 124; 4 *ABA Rep* 41-84 (1881); Radin, 908; 5 *ABA Rep* 363 (1882).

25. 5 *ABA Rep* 18-102 (1882); 26 *Alb. Law J.* 141 @ 142 (August 19, 1882); 5 *ABA Rep* 101 (1882).

26. *New York Times*, May 6, 1882, 1; Walter B. Hill, "The Federal Judicial System," 12 *ABA Rep* 289 @ 319 (1889); Walter George Smith, 12 *ABA Rep* 9 (1889); Cortlandt Parker, "Address of the President," 7 *ABA Rep* 147 @ 199 (1884); Frankfurter and Landis, 96-97.

the matter in his state of the union address.[27] Meanwhile, William Evarts—a member of the ABA committee, a ranking member of the Judiciary Committee, and a convert to the circuit court plan—led the fight in the Senate. Evarts even invited the ABA's Committee on Judicial Administration and Remedial Procedure to consult with a joint subcommittee of the House and Senate Judiciary Committees in fine-tuning the proposed legislation. The measure received the President's signature on March 3, 1891, and the number of docketed cases before the Supreme Court dropped almost immediately.[28]

The Judiciary Act of 1891 was the first major legislative victory for the American Bar Association, boosting morale and organizational prestige. Still, the triumph was largely fortuitous. Congress would have had to have taken action regardless of the Association's recommendation, and both the appeal of the Supreme Court justices and the Republican sweep of 1888 were more important factors in securing passage of the bill.

Fortunately for the ABA, it had chosen the winning side at a moment when it was being challenged by its only serious competitor. The National Bar Association (1888-1891) had been conceived by members of the Bar Association of the District of Columbia and organized in Washington on May

---

27. Frankfurter and Landis, 97; Walter B. Hill, "The Federal Judicial System," 12 *ABA Rep* 289 @ 322 (1889); John F. Dillon, 13 *ABA Rep* 36 (1890); Henry Hitchcock, "Address of the President," 13 *ABA Rep* 147 @ 155 (1890).

28. Frankfurter and Landis, 98-102; Chester L. Barrows, *William M. Evarts: Lawyer, Diplomat, Statesman* (Chapel Hill: University of North Carolina Press, 1941), 480-82.

22, 1888. Curiously, just four years before, the New York-based American Chemical Society had been challenged in virtually the same way (and with the same ultimate lack of success) by the Chemical Society of Washington.[29]

The National Bar Association attempted to distinguish itself from the American Bar Association in three ways. First, the founders of the new organization emphasized that its primary mission would be the drafting of uniform state laws to promote uniformity, especially in commercial law. Second, membership in the new body was to be "purely representative," that is, it was to be composed of delegates elected by state and local bar associations. Third, despite the desire of the Washington men to create a permanent home for the organization in the nation's capital, they decided—temporarily at least—to hold meetings in a different place each year in order to tap potential interest in other parts of the country.[30]

---

29. National Bar Association, *Preliminary Statement* (Washington, D. C.: McQueen & Wallace, 1888), 5-6. The National Bar Association (1888-1891) is not to be confused with the predominantly black National Bar Association, Inc., founded in 1925. Reese, "American Chemical Society," 23-24.

30. National Bar Association, *Preliminary Statement*, 16, 18, 23, 27-30; *Washington Star*, May 22, 1888, 5; *Washington Post*, May 22, 1888, 3; letter from G. A. F.[inkelnberg], 26 *Central Law Journal* 487 (May 1, 1888). There had been attempts to have the ABA organize (or reorganize) itself along similar lines, but the leadership was cool to the idea. "Current Topics," 20 *Albany Law Journal* 161 (August 30, 1879); Simeon E. Baldwin, "The Founding of the American Bar Association," 3 *ABAJ* 658 @ 668, 678-79 (1917); E. F. Bullard, 5 *ABA Rep* 17 (1882). At the annual meeting of 1888, Rufus King, the founder of the Cincinnati Law School, argued that had the ABA adopted a representative scheme of organization, the "other, styled the National, would not have been formed." 11 *ABA Rep* 14 (1888); see also 32 *Am. L. Rev* 596-97 (1898); 31 *Am. L. Rev.* 749 (1897); 34 *Am. L.*

The National Bar Association made repeated professions of good will towards the ABA, but suspicion remained that the rivalry was more than friendly competition. From Ohio to Georgia, local bar association members noted the "ill-feeling."[31] For instance, the NBA elected as its first president James O. Broadhead, who had been the first president of the American Bar Association as well; and in his acceptance speech, Broadhead implied that the ABA was incapable of spearheading serious reform because of its clubby atmosphere.[32]

Just as the American Chemical Society had been challenged in the mid-1880s during a period of waning

---

Rev. 573 (1900). While ABA by-laws gave temporary "privileges of membership" to delegates from state and local bar associations, there had been little interest in exercising them. Alfred Z. Reed, *Training for the Public Profession of the Law* (New York: Carnegie Foundation for the Advancement of Teaching, 1921), 210. 2 *NBA Proc.* 36 (1889); *Washington Post,* December 10, 1891, 7; *Dinner Given by the Committee of Arrangements Appointed by the Bar Association of the District of Columbia to the Fourth Annual Meeting of the National Bar Association of the United States* (Washington, D. C.: The Arlington Hotel, 1891), 41-42.

31. *Preliminary Statement,* 34; 2 *NBA Proc.* 33-35 (1889); John D. Sullivan, 9 *Ohio State Bar Association Proceedings* 86 (1888), John J. Hall, *OSBA Proc.* 82 (1888); "Major Bacon," 5 *Georgia State Bar Association Proceedings* 26 (1888). In 1886, the American Medical Association was challenged by the "Congress of American Physicians and Surgeons," the organizers of which announced that they had no "intention of offering any obstacle or opposition to any other association in America"; quoted in Samuel Haber, *The Quest for Authority and Honor in the American Professions* (Chicago: University of Chicago Press, 1991), 340.

32. On accepting the presidency of the National Bar Association, Broadhead damned the ABA with faint praise: "The American Bar Association, I think, has established itself. It may not be as efficient as it ought to be, but it has done some good." *Preliminary Statement,* 20-21; Report of the Secretary, 2 *NBA Proc.* 33-37 (1889).

interest in the organization, so too had the ABA meetings of 1887 and 1888 been less than successful. Luke Poland died six weeks before the convention of 1887, and neither Baldwin nor Rawle had attended. Apparently the meeting of 1888 was not much better. Registered attendance was officially 121; but the *American Law Review* reported that it had "dwindled down to about sixty."[33]

Though ABA leaders did not panic, they appreciated the threat.[34] To counter interest in the National Bar Association, Hinkley ostentatiously urged delegates from state and local bar associations to attend ABA meetings. He also tried to arrange reduced railroad fares to Saratoga because the two annual meetings were scheduled so closely together as to put them in virtual competition.[35] At the 1888 meeting, President George Wright took conspicuous note of the representatives of state and local associations, and Simeon Baldwin proposed a less-than-subtle measure to court their favor—a maneuver similar to that in which the leaders of the American Historical Association tried to squelch an attempt to establish an organization of local historical societies.[36]

---

33. C. C. Bonney to Baldwin, July 27, 1888; Rawle to Baldwin, January 17, 1888; Daniel H. Chamberlain to Baldwin, September 13, 1888, Baldwin Papers. Baldwin, Rawle, Field, and E. J. Phelps were in Europe attending the conference of the International Law Association. "The American Bar Association," 22 *Am. L. Rev.* 929 (1888).

34. Rawle to Baldwin, January 17, 1888; Baldwin to George C. Wright, July 9, 1888, Baldwin Papers.

35. Hinkley to Baldwin, June 11, 1888; Baldwin to Hinkley, June 12, 1888, Baldwin Papers; *Washington Star*, May 23, 1888, 1; Reed, 211.

36. 11 *ABA Rep* 13-14, 29, 33, 43 (1888); 12 *ABA Rep* 5-6 (1889); Van Tassel, "From Learned Society to Professional Organization," 949. Baldwin proposed the amendment of a bylaw that forbade representation

The National Bar Association had its own weaknesses. Its leaders grossly underestimated the commitment in time, effort, and money that would be necessary to secure even small changes in the statute law. Discussions about model laws degenerated into petty squabbling, and the five short pieces of legislation actually approved by the association were ignored by legislatures everywhere.[37] Unlike the ABA, the National Bar Association could not afford to hold quasi-professional meetings with high-toned recreation as their true purpose. The new association had been formed, at least in part, in reaction to just such aspects of the ABA. If it could not register timely legal reforms, it would disappear. Furthermore, reforms in legal education and in admission to the bar were at least as important to elite lawyers as were conflicts in state commercial codes. Yet the National Bar Association took no official interest in these questions.[38]

---

by city and county bar associations in a jurisdiction where a state bar association had been organized. Baldwin's amendment would have allowed two delegates from any local association regardless of the existence of a state organization. Since most support for the National Bar Association came from local rather than state bar associations, and since delegates to the NBA would pay dues while those accredited to the ABA would be guests, the change in the bylaw might have sparked open competition between the two associations. But after vigorous debate, the bylaw change was recommitted to the Executive Committee and eventually withdrawn.

37. *Preliminary Statement,* 19. The suggested uniform acts concerned the negotiability of promissory notes, acknowledgments affecting real estate and married women, and limitations of actions, wills, and interstate extradition. 3 *NBA Proc.* 85-89 (1890).

38. Hobson, 253; Norbert Brockman, "The National Bar Association, 1888-1893: The Failure of Early Bar Federation," 10 *American Journal of Legal History* 122 (1966), 125-26. However, contrary to the implication of Brockman's article, the National Bar Association did have a Committee on

Most importantly, the National Bar Association was handicapped by its inability to attract leaders from the highest stratum of the legal profession or even to find an equivalent to the Saratoga clique to guide its affairs. When, in its second year, the association could not replace Broadhead with a president of similar stature, the delegates reelected him over his own objection and in violation of a constitutional provision expressly forbidding it.[39] Most of the original NBA officers were competent if undistinguished, but by 1890, a nonentity was serving as president and a rude egotist as secretary.[40]

Support for the NBA rapidly eroded, and the organization nearly expired during the summer of 1891.[41] Having learned

---

Legal Education and Admission to the Bar that presented reports to the Association in 1889 and 1890.

39. 20 *Weekly Law Bulletin* 132 (August 13, 1888).

40. The president was Charles Marshall, whose chief attribute seems to have been that he was the grandnephew of Chief Justice John Marshall. *Indianapolis News,* August 7, 1890, 1. The secretary was Lewis H. Pike; *National Cyclopaedia of American Biography,* 2: 176; *Indianapolis News,* August 6, 1890, 1, August 7, 1890, 2; 11 *OSBA Proc.* 31 (1890). In the only, scholarly article ever written about the National Bar Association, Norbert Brockman asserts that "the National Bar Association had drawn to its [first] meeting as prominent a group of lawyers as the American Bar Association could boast." "The National Bar Association," 125. Brockman provides as examples future Vice-President Adlai Stevenson, Senator Lyman Trumbull, and Richard Venable of Maryland. Of these, Venable, a professor of law at the University of Maryland, was an ABA member and not an especially notable one. In 1888, Stevenson was only first assistant Postmaster and better known as a politician than a lawyer. Trumbull, another ABA member, never attended an NBA session.

41. In 1889, twenty-four state and local bar associations contributed $1,190 to the treasury. The next year, however, only $654 arrived from eighteen associations. "At every meeting," the last secretary confessed, "we had fewer delegates and less enthusiasm." 20 *Weekly Law Bulletin* 134

a lesson about elitism at the bar, an NBA founder proposed a "senate" composed of the most eminent members of the profession, and the District bar hosted a promotional dinner that featured saddle of mutton, terrapin, and boiled pheasants. The money and amiable speeches were wasted. The National Bar Association never held a fifth meeting.[42]

This brush with a rival encouraged ABA leaders to schedule meetings outside Saratoga. So long as the American Bar Association conceived of itself as a private club, the relatively inaccessible and expensive Saratoga admirably suited its purpose.[43] Although the Association grew from 289 members in 1878 to 751 ten years later—that is, about one percent of all American lawyers—the social status of members remained uniformly high. For instance, of the 94 members from Massachusetts in the years 1878 to 1887, at least 56 were college educated, and 49 had some law school training (almost all at Harvard). At least seventeen were mayors and other local officials, 24 were state representatives or senators, and eight were congressmen, senators, or cabinet members.[44]

(August 13, 1888); "Report of the Treasurer," 2 *NBA Proc.* 82 (1889); 3 *NBA Proc.* 77 (1890). In 1891, the Treasurer did not appear, and there was no treasurer's report. *Washington Post,* December 10, 1891, 7; *Dinner Given by the Committee,* 42; *Washington Post,* December 9, 1891, 6; 15 *Alabama State Bar Association Proceedings* 197-99 (1892).

42. *Dinner Given by the Committee,* 42, 44; *Washington Star,* December 9, 1891, 6; *New York Times,* December 11, 1891, 4.

43. Sunderland, 36. There had been numerous complaints about the Executive Committee's "Saratoga policy." The American Bar Association," 19 *American Law Review* 777 @ 778 (1885); 19 *American L. R.* 717 (1885); 21 *Cent. L. J.* 241 (1885); W. L. Gross, "Presidential Address," 7 *Illinois State Bar Association Proceedings* 50-51 (1884).

44. Only four of the ninety-four ABA members from Massachusetts are not listed in William T. Davis, *Bench and Bar of the Commonwealth of Massachusetts* (Boston: Boston History Company, 1895), 2 vols. There

In 1882, Edward Hinkley actually suggested excluding younger lawyers from Association membership so as to limit participants at the annual banquet to about a hundred, "a good round number," he thought, "ordinarily sufficient for social purposes."[45]

After the founding of the National Bar Association, perceptions changed. Between 1882 and 1887, the Association grew at the rate of approximately fifty members a year; but in the year that the National Bar Association was organized, membership rose by precisely one. A change of meeting site was endorsed by the annual meeting of 1888, and the Executive Committee chose Chicago. Thereafter Saratoga alternated with larger cities until 1902, when the final break was made.[46]

By leaving Saratoga, the ABA also increased the diversity of its membership. At the 1889 Chicago meeting, the ABA admitted 279 new members, most from the Midwest.[47] One of these was Adolph Moses (1837-1906), a highly successful Chicago lawyer and founder of the *National Corporation Reporter*, a weekly legal newspaper. Moses was also a Jew.[48] During the 1880s, Saratoga had been battleground between those hotels that excluded Jews and those that had catered to

---

were never more than 61 Massachusetts members in any one year (1881), and the average was 46.

45. 5 *ABA Rep* 15 (1882). By 1883, Hinkley had completely reversed himself. 6 *ABA Rep* 53 (1883).

46. 11 *ABA Rep* 93 (1888); Sunderland, 38-39.

47. 12 *ABA Rep* 74 (1889).

48. "Adolph Moses," 29 *ABA Rep* 654 (1906); "Adolph Moses," 38 *Chicago Legal News* 100 (1906). Though it is possible that the ABA admitted other Jews to membership before 1889, Moses was certainly the first influential member of obvious Jewish descent. In other words, it is difficult to believe his Jewishness went unnoticed.

an exclusively Jewish clientele.[49] Although by the latter years of the decade the ABA was holding its meetings at Putnam Music Hall, rather than at a hotel, the atmosphere at Saratoga was poisoned. It would have been difficult for a Jewish member to have found welcome in the social activities that were so much a part of the contemporary Association. In Chicago, Moses was admitted without recorded protest. The American Bar Association was still very much a private club—as were the contemporary American Chemical Society and the American Historical Association, for that matter—but by 1891, the ABA's definition of "elite" had enlarged slightly to include lawyers who would never have taken vacations at a fashionable spa.

Other harbingers of professionalism appeared. The list of banquet toasts was dropped from the *Report*, and the Annual Address became less flowery oration, more prosaic lecture. Committees were reimbursed for their expenses, and their reports were printed. The Executive Committee began a gradual expansion. Even the increasingly heated debates at annual meetings, and their coverage by the legal press, testified to the organization's growing seriousness of purpose.

---

49. John Higham, *Send These to Me: Jews and Other Immigrants in Urban America* (New York: Atheneum, 1975), 148-149; Hugh Bradley, *Such Was Saratoga* (New York: Doubleday, Doran and Company, Inc., 1940), 135-159.

Chapter **3**

The "Noiseless, Unobtrusive Way" ***1891-1911***

In the twenty years that separated the passage of the Judiciary Act of 1891 from the Association's first coordinated lobbying effort in 1911, the ABA came to be increasingly viewed as the representative of the American legal profession. Association membership rose, the influence of the Saratoga clique declined, and the Association subdivided itself along lines of professional interest. Meanwhile, the organization continued to shun political controversy. In 1906, President George R. Peck accurately observed that the Association had conducted its public affairs in a "noiseless, unobtrusive way, not joining very conspicuously in the clash of opinions, or fighting in the battle lines of real or imaginary issues."[1]

Of course, Peck was referring only to public controversies. But even internal squabbles were usually resolved decorously, and in private, at a time when the internal feuds of the American Medical Association and the American Library Association were vicious by comparison.[2]

---

1. George R. Peck, "Address of the President," 29 *ABA Rep* 297 @ 298 (1906).

2. Wayne A. Wiegand, *The Politics of an Emerging Profession: The American Library Association, 1876-1917* (New York: Greenwood, 1986), 98-99, 166;

An exception to this rule occurred in 1891 when Simeon Baldwin and other members of the Saratoga clique created an award to be given to some lawyer who had distinguished himself as an author, legislative draftsmen, or originator of "a good reform." Unfortunately for the creators, the irrepressible David Dudley Field lobbied to have the medal awarded to himself—even though he was a member of the awards committee.[3] The medal brouhaha would have been only an amusing trifle had it not been perceived as a defeat for the Saratoga clique. Members of the inner circle had assumed that the annual meeting would rubber-stamp their nominee. Instead, they discovered that the Association had outgrown their control.[4]

Baldwin took the long view. After serving a final term on the Executive Committee, he put formal guidance of Association affairs behind him. He was, he wrote in his diary, "both relieved and half regretful at parting with all active control of the Bar Association [but] it will get along as well, if not better, without me."[5] By this time, the other members of

---

Samuel Haber, *The Quest for Authority and Honor in the American Professions, 1750-1900* (University of Chicago Press, 1991), 338-40.

3. The clique wanted the first medal to go to Sir Roundell Palmer, Lord Selborne (1812-1895), the author of the English Judicature Act of 1873. Eventually a compromise was reached whereby two medals were awarded in 1891. The Association then voted to strike the debate from the *Report.* The bylaw authorizing a medal was repealed, and the ABA made no more awards until 1929. John Hinkley, "Reminiscences of the American Bar Association," 21 *ABAJ* 452 @ 455-56 (1935); *Boston Globe,* August 29, 1891, 9; 55 *ABA Rep* 149-155 (1929); "The American Bar Association Medal," 25 *Amer. L. Rev.* 975 (1891).

4. James Grafton Rogers, "Fifty Years of the American Bar Association," 53 *ABA Rep* 518 @ 528 (1928).

5. Baldwin Diary, August 28, 1892, Baldwin Papers. Unlike Baldwin, Melvil Dewey, the founder of the American Library Association, refused

the leadership group were mostly in their sixties and seventies. Only two served as president after 1891, and only Baldwin, Rawle, and Carleton Hunt were still alive in 1904.

Still, the break with the old order was gradual. Baldwin continued to attend ABA meetings and was, in his own words, "treated with great respect." The position of Secretary was passed from Edward Hinkley to his son and assistant, John Hinkley (1864-1940), before the father's death; and John Hinkley served as a member of the Executive Committee until 1912. Likewise, Francis Rawle served as Treasurer and unofficial editor of the Reports until 1902 and provided advice—solicited and unsolicited—well into the 1920s.[6]

The gradual transformation of the Association between 1891 and 1911 was more a result of organizational growth than a change of leadership. Membership rose from 1,102 in 1891 to 1,720 in 1901, then nearly tripled in the succeeding decade. Baldwin admitted as early as 1891 that approval by an applicant's local council had become a "matter of form"—at least for the proper sort of lawyer.[7]

Membership declined after four of the seven Saratoga meetings between 1889 and 1902. Membership rose when

---

to go quietly and finally was ousted from power by his colleagues. Wayne A. Wiegand, 167.

6. Baldwin Diary, August 28, 1892; Rawle to Baldwin, January 14, 1893, May 4, 1894, August 22, 1898, Baldwin Papers; Rawle to W. Thomas Kemp, September 21, 1922, John W. Davis Papers, is an example of unsolicited advice; see also the correspondence of Henry St. G. Tucker with John Hinkley from November 1904 to May 1905, Tucker Papers.

7. In 1901 the Local Council of Colorado unanimously rejected the application of Senator Thomas MacDonald Patterson (1839-1916), an Irish-born millionaire populist, but then Patterson had gone out of his way to make personal and political enemies. *Denver Post*, August 23, 1901, 1; "Thomas MacDonald Patterson," *DAB*, 8: 308-09.

the Association met in other cities. By the turn of the century, Saratoga had passed its prime as a fashionable resort, and its Convention Hall now seemed "inconvenient, uncomfortable and unpleasant."[8] Except for the Association's fortieth anniversary in 1917, the ABA abandoned Saratoga for good. In any case, Association meetings were so well attended by this period that a resort like Saratoga could no longer provide enough first-class accommodations and a suitable auditorium at the peak of the season.[9]

Nationally known lawyers such as Thomas Cooley, James C. Carter, Moorfield Storey, Joseph Choate, and Alton Parker served as presidents of the Association during this period, and annual banquets were frequently enlivened by facile after-dinner speakers and the appearance of the politically powerful. For instance, in 1897, newly-inducted ABA member and President of the United States, William McKinley, was induced to say a few words to those attending

---

8. Rome Brown, President of the Minnesota Bar Association, in welcoming remarks to the ABA, 20 *ABA Rep* 4 (1906); H. H. Ingersoll, 25 *ABA Rep* 29 (1902).

9. In 1919 the Association was forced to substitute Boston for New London, Connecticut, only three months before the annual meeting, in order to assure adequate hotel accommodations. W. Thomas Kemp to William Howard Taft, June 25, 1919, Taft Papers. The American Library Association moved in the opposite direction. During its first decade it held conventions in major eastern cities; in its fifth decade, it met at resorts. Wiegand, 246-49.

The selection of an annual meeting site was a time-consuming chore for the ABA leadership. Geographical balance and the availability of hotel accommodations were primary considerations. Some attractions in the host city were welcome but not so many that members would ignore the Association meetings. Cool temperatures were preferred.

a dinner at which he, Senator Mark Hanna, and Secretary of War Russell Alger were guests of honor.[10]

Prime acquisitions of program planners were influential British attorneys and judges like Sir Frederick Pollock (1903) and James Bryce (1906). Their visits occurred during a period of growing amity between elites in Great Britain and the United States, and notably among legal scholars who were able to squint Anglo-American common law into a verisimilitude of unity.[11]

The business side of the ABA meetings settled into conventionality, and Association affairs were committed to another inner circle. Composed mainly of former presidents

---

10. 20 *ABA Rep* 99 (1897); 56 *Albany Law Journal* 173 (1897); U. M. Rose, "Address of the President," 25 *ABA Rep* 199 @ 200 (1902); Frances Casey Meldrim, "How the 7th Army Corps Happened to Encamp in Savannah," Peter Meldrim Papers, Box 3. In its earliest days the Association "carefully eschewed any political connection." For instance, Edward Hinkley once advised Rawle not to invite Benjamin Harrison to make a banquet speech "because he was then in politics." Rawle to John W. Davis, June 18, 1923, Davis Papers, Series III, Box 15. Four Supreme Court Justices—White, Peckham, McKenna, and Brown—attended the 1907 meeting at Narragansett Pier. *New York Times*, August 24, 1905, 6.

11. Richard A. Cosgrove, *Our Lady the Common Law: An Anglo-American Legal Community* (New York University Press, 1987), 6-22; *New York Times*, August 20, 1896, 3; Rogers, *American Bar Leaders*, 123; Wadhams to Hinkley, October 25, 1904, Tucker Papers. Lord Russell of Killowen, the Lord Chief Justice, was the first and probably the most handsomely feted of these Englishmen. The idea of inviting him was Francis Rawle's, and he carried off the scheme with a flourish, meeting the Lord Chief Justice in New York harbor and then seeing "him through a round of entertainment furnished by Henry Villard, the elder Pierpont Morgan, the Canadian bar, James Coolidge Carter and the President, Moorfield Storey." The convention of 1896, where Russell appeared, was the last assembly in Saratoga to attract any appreciable number of new members.

and executive committee members, this new group was more fluid than the old Saratoga clique and by necessity shared guidance of the Association with current officeholders, especially the secretaries, treasurers, and the chairmen of the more important committees.[12] The life of the Association gradually passed from the business sessions of the annual meeting to the smaller forums provided by the ABA conventions—the "sections" and other associated bodies, such as the Conference of Commissioners on Uniform State Laws.

Sections were another product of Simeon Baldwin's penchant for creating organizations. In August 1892, a year after the medal debacle, Baldwin met informally at Saratoga with members interested in legal education, and they agreed to create a legal education society at the next ABA convention. At first, Baldwin was uncertain whether this new group would be organically related to the American Bar Association. The idea of calling the group a "section" of the Association came from Baltimore attorney George M. Sharp (1851-1911), a former law student and sometime colleague of Baldwin's at Yale Law School, Sharp being reminded of the sections in medical societies that represented professional specialties.[13]

---

12. Roscoe Pound said that the inner group included Moorfield Storey, Alfred Hemenway, Simeon Baldwin, Jacob M. Dickinson, Frederick W. Lehmann, James Hagerman, Alton B. Parker, George R. Peck, Everett P. Wheeler, and Henry D. Estabrook. Roscoe Pound to Norbert Brockman, May 24, 1960, copy in possession of author. Pound refers to these men only as "those particularly active in the Association." However, there were other active members, such as William A. Ketcham, Walter S. Logan, and R. S. Taylor, to name three, who did not participate in the general direction of the Association to the degree in which Pound's gentlemen did.

13. 16 *ABA Rep* (1893); George Sharp to Baldwin, April 27, 1893, Baldwin Papers; "George Matthews Sharp," 26 *ABA Rep* 509 (1911). At the

With a typically sure hand, Baldwin secured the creation of a Section of Legal Education in 1893, suggesting that the new entity would "serve as an important feeder to the Association."[14] He was right. The following year the Section meeting attracted almost as much attention as the convention itself and boasted as speakers Baldwin of Yale, William Keener of Columbia, Woodrow Wilson of Princeton, and John H. Wigmore and Henry Wade Rogers of Northwestern. At the same meeting Baldwin successfully moved the creation of a second section, that of Patent Law.[15]

Unlike committees of the Association, which were usually appointed by the president with the assistance of the inner circle, sections were virtually autonomous professional societies. Although dependent on the Association for the choice of meeting site and the printing of their proceedings, they elected their own officers, adopted their own bylaws, and scheduled their own programs.[16] In effect, sections restored some of the intimate atmosphere of the earliest

---

organizational meeting, Sharp was named secretary of the Section, and he served as chairman from 1888 to 1906. Roger W. Tuttle, comp., *Biographies of Graduates of the Yale Law School, 1824-1899* (New Haven: The Tuttle, Morehouse & Taylor Company, 1911), 321.

14. The ABA's official history of the Section of Legal Education, published in honor of its centennial, is Susan K. Boyd, *The ABA's First Section: Assuring a Qualified Bar* (Chicago: American Bar Association, 1993).

15. Baldwin to James B. Thayer, May 23, 1893, Baldwin Papers; 16 *ABA Rep* 7 (1893); *New York Times*, August 24, 1894, 5, August 25, 1894, 8; 17 *ABA Rep* 351-493 (1894); 17 *ABA Rep* 51-52 (1894). The name of the section was changed in 1899 to the Section of Patent, Trademark and Copyright Law—today the Section of Intellectual Property Law.

16. Glenn R. Winters, "Bar Association Activities: Suggestions for Bar Association Executives." 36 *ABAJ* 546 @ 548 (1950); Sunderland, *History of the ABA*, 31-33; Edward O. Hinkley, 17 *ABA Rep* 67 (1894).

Association meetings, and their narrower focus promised greater effectiveness as deliberative bodies.

Some Association members grew uneasy at the success of the Section of Legal Education and were even more wary of a section dedicated to the arcane specialty of patent law. The Section of Legal Education had been required to have its recommendations approved by both the Committee on Legal Education and the full Association, a process guaranteeing years of delay for any matter of substance. The Section of Patent Law, on the other hand, was allowed to take any action it deemed "wise in regard to any legislation concerning patent laws in Congress" so long as the Section proposed no new laws without Association approval. In other words, while the Section could not promote its own legislation, it remained free to oppose any it disliked.[17]

When, in 1896, a Section of Insurance was proposed, some members, including former president James C. Carter, feared that creating another section would be "a step in the line of disintegrating this entire body and dividing it up into a number of small useless bodies." One member suggested that large insurance companies might have friendly legislation adopted at Section meetings and then imply that the Association had endorsed it. The resolution to establish a Section of Insurance Law was defeated, and no more sections were organized until 1913.[18] When Baldwin next felt the

---

17. By-Law XII, 16 *ABA Rep* 89 (1893); 17 *ABA Rep* 51-52 (1894); John F. Dillon, 17 *ABA Rep* 58 (1894). Former president Dillon called the delegation of this power "entirely wrong and ill-advised."

18. 19 *ABA Rep* 29-40 (1896); 17 *ABA Rep* 54-67 (1894); George M. Foster, 19 *ABA Rep* 39-40 (1896). A Judicial Section was organized in 1913, but

organizational urge in 1907, he proposed creating a Comparative Law *Bureau* to study foreign and historic laws. The Bureau was a section in all but name but so academic in propose that its creation was easily approved.[19]

Only the American Bar Association's renewed interest in legal education proved more important than its increased interest in promoting uniformity of state laws. During the final decades of the nineteenth century, "conflicts of law," especially in commercial matters, annoyed elite lawyers. Improvements in transportation and communication and the rise of finance capitalism made state boundaries a nuisance. Further, the conviction that parochial legal differences were unscientific, and thus out-of-step with a scientific age, heightened irritation even with anomalies that had minimal consequences for the profession. Then too, as Grant Gilmore has suggested, the nationalizing principle of *Swift* v. *Tyson,* which had provided solutions to such conflicts in the past, may have been breaking down because of the increasing number of state judges who "took the *stare decisis* business seriously."[20]

During its first decade, the ABA tended to treat conflicts of laws as an incidental problem. The danger of this casual approach was revealed in the National Bar Association challenge of 1888. The following year the ABA established a Committee on Uniform State Laws consisting of forty-three members, one from each state. Two attempts to call a

---

since judges are an obviously distinct group of lawyers, perhaps the next "true" section organized was the Section of Public Utility Law in 1917.

19. 31 *ABA Rep* 1001-1009 (1907). In 1919 the Bureau changed its name to the Section of Comparative Law.

20. Grant Gilmore, *The Ages of American Law* (New Haven: Yale University Press, 1977), 70.

meeting of this unwieldy group resulted in respective attendances of ten and seven. Although disposed to concede defeat, the seven discovered that New York had recently created a board of "Commissioners for the Promotion of Uniformity of Legislation in the United States," apparently at the instigation of state legislators who were members of the ABA. The committeemen recommended that the Association endorse such legislation in other states. Thus, by 1892, the ABA was able to organize a meeting of a National Conference of Commissioners on Uniform State Laws (NCCUSL) with commissioners representing nine jurisdictions.[21]

Although technically a separate organization, the Conference of Commissioners maintained such an intimate relationship with the American Bar Association that ABA members occasionally had to be reminded of the distinction. Meetings of the NCCUSL were held just before the annual meetings and in the same city, the proceedings of the Conference were published for a time in the *Report*, and gradually the members of the Association's Committee on Uniform State Laws became nearly identical with the State Commissioners. Furthermore, because active members of the Conference were likely to be active members of the Association as well, the tie between the two organizations was stronger than between the Association and some of its sections. James Grafton Rogers described the Conference as "the main axis of the social life of the American Bar

---

21. Sunderland, 50-52;12 *ABA Rep* 50-51 (1889); Rufus King, 13 *ABA Rep* 29-30, 336-37 (1890); Max Radin, "The Achievements of the American Bar Association: A Sixty Year Record," 25 *ABAJ* 1008 (1939).

Association," and it therefore wielded considerable influence in the organization's internal politics.[22]

Although not all states were represented in the NCCUSL until 1912, much of its most important work was accomplished during its first twenty years. In fact, the first uniform act drafted by the NCCUSL, the Negotiable Instruments Act or N. I. L. of 1896, was more successful in terms of legislative adoptions than any that followed. By 1908, thirty-two jurisdictions had adopted it, and by 1928 it had been passed, with minor modifications, in all the states and territories.[23] Almost fifty years later, legal realist Karl Llewellyn (1896-1962) effusively praised the N.I.L. as "a job

---

22. Walter George Smith, 35 ABA Rep 19-20 (1910); Radin, 1008; Sunderland, 54; Rogers, *American Bar Leaders*, 197; Rogers, "History of the American Bar Association," 30 *ABAJ* 659 @ 661 (1953). Samuel Williston, who was an important member of the NCCUSL and the draftsman of the Uniform Sales Act, described his colleague on the NCCUSL Committee on Commercial Laws, John Hinkley, as "a careful lawyer, a baseball enthusiast, a good story teller, and a delightful companion. Many a game of cards in which he was a party have I had on railroad trains or in hotels when our work was not occupying our attention." Samuel Williston, *Life and Law: An Autobiography* (Boston: Little, Brown and Company, 1940), 229; see also Thomas Kilby Smith to Hampton L. Carson, August 13, 1919, Carson Papers.

23. Other commercial statutes followed, including those covering sales (1906), warehouse receipts (1906), bills of lading (1909), and the transfer of stock share certificates (1909). While less successful in terms of adoptions than the N.I.L., they were generally received by the states with more enthusiasm than the noncommercial uniform acts promulgated concurrently by the NCCUSL. Lawrence M. Friedman, *A History of American Law* (New York: Simon and Schuster, 1985), 540, 674-76; Radin, 1008; Morton Keller, *Regulating a New Economy: Public Policy and Economic Change in America, 1900-1933* (Cambridge: Harvard University Press, 1990), 95-96.

well designed and sweetly drafted. There is no fat on its words.... *Each* word of the N. I. L. *counts.*"[24]

Laws relating to interstate business practice, especially those regulating the transfer of commercial paper, were in genuine need of codification. Even extreme opponents of codification admitted as much. Resistance continued more from legal particularism than from antagonism to the idea of uniformity per se. When the generally progressive-minded Chief Justice Charles Doe (1830-1896) of New Hampshire was asked if he supported more uniformity, he replied, " Yes.... Just let all the other states copy our New Hampshire laws and the thing is done."[25]

The ABA's interest in uniform laws did not primarily spring from a desire "to aid the large corporations," as one modern commentator would have it—though uniform laws certainly benefited corporations. At least in the earlier years of the uniform laws movement, its proponents believed that eliminating legal technicalities would help raise standards of the legal profession by suppressing "pettifoggers"—the lower stratum of the bar. As one ABA member wrote, the more the law remained "a mass of unorganized and arbitrary detail, the

---

24. Karl Llewellyn, "Meet Negotiable Instruments," 44 Columbia Law Review 300-301 (1944), quoted in Jennifer Trost, "The Imposter Rule and Identity Theft in America, *Law and History Review* 35: 2 (May 2017), 431.
25. Doe quoted in Lyman D. Brewster, "Uniform State Laws," 21 *ABA Rep* 315 @ 330 (1898). Even a breezy article critical of the uniform laws movement agreed that uniformity of state laws in commercial matters was "advantageous, perhaps even necessary." John Hemphill, "The Uniform Laws Craze," *American Mercury* 5 (May 1925), 59. Richard M. Venable, "Growth of Evolution of Law," 23 ABA Rep 278@291-92 (1900); Lawrence Friedman, "Law Reform in Historical Perspective," 13 *St. Louis University Law Journal* 351 @ 358-59 (1969).

more will the mere digest-manipulating and precedent-hunting type of lawyer be given the advantage."[26] Uniform marriage laws seem to have originated, at least in part, from the desire of the legal elite to hobble the practice of divorce lawyers. In Michigan, opposition to the passage of the N. I. L. arose from collection lawyers who grumbled that legal simplification would be bad for business.[27]

During the progressive era, proponents of uniform laws also claimed that they would retard the growth of the federal government, though their pronouncements seem as much intended to justify the uniform law establishment itself as to check creeping federalism. Despite some brave talk and the promulgation of a Uniform Child Labor Act, neither the ABA nor the state legislatures had much interest in uniform laws that might result in significant social change.[28]

---

26. Charles Rembar, *The Law of the Land* (New York: Simon and Schuster, 1980), 237fn; Friedman, "Law Reform," 358; Henry T. Terry, 12 *ABA Rep* 327 @ 332 (1889); John W. Stevenson, "Address of the President," 8 *ABA Rep* 149 @ 184-85 (1885); John Ruhm, "A Plea for Uniform Laws," 2 *Proceedings of the Bar Association of Tennessee* 79 @ 84 (1883); Report of the Committee on Jurisprudence and Law Reform, 5 *ABA Rep* 295 (1882); 11 *ABA Rep* 308-09 (1888). However, prominent Philadelphia lawyer and ABA leader Walter George Smith, who was a devout Catholic, became a strong proponent of uniform divorce laws for religious reasons. Thomas A. Bryson, *Walter George Smith* (Washington, D.C.: Catholic University Press, 1977), 40-41.

27. George M. Bates, "Negotiable Instruments Act in Michigan Legislature, 37 *American Law Review* 876-879 (1903); Wayne Karl Hobson, *The American Legal Profession and the Organizational Society, 1890-1930* (New York: Garland Publishing, 1986), 246-247.

28. Alton B. Parker, "Uniform State Laws," 43 *Chicago Legal News* 314-315 (May 7,1910); "Report of the Committee on Uniform State Laws", 14 *ABA Rep* 365 (1891); Charles F. Libby, "Address of the President," 33 *ABA Rep*

For uniformity in bankruptcy law, the American Bar Association had to look to Congress because the Constitution specifically authorized national bankruptcy laws. A federal bankruptcy act had been repealed without replacement in 1878, and although Association members tended to favor passage of new legislation, the organization remained predictably cautious. In 1887, it endorsed the *idea* of a national bankruptcy law, though not any of the bills drafted by its Committee on Commercial Law in particular. There the matter rested for nine years. Not until 1898, after Congress had actually passed a new bankruptcy act, did Association interest revive.[29]

Almost immediately its Committee on Commercial Law, chaired by influential patent lawyer Walter S. Logan (1847-1906), began to lobby for changes in the law. Now armed with Association approval of his committee report, Logan enjoyed considerable success in Washington. He received the cooperation of the chairmen of appropriate committees in

---

331 @ 350 (1910); John Lowell, 14 *ABA Rep* 4 (1891); Charles Thaddeus Terry, 42 *ABA Rep* 77 (1917); Lawrence E. Sommers, "Lawyers and Progressive Reform: A Study of Attitudes and Activities in Illinois, 1890 to 1920," Ph.D. dissertation, Northwestern University, 1967, 151; Friedman, "Law Reform," 359: "Modern law reform (in the technical sense) is presented as the program of 'the bar,' and it is presented as scientific and objective; to be credible, it must be socially innocuous." See also Edgar H. Farrar, "Address of the President," 36 *ABA Rep* 229-258 (1911) and a fitting reply by Frank B. Kellogg, "New Nationalism" 37 *ABA Rep* 341 @ 362 (1912).

29. National bankruptcy laws had been in effect in the United States in 1800–1801, 1841–43, and 1867–1878. Samuel Wagner, "The Advantages of a National Bankruptcy Law," 4 *ABA Rep* 223-235 (1881); *New York Herald*, August 19, 1880, 4; 10 *ABA Rep* 344-358 (1887); 12 *ABA Rep* 29, 35 (1889); Charles Warren, *Bankruptcy in United States History* (Cambridge: Harvard University Press, 1935), 133–141.

both houses of Congress, and his report was quoted extensively and "with unqualified commendation" by the Attorney General. In 1903, the recommendations of the ABA committee were in substance approved by Congress, and Logan boasted that the bankruptcy law, "as it stands today as amended, is practically the work of this Association." For the next two decades, the Committee on Commercial Law and its successors successfully fended off dozens of attempts to amend or repeal.[30]

The minor success of the Association in amending the bankruptcy law was significant because it was so unusual. Before 1912, the Association exercised little influence on either state or national legislation and, except in the area of legal education, it had almost negligible effect on the legal profession as well. In an attempt to catalogue Association achievements at the beginning of its fourth decade, President J. M. Dickinson listed the ABA's promotion of higher standards in legal education, the enactment of uniform state laws, and the encouragement that the ABA had rendered to state and local bar associations. Otherwise, Dickinson was reduced to claiming that the Association had "justified its existence...in many other ways not necessary to recapitulate."[31]

To be fair, one cause of Association inaction was that the problems it might have tackled had no easy solutions, as for

---

30. 21 *ABA Rep* 14, 411 (1898); 22 *ABA Rep* 25-27, 414-416 (1899); M. Louise Rutherford, *The Influence of the American Bar Association on Public Opinion and Legislation* (Philadelphia: privately printed, 1937), 332; Sunderland, 64, 117-18; Charles F. Manderson, "Address of the President," 23 *ABA Rep* 179 @ 183 (1900); 26 *ABA Rep* 11-12 (1903).

31. Jacob M. Dickinson, "Address of the President," 33 *ABA Rep* 341 @ 355 (1908).

example, the profusion of reported court decisions that threatened to swamp the profession in unindexed words.[32] As early as 1821, Justice Story complained that lawyers could not contemplate without discouragement the volumes of new cases issuing annually from the printers.[33] While every scrap of precedent might be useful to some lawyer somewhere, the elite suspected that the lower echelons had the advantage at grubbing through reported decisions. The law, said one bar leader, was in danger of being reduced from a science "ruled by intellect and learning into a merely speculative, laborious and mechanical pursuit, in which endurance, shrewdness, accident and, often influence, win the day."[34]

The difficulty was in finding a way to diminish the volume of case law being produced at the rate of two or three hundred volumes a year. Some members suggested that judges or court reporters might shorten the reports by summarizing cases. Other saw dangers in committing this power to either of these special groups of lawyers. In the end, the ABA was reduced to endorsing a bootless plea that judges write shorter opinions.[35]

---

32. John F. Dillon, "Annual Address," 7 *ABA Rep* 223-24 (1884); William P. LaPiana, *Logic and Experience: The Origin of Modern American Legal Education* (New York: Oxford University Press, 1994), 105-06.
33. Joseph Story, "Address before the Suffolk Bar," 1 *American Jurist* 31 (1829).
34. John Ruhm, "A Plea for Uniform Laws," 2 *Proceedings of the Bar Association of Tennessee* 79 @ 84 (1883).
35. Emlin McClain, "The Evolution of Judicial Opinion," 25 *ABA Rep* 373 @ 386, 396-97 (1902); 19 *ABA Rep* 398-404 (1896); 21 *ABA Rep* 437-450 (1898); 23 *ABA Rep* 377-378 (1900); 26 *ABA Rep* 456-459 (1903); 27 *ABA Rep* 450 (1904); 28 *ABA Rep* 460-464 (1905); 35 *ABA Rep* 532 (1910); Sunderland, 70-71, 138-39; John F. Dillon, "Law Reports and Law

Appropriately, the problem of burgeoning case law was ameliorated via the capitalistic system that had created it. The West Publishing Company began to index all new cases in its "key number" system. In 1914, five years before the Committee on Law Reporting was abolished as unnecessary, its members announced that although they would not trust judges or court reporters to decide which cases to eliminate from the published record, they *would* trust the West Publishing Company to make such decisions.[36]

Another cause of Association inaction before 1912 was the organization's reluctance to offend even a minority of its members. The Association repeatedly exercised caution—sometimes excessive caution—in its public pronouncements and legislative recommendations. For instance, in 1892, the Committee on Judicial Administration reported that while a resolution recommending a code of federal procedure for federal courts had been adopted unanimously by the Association in 1888, the Committee had detected a lack of consensus about the necessity for such a code. The Committee therefore suggested that the Association confine itself "at present to that part of the resolution which will not be likely to create any division of opinion."[37]

On August 14, 1899, two weeks before the annual meeting, the French lawyer Fernand Labori, counsel for Alfred Dreyfus, was shot in the back by an unknown assailant. During the convention, an ABA member moved a

---

Reporting," 9 *ABA Rep* 257 @ 271 (1886); 25 *ABA Rep* 14-18 (1902); 35 *ABA Rep* 532 (1910); 39 *ABA Rep* 24 (1914); 41 *ABA Rep* 51 (1916); 42 *ABA Rep* 58-60 (1917).

36. Friedman, *A History of American Law*, 409-10; 39 *ABA Rep* 24 (1914).

37. 15 *ABA Rep* 314-15 (1892); 16 *ABA Rep* 53, 60 (1893); Walter George Smith, 28 *ABA Rep* 121 (1905).

resolution of sympathy to Labori for the assault made on him "while in the discharge of his duty to his client." The resolution was watered down by the excision of a pro-Dreyfus sentence and the inclusion of a disclaimer declaring the Association's unwillingness to pass on the merits of the case. Still, there were objections. One member cautioned the Association to go "slow in passing resolutions. Matters political should be eschewed." In this case, however, the Association's hand was forced by some adverse publicity generated the previous day when the resolution had been temporarily tabled as out of order. One Stephen Hoye warned that the organization's image would suffer if "it should...go out to the world that the American Bar Association is a pack of cowards." Eventually the resolution was adopted by a vote of 130 to 69.[38]

One member found it "remarkable that whenever a report of a committee is made, it is at once followed by a proposition to postpone its consideration." Postponements were especially ludicrous (and were seen as such) when the Association considered the delays on the Supreme Court docket.[39] Some committees made no report at all. The most extreme case was that of the Grievance Committee, which though created in 1878, issued no report until 1904. The Committee on Taxation made no report in 1911 except to ask

---

38. 22 *ABA Rep* 70-81 (1899); *Buffalo Evening News*, August 30, 1899. Labori's attacker was never identified.

39. W. O. Hart, 33 *ABA Rep* 59 (1908): "Why, gentlemen, the report of the Committee on Commercial Law presented by our lamented brother, Mr. Logan of New York, in 1903, was postponed so long that he died before it even got before the Association." George G. Wright, 12 *ABA Rep* 17 (1889); A. A. Ferris, 12 *ABA Rep* 31 (1889); *New York Times*, August 31, 1889, 5.

for an appropriation of $1000 to continue its work. This inactivity reminded one member of lyrics from Gilbert and Sullivan's *Iolanthe*:

> When Wellington thrashed Bonaparte,
> As every child can tell,
> The House of Peers, throughout the war,
> Did nothing in particular,
> And did it very well.[40]

In a letter to the Chairman of the Committee on Federal Courts, Alexander Campbell Botkin (1842-1905), a federal commissioner tasked by President McKinley with the revision of criminal laws, chided the American Bar Association for its lack of cooperation with his Commission, but he did so with a measure of understanding, noting that "the season of the year and the conditions attending the annual meetings" were not "conducive to the mature consideration of questions that inevitably invite differences of opinion and debate." [41] That is, Botkin understood that the American Bar Association remained largely a social, rather than a professional, organization.

In fact, the social activities surrounding the annual meetings became even more important than they had been when the ABA was a society of intimates. Banquets could never again be as private as they had been in Saratoga, but what they lost in exclusivity, they gained in sumptuousness. For instance, the 1906 banquet in the Minneapolis

---

40. 36 *ABA Rep* 42 (1911).

41. 36 *ABA Rep* 42 (1911). Alexander C. Botkin to Charles F. Libby, June 16, 1902, @ 25 *ABA Rep* 482-83 (1902).

Auditorium featured a table extending the width of the hall covered in red roses. Four hundred guests entered to the strains of *Tannhäuser* being played by the Minneapolis Symphony. Modifying its earlier closed-door policy at banquets, the Association also grudgingly allowed women to attend after-dinner speeches once plates had been cleared and cigars and champagne had been served.[42]

Most of one day of the three-day annual convention was devoted to a semi-official sightseeing trip, usually arranged by the local bar association. Hotels, railroads, and traction companies provided favors. The Association brushed aside the uneasiness of a few members on this score.[43]

Receptions, luncheons, and evening affairs occupied Association members during the convention, not to mention

---

42. *Minneapolis Tribune*, September 1, 1906; *Denver Post*, August 23, 1906, 1; [Chattanooga] *Daily Times*, September 2,1910, 3. Reporters were sometimes admitted with the ladies, sometimes excluded completely. *New York Times*, August 22, 1896, 3; *Buffalo Evening News*, August 30, 1899, 1; *Denver Post*, August 22, 1901, 2; *Detroit Free Press*, August 28, 1909, 12; Francis Rawle to Simeon Baldwin, August 22, 1898, Baldwin Papers. Charles Whitman, ABA president in 1927, referred to Association members of this period as "a parcel of extinct volcanoes, which met once a year, listened to one of their number (not yet quite extinct) in feeble eruption, dined together and separated for another year, when the performance was repeated." Charles Whitman, "Annual Address," 52 *ABA Rep* 154 (1927).

43. 12 *ABA Rep* 53 (1889); *New York Times*, August 22,1889, 8; 23 *Amer. L. Rev.* 663 (1889); 14 *ABA Rep* 6 (1891); 16 *ABA Rep* 5 (1893); *New York Times*, August 29, 1895, 14; August 26, 1897, 1; 29 *ABA Rep* 7 (1906); 31 *ABA Rep* 82 (1907); *Detroit Free Press*, August 26, 1909, 9; *Boston Globe*, August 30, 1911, 5; Hinkley, 454, 457; 27 *ABA Rep* 56 (1904) "The Great Expedition," 8 *ABAJ* 533-534 (1922); *Minneapolis Journal*, August 30, 1923, 8; A. H. Tillman, 20 *ABA Rep* 73-74 (1897).

side trips and house parties coming and going. An atypical member complained that half the meeting was taken up in "being feted and magnificently entertained" and wondered if not more of the convention ought to be devoted to business. The Association answered him indirectly a few moments later with a resolution that praised the host city for "the generous manner of our entertainment [that] has tended in a great degree to make this one of the most successful meetings in the history of the Association."[44]

Ironically, the American Bar Association, founded with reformist aspirations, had grown in membership and prestige in part precisely because it had achieved so little of substance during its more than thirty years of existence. Yet, that very growth also made it increasingly likely that the American Bar Association would eventually have to abandon its "noiseless, unobtrusive way.

---

44. John C. Richberg, 29 *ABA Rep* 73 (1906); 29 *ABA Rep* 78 (1906); Michael de. L. Landon, *The Honor and Dignity of the Profession: A History of the Mississippi State Bar, 1906-1976* (Jackson: University Press of Mississippi, 1979), 35. Social activity encouraged attendance at other professional gatherings as well, though amusements provided for contemporary Iowa pharmacists were both less sophisticated and more family oriented than those at the ABA—including a fishing contest, a wheelbarrow race, and a ladies' potato throw. Wiegand, 226-27; Lee Anderson, *Iowa Pharmacy, 1880-1905: An Experiment in Professionalism* (Iowa City: University of Iowa Press, 1989), 105.

Chapter **4**

Conservative Reformers

ABA Ideologies, 1878–1914

At least as important as the actions (or non-actions) of the early American Bar Association are the resolutions, committee reports, and the 159 speeches made at the annual meetings between 1878 and 1914, which illustrate the thinking of elite lawyers as they grappled with the social and professional problems of their day. Only in the most general sense could there have been a united point of view in the attempts to blend reformist impulses with the conservative "search for order."

By necessity, elite lawyers had to be conservatives of some sort because they relied on the social order to preserve their status, wealth, and power. During the Gilded Age and Progressive Era, lawyers were challenged by what they perceived as an increased disrespect for the law and the legal profession. They viewed with increasing alarm public attacks on the judiciary, injunctions met with contempt, lynch mobs settling private scores, labor disturbances crushed by force, and corporate monopolies acting as law unto themselves.[1]

---

1. Benjamin Cardozo observed in a memorial address for a colleague that the "existing social order had brought him opulence and fame and happiness. He did not share the views of those who would supplant it by

The solution, the elite concluded, lay in the restoration of a political order in which legal professionals rather than capitalists, labor unions, lynch mobs—or even legislators—made the law.

Elite lawyers were not being cynical when they claimed to buttress the social order by improving the status of their own profession. Most sincerely believed that what benefited the profession would also benefit the country. In the Annual Address of 1899, Senator William Lindsay (1835-1909) of Kentucky declared that the influence of lawyers had "always been for good."[2] Nor were Association pronouncements doctrinaire. Systematic philosophizing was rare, and even fumbling for first principles unusual. Speeches were sometimes not even internally consistent, let alone consistent with each other.

The few scholars who have studied the *ABA Reports* of this period have exaggerated its support for laissez-faire economics.[3] One can certainly find promotion of free-market

---

another or even greatly change it." 45 *Association of the Bar of the City of New York Reports* 337 @ 441, quoted in George Martin, *Causes and Conflicts: The Centennial History of the Association of the Bar of the City of New York* (Boston: Houghton, Mifflin Company, 1970), 203; William M. Wiecek, *The Lost World of Classical Legal Thought: Law and Ideology in America, 1886-1937* (New York: Oxford University Press, 1998), 72.

2. William Lindsay, "Annual Address," 22 *ABA Rep* 327 @ 329 (1899).

3. Benjamin Twiss, *Lawyers and the Constitution* (Princeton: Princeton University Press, 1942) argued that the American Bar Association had served as an intellectual bridge between capitalists and judges by introducing the doctrine of laissez faire to the courts. While Twiss admitted that the addresses cited in his study were specifically chosen to illustrate his thesis and that approval of laissez-faire thought "was not universally shared" within the Association, he nevertheless contended that the "doctrine represented a consensus among members of the bar" and that "disagreement was the exception which proved the rule."

Nearly twenty years later, Arnold M. Paul, *Conservative Crisis and the*

capitalism in the *Reports,* but careful examination suggests a considerable ratio of pitchblende to radioactive ore. More often, the *Reports* reveal a conservatism that, in the words of Arnold Paul, assigned a high status to the protection of private property but "was especially concerned with the problems of maintaining an ordered society."[4]

Nowhere was the social vision of the American Bar Association more evident than in the members' collective opinion of the large corporation. Perhaps many late nineteenth-century lawyers did believe that the common good was best served by huge business combinations, but more often the reverse of that sentiment was heard at American Bar Association meetings. Nor was antipathy to corporate power con-

---

Rule of Law: Attitudes of Bar and Bench, 1887-1895 (Ithaca: Cornell University Press, 1960), concluded that "traditional legal conservatism" had given way to "laissez faire conservatism" with the "hardening of conservative attitudes" during the 1890s. Since this thesis necessitated a close integration of political, economic, and intellectual history over a comparatively short period, Paul emphasized the "laissez-faire" speeches presented to the Association during the 1890s but slighted those with similar tendencies delivered in the previous decade. Paul did not dispute Twiss's findings but expressed doubt that early ABA speeches were representative of the legal profession as a whole.

Norbert Brockman, "Laissez-Faire Theory in the Early American Bar Association," 39 *Notre Dame Lawyer* 270 (1964) agreed that laissez-faire conservatism grew more influential during the Association's first decade and reached "eventual dominance" in the Association during the 1890s. But Brockman disputed Twiss's thesis that the ABA had played a large role in the transmitting Spencerian ideology to the courts. He also emphasized the point, conceded by Twiss, that members of the ABA did not universally share a belief in laissez-faire theory and that there were "voices of dissent" within the Association.

4. Arnold Paul, *Conservative Crisis and the Rule of Law,* 4-5.

fined to any particular segment of the 35-year period between 1878 and 1914.

As early as 1884, ABA President Cortlandt Parker (1818-1907) denounced the "sins of corporations," which he feared might soon bring down on the nation the horrors of class conflict. Even earlier, Edward J. Phelps (1822-1900), an able defender of limited government, warned that the growth of large corporations was the "subject of the gravest foreboding among reflecting men." Even during the early 1890s, a period that according to Arnold Paul witnessed "the hardening of conservative attitudes," speakers continued to warn their colleagues about the dangers of industrial combinations. In 1893, U. M. Rose (1834-1913), a founding member of the ABA and a leader of the Arkansas bar, asked rhetorically (via the words of Thomas Cooley) "whether the trust as we see it is not a public enemy, whether it is not teaching the laborer dangerous lessons, whether it is not helping to breed anarchy!"[5]

---

5. Cortlandt Parker, "Address of the President," 7 *ABA Rep* 147 @ 160, 175 (1884); Rogers, *American Bar Leaders*, 29-32. Edward J. Phelps, "Address of the President," 4 *ABA Rep* 141 @ 142-47, 160-61 (1881); see also Edward J. Phelps, 5 *ABA Rep* 46 (1882); Edward J. Phelps, "Chief Justice Marshall and the Constitutional Law of his Time," 2 *ABA Rep* 173 @ 184 (1879); Twiss, 149-51; Brockman, 280. Phelps advocated regulation of firearms, fire and safety inspections, destruction of diseased cattle, and the elimination of medical quackery by licensing physicians. He complimented the state of New York for enacting "a statute so humane that it ought not to have been necessary, requiring the proprietor of stores to provide seats for the use of their shopwomen." Phelps was especially critical of railroads: "[T]heir power, their vast accumulation of capital and influence, the disregard some of them have occasionally manifested for the public convenience, and the irritating discriminations they have imposed, have furnished facile material to the demagogues with which to inflame public sentiment against them." It should be added that Phelps had been a

Only at the turn of the century did the trusts gain defenders, and even then, defenders remained a minority.[6] U. M. Rose, president in 1901, scoffed at the notion of "benevolent industrial feudalism," equating it to "benevolent smallpox." Frederick Lehmann (1853-1931), an attorney for the Wabash Railroad and later Taft's Solicitor General, warned in his presidential address of 1909 that the American people had "no faith in a benevolent despotism. They know that [corporate] power tends to abuse." Thomas J. Kernan (1854-1911), another railroad lawyer, charged that the antagonism of the people against corporations and men of wealth could be attributed to "the establishment of plutocracy in this country" that would eventually result "in a few vulgar masters and a horde of overworked and underfed slaves."[7]

If anything, these anti-corporation sentiments intensified as the Association moved into its fourth decade. Two years before Woodrow Wilson was elected President of the United

---

Copperhead during the Civil War, and he remained an unabashed racist for the rest of his life. *New York Times*, September 6, 1880, 1.

U. M. Rose, "The Law of Trusts and Strikes," 16 *ABA Rep* 287 @ 319 (1893); see also Alan Jones, "Thomas M. Cooley and 'Laissez Faire Constitutionalism': A Reconsideration," *Journal of American History* 53 (March, 1967), 751-771.

6. The following are probably the best examples of "pro-trust" sentiment, with the last example being the strongest defense of corporations though the weakest speech: Charles F. Manderson, "Address of the President," 22 *ABA Rep* 219 @ 252-53 (1899); Edward Quinton Keasbey, "New Jersey and the Great Corporations," 22 *ABA Rep* 379 @ 393, 413 (1899); William A. Glasgow, Jr., "A Dangerous Tendency of Legislation," 26 *ABA Rep* 376 @ 386 (1903).

7. U. M. Rose, "Address of the President," 25 *ABA Rep* 199 @ 234 (1902); Frederick W. Lehmann, "Address of the President," 34 *ABA Rep* 347 @ 365 (1909); Thomas J. Kernan, "The Jurisprudence of Lawlessness," 29 *ABA Rep* 450 @ 464 (1906).

States, he spoke to the ABA convention in Chattanooga and there called for cutting away "the undergrowth of law that has sprung so rankly about the corporation and made of it an ambush and covert." Likewise, in his 1911 presidential address, Edgar H. Farrar (1849-1922) described the "great aggregations of capital" as "armed colossuses astride the gateway of commerce" destroying "every entrant who presumes to compete with them."[8]

Critics of corporate power differed in their reasons for condemning it. When Frederick Lehmann censured the financial manipulations of railroad magnates, he referred disdainfully to their private fortunes "squandered with lavish hand and vulgar ostentation"—as if bad taste were on a level with corporate thievery.[9] More commonly, the wealth and power of large corporations was believed to jeopardize the lawyers' independence of action. Woodrow Wilson asked rhetorically if the lawyer "had not been sucked into the

---

8. Woodrow Wilson, "The Lawyer and the Community," 35 *ABA Rep* 419 @ 438 (1910); Edgar H. Farrar, "Address of the President," 36 *ABA Rep* 229 @ 232, 239 (1911); Rogers, *American Bar Leaders*, 163; see also Peter S. Grosscup, "How to Save the Corporation," *McClure's*, 24 (February, 1905), 443-48; N. Charles Burke, "The Struggle for Simplification of Legal Procedure: Legal Procedure and Social Unrest," 38 *ABA Rep* 445 @ 448, 451 (1913); George R. Peck, "Address of the President," 29 *ABA Rep* 297 @ 314, 318 (1906): "I do not believe in laissez faire. I do not believe the infinitely complicated affairs of our modern life can be safely left to the unregulated instincts of those who are interested in or profit by them."
9. Frederick Lehmann, "Address of the President," 34 *ABA Rep* 347 @ 369 (1909); Rogers, *American Bar Leaders*, 151-156; see also Alexander R. Lawton, "Address of the President," 6 *ABA Rep* 137 @ 176 (1883). Lawton was annoyed at "the self-prostration of society" before great wealth as a "dignity, a principality, a power"--terms used in the Bible to refer to evil.

channels of business" and been "turned away from his former interests and duties?"[10]

ABA speakers believed the most sinister aspect of corporate wealth was its power to command special favors from government, especially from legislatures. In 1883, John M. Shirley (1831-1887), a leader of the New Hampshire bar, denounced the great corporations as "highwaymen of speculative finance" who had purchased their political influence. Shirley's opinion was seconded in 1884 by Simon Sterne (1839-1901), later a draftsman of the Interstate Commerce Act. Sterne charged that for thirty years legislation had been "whatever the strong nets and long purses of our builders-up of corporate wealth chose to have."[11]

---

10. Woodrow Wilson, "The Lawyer and the Community," 35 *ABA Rep* 419 @ 435 (1910). Other elite lawyers agreed with Wilson: Cortlandt Parker, "Alexander Hamilton and William Wirt," 3 *ABA Rep* 149 @ 165 (1880); Robert T. Platt, "The Decadence of Law as a Profession and its Growth as a Business," 12 *Yale Law Journal* 441-45 (1902-03); Walter George Smith, "Address of the Chairman," [Section of Legal Education] 38 *ABA Rep* 761 (1913); Clarence A. Lightner, "A More Complete Inquiry into the Moral Character of Applicants for Admission to the Bar," [Section of Legal Education] 38 *ABA Rep* 779 (1913); Andrew A. Bruce, 40 *ABA Rep* 737 (1915). Hofstadter, *The Age of Reform*, 160, fn.6, provides a brief listing of contemporary journal articles decrying the lawyers' loss of independence to the corporation, "this artificial creature of his own genius, for whom he is now simply a clerk on a salary."

11. John M. Shirley, "The Future of Our Profession," 6 *ABA Rep* 195 @ 218 (1883); see also William P. Wells, "The Dartmouth College Case and Private Corporations," 9 *ABA Rep* 229 @ 238 (1886); Simon Sterne, "The Prevention of Defective and Slipshod Legislation," 7 *ABA Rep* 275 @ 284 (1884); "Simon Sterne," 24 *ABA Rep* 639 (1901); Robert C. Bannister, *Social Darwinism: Science and Myth in Anglo-American Social Thought* (Philadelphia: Temple University Press, 1979), 66-68.

ABA leaders maintained no illusions about lawyers' ability to preserve the social order if predatory wealth could not be checked. "If governmental policy, directly or indirectly, helps one to make a billion out of the many," said J. Randolph Tucker in 1892, "why not, in turn help the many to distribute his excess? . . . Privilege sows the wind, the commune will bring the harvest of the whirlwind!" Even more forceful was that respected but unloved Boston Brahmin, Moorfield Storey (1845-1929). In the Annual Address of 1894, Storey lashed out at corporations that could "secure or defeat legislation at will and dominate the politics of whole states [by] corruption."[12] Storey claimed the speech was received so favorably he was elected ABA president the following year without his having sought the office.[13]

ABA leaders encouraged professional brethren to stand against both corporate wealth and labor radicalism to prove that lawyers were not "merely conservative" but rather "the best and safest organizers of improvements."[14] "If lawyers do

---

12. J. Randolph Tucker, "British Institutions and American Constitutions," 15 *ABA Rep* 213 @ 233 (1892); see also Charles Claflin Allen, "Injunction and Organized Labor," 17 *ABA Rep* 299 @ 323, 325 (1894); Paul, 146-49. Moorfield Storey, "The American Legislature," 17 *ABA Rep* 245 @ 256-57 (1894). Paul does not discuss this speech in *Conservative Crisis and the Rule of Law.* See also the similar sentiments expressed by Elihu Root in his commencement address at Hamilton College in 1879, *Utica Morning Gazette,* June 26, 1879, quoted in Philip C. Jessup, *Elihu Root* (New York: Dodd, Mead and Company, 1937), I, 207.

13. M. A. DeWolfe Howe, *Portrait of an Independent: Moorfield Storey, 1845-1929* (Boston: Houghton Mifflin, 1932), 187.

14. John Lowell, President of the Boston Bar Association, in welcoming remarks to the ABA annual meeting, 14 *ABA Rep* 4 (1891). In 1898 Elihu Root wrote, "No amount of professional employment by corporations has blinded me to the political and social dangers which exist in their relations

not take the initiative," said Walter Logan in 1903, "the demagogues will." Frank Kellogg (1856-1937), whom Theodore Roosevelt had called "the best trust-buster of them all," warned the Association that blind opposition to change was "the surest way to destroy our form of government." Lawyers, he said, must champion reform in order to maintain their influence.[15]

How lawyers could supervise corporations in the interest of an ordered society remained a conundrum. Association speakers occasionally suggested regulating them through state law, but that strategy seemed unlikely when corporations were able to migrate "like divorce hunting wives to the laxest of states."[16] Other speakers suggested enacting uniform state laws. But Frank Kellogg, who had prosecuted Standard Oil from its lair in New Jersey, correctly regarded the hope of uniform state action as an "idle dream impossible of accomplishment."[17]

---

to government and public affairs." Root to James B. Reynolds, quoted in Jessup, I, 206; see also Nathan William MacChesney, 30 *ABA Rep* 8 (1906); U. M. Rose, "Address of the President," 25 *ABA Rep* 199 @ 230 (1902); Alexander R. Lawton, "Address of the President," 6 *ABA Rep* 137 @ 176-77 (1883).

15. Walter S. Logan, 26 *ABA Rep* 12 (1903); Frank B. Kellogg, "New Nationalism," 37 *ABA Rep* 341 @ 370 (1912); Rogers, *American Bar Leaders*, 171; see also Robert T. Swayne, "The Impact of Big Business on the Profession: An Answer to Critics of the Modern Bar," 35 *ABAJ* 89 @ 171 (1949); Roscoe Pound, "The Need of Sociological Jurisprudence," 31 *ABA Rep* 911 @ 925-926 (1907); Emory A. Storrs, 6 *ABA Rep* 37 (1883).

16. Lawrence M. Friedman, *A History of American Law* (New York: Simon and Schuster, 1985), 523.

17. Edgar H. Farrar, "Address of the President," 36 *ABA Rep* 229 @ 244 (1911); see also Charles F. Libby, "Address of the President," 35 *ABA Rep* 331 @ 351 (1910); Alton B. Parker, "Address of the President," 31 *ABA Rep* 339 @ 344 (1907); Frank B. Kellogg, "New Nationalism" 37 *ABA Rep* 341 @ 362 (1912).

In 1905, the newly created Committee on Insurance Law recommended that the ABA endorse federal regulation of interstate insurance transactions. Some larger insurance companies, frustrated by hostile state legislation, had also concluded that federal supervision would be in their best interest. Nevertheless, the Supreme Court had ruled in *Paul* v. *Virginia* (1869) that insurance was not commerce as defined by the Constitution. Therefore, ABA approval of the Committee report might imply disagreement with the Court—four of whose members were present at the meeting. Opponents of the measure also warned that if the Association endorsed federal regulation of insurance while it remained a live political issue, the resulting controversy might divide the Association.[18]

Although the Committee chairman insisted that his report treated the subject "from the standpoint of the people," in the corridors it was whispered that it had been written for an insurance company's fee. (Worth noting is that in 1905, insurance companies considered a pronouncement of the Association significant enough to dispatch lobbyists.) In the end, the Association took refuge in inaction, sending the matter back to committee.[19]

---

18. 28 *ABA Rep* 92-122 (1905); John F. Dryden, "The Federal Regulation of Insurance," *World's Work* 10 (1905), 6782-4; *New York Times*, August 24, 1905, 6.

19. Ralph Breckenridge, 28 *ABA Rep* 144 (1905); James M. Beck, 28 *ABA Rep* 116 (1905). The report was recommitted by a vote of 113 to 29. Gabriel Kolko noted the conclusion of the Committee on Insurance Law that federal regulation of insurance "was constitutional and desirable"; he did not mention the ABA's inaction on the matter. Gabriel Kolko, *The Triumph of Conservativism: A Reinterpretation of American History 1900-1916* (New York: Macmillan Company, 1963), 95.

An even more heated controversy erupted when the Committee on Commercial Law presented its 1903 report. Having recently won congressional approval for ABA recommendations that modified federal bankruptcy law, the Committee arrived at the meeting convinced that the American Bar Association was ready to wield "a power for good and an influence for wisdom and conservatism far beyond what any of us has heretofore supposed.... The American people and their representatives are ready to heed its views and to follow its lead."

Committee chairman Walter Logan sought ABA endorsement for vigorous governmental action to solve the perceived problem of the trusts, legislation that would tax trusts to death or at least impose tax rates high enough to inhibit their growth. The report further suggested that the federal government could undercut the Meat Trust by using federal lands for pasture and could destroy the Coal Trust by taking coal fields through eminent domain. "This might be called socialism," wrote Logan, "but it is not."[20]

Though this remarkable report was signed by five "lawyers of distinction" (as the *American Law Review* called them), their reputations did not win approval from the Association. Former president Charles Manderson confessed that the report filled him "with amazement and indignation." Another member said that if it had been made at a recent Populist convention, "by unanimous vote it would have been thrown out as too radical." Yet a surprising number of ABA members spoke in its favor. Even those who opposed the report

---

20. "Report of the Committee on Commercial Law," 26 *ABA Rep* 12, 429-448 (1903).

seemed less concerned with its effect on the nation than its effect on the Association.[21]

Debate was heated. One Logan supporter was hooted down. Finally the controversial portion of the report was returned to the Committee with instructions to draft "specific remedies in legislative form" to deal with the trusts. Then, incoming president James Hagerman (1848-1913)—ironically, a former supporter of Bryan and Free Silver—replaced three members of the Committee with three opponents of the 1903 report. The majority of the reconstituted Committee then concluded that federal action against trusts was unnecessary.[22]

---

21. 37 *Am. L. Rev.* 728 (1903) also called Logan's report "one of the ablest documents which had ever been presented before that association." Logan was typical of early ABA leaders. He had graduated from Yale, Harvard, and Columbia; had been associated with the firm of the noted New York lawyer Charles O'Conor; had been a leader in various reform movements; and had served as president of the New York State Bar Association. The other signers were Henry Budd, a wealthy Philadelphian and ABA vice-president for Pennsylvania; Gardiner Lathrop, solicitor for the Atchinson, Topeka and Santa Fe; George Whitelock, a leading Baltimore lawyer and a candidate for the office of Maryland Attorney General; and John Morris, Jr., a member of the ABA's local council for Indiana. The debate is reported at 26 *ABA Rep* 11-53 (1903). Everett P. Wheeler called the trust question a "distinctly a political subject" that the Association should avoid. Oscar R. Hunley of Alabama urged the Association to throw out any question that might "bring discredit upon it; anything . . . bound to be merely political." Even Manderson's chief complaint was that the Committee had turned the Association meeting into "a political hustings."

22. 37 *Am. L. Rev.* 728-730 (1903); Waldo G. Morse, 26 *ABA Rep* 45-48, 53 (1903); Rogers, *American Bar Leaders*, 130; 27 *ABA Rep* 391-413 (1904). Francis Rawle thought the Logan report "a catastrophe," especially since Rawle feared that Logan, a "copper speculator"—he was the treasurer of a company with copper mines in Sonora, Mexico—was lowering the prestige of the ABA in New York City where "the bar is somewhat

Undeterred, Logan issued a series of minority reports that recommended national incorporation laws and the progressive taxation of corporations. In 1905, the year before his death, his proposals finally reached the floor of the annual meeting and precipitated another spirited debate. Logan remained convinced that by passing his bill "Congress would be doing God's holy work," and apparently many members sympathized with him. His draft legislation failed of Association endorsement by only three votes.[23]

Although Association leaders viewed labor unions with as much suspicion as big corporations, ABA speakers rarely attacked unions *per se*. Indeed, most speakers displayed understanding of, and occasional sympathy for, the goals of labor unions. In their addresses, ABA presidents took note of state legislation that prohibited wage payments in scrip, required weekly paydays, regulated working hours, and banned "yellow dog" contracts that prevented workers from joining unions. Rarely did the presidents criticize these laws.[24]

---

skeptical of the value of our Association." Rawle to H. St. G. Tucker, October 10, 1904, Tucker Papers.

23. 28 *ABA* Rep 63, 70 (1905); *Providence (RI) Journal,* August 24, 1905, 2. The vote on Logan's minority report was 68 to 70. Ironically, Logan died in 1906 immediately after dictating a letter concerning committee business to George Whitelock, the only other member of the 1903 Commercial Law Committee continued in office. James M. Beck, 29 *ABA Rep* 299 (1906).

24. Only Alexander R. Lawton, president in 1883, questioned the legitimacy of labor unions; "Address of the President," 6 *ABA Rep* 137 @ 138 (1883); Henry B. Brown, "The Distribution of Property," 16 *ABA Rep* 213, 214 (1893); William Howard Taft, "Recent Criticism of the Federal Judiciary," 18 *ABA Rep* 237 @ 265-66 (1895); U. M. Rose, "The Law of Trusts and Strikes," 16 *ABA Rep* 287 @ 297 (1893); N. Charles Burke, "The Struggle for Simplification of Legal Procedure: Legal Procedure and Social Unrest," 38 *ABA Rep* 445 @ 450, 452-53 (1913); John W. Stevenson,

Labor violence was another matter. Organized violence of any sort threatened the social order and the rule of law. Although ABA leaders remained sensitive to the claims of workers as individuals, they shuddered at strikes, pickets, and boycotts.[25] In the wake of the Haymarket Incident and a major railroad strike, ABA President William Allen Butler warned that "organizations ostensibly in the interest of the working people [were] in their practical effects at war with the good of society." After the Pullman strike of 1894, William Howard Taft said that labor unions, just like corporations, were capable of "great good and much evil."[26]

That this fear of labor violence reflected more than simple antagonism between economic classes is demonstrated by the reaction of ABA leaders to another violent combination of the period, the lynch mob. Elite lawyers were even more dismayed with lynch law than with labor violence because lynch mobs often included men of status and reputation, even lawyers. One ABA speaker said vigilante justice struck "at the very roots of all social order and opened wide...the road to anarchy with the gaunt, grim figure of the red specter grinning in the dis-

---

"Address of the President," 8 *ABA Rep* 149 @ 171 (1885). Morton Keller, *Affairs of State: Public Life in Late Nineteenth Century America* (Cambridge: Harvard University Press, 1977), 397, 399.

25. Samuel P. Hays, *The Response to Industrialism, 1885-1914* (Chicago: University of Chicago Press, 1957), 85; Keller, *Affairs of State*, 404.

26. William Allen Butler, "Address of the President," 9 *ABA Rep* 153 @ 168 (1886). During his lifetime, Butler, a wealthy but public-spirited New York corporation lawyer, was best known for a piece of satirical verse, "Nothing to Wear," which pointedly compared a society girl's lack of a stylish dress—what we would call "a first world problem"—to the real material needs of the urban poor. William Howard Taft, "Recent Criticism of the Federal Judiciary," 18 *ABA Rep* 237 @ 266 (1895); Charles Claflin Allen, "Injunction and Organized Labor," 17 *ABA Rep* 299 @ 324 (1894).

tance."[27] Thomas Cooley reminded the respectable lynch mob participant that when the disorder he had encouraged became general, it would not be "the vagabond or the beggar that the lawless classes [would] select for victims."[28]

While ABA speakers generally agreed that resort to lynch law could be curbed by speedier criminal court procedure, they found it more difficult to reach a consensus about how to solve the problem of labor violence. A popular notion during the 1880s was that arbitration might be the solution, and nearly every industrial state passed laws encouraging collective bargaining and arbitration.[29] For the legal elite, one advantage of arbitration was that it removed controverted social questions from the courts and thus protected judges from the charge that they were simply tools of capitalists. Nevertheless, lawyers were reluctant to endorse the notion that decisions rendered by panels of laymen were preferable to decisions rendered by legal professionals.[30]

---

27. Thomas J. Kernan, "The Jurisprudence of Lawlessness," 29 *ABA Rep* 450 @ 455-56 (1894). Kernan's chief concern was not the victim. To remedy the problem of lynching, he suggested censorship of courtroom testimony, hasty trials with no appeals, and public execution "by some form of death so supremely horrible as to strike terror even to the hearts of fiends themselves." (458) See also Henry B. Brown, "Judicial Independence," 12 *ABA Rep* 265 @ 286 (1889); "Report of the Committee on Delay and Uncertainty in the Law," 9 *ABA Rep* 351 (1886). In 1915, the ABA unanimously adopted a resolution condemning the Leo Frank lynching as "a willful and deliberate murder by mob violence, concerted and accomplished in a spirit of savage and remorseless cruelty unworthy of our age and time." *New York Times*, August 20, 1915, 4.
28. Thomas Cooley, "Address of the President," 17 *ABA Rep* 181 @ 219 (1894).
29. William E. Akin, "Arbitration and Labor Conflict: The Middle Class Panacea, 1886-1900," *Historian* 29 (1967), 565-583; Keller, 400.
30. E. B. Sherman, 10 *ABA Rep* 32-33 (1887); Moorfield Storey, "The

The general railroad strike beginning at the Pullman works in 1894 ended serious interest in arbitration. Most members of the American Bar Association were angered and frightened by the strike and sided firmly with President Grover Cleveland in his decision to send federal troops to Illinois against the wishes of Governor John P. Altgeld. Thomas Cooley spoke for the overwhelming majority of elite lawyers when, in his presidential address of 1894, he denounced the illegality of the Pullman boycott and the violence that "almost immediately" became "its leading characteristic." Cooley castigated strike leaders for ignoring the effects of coercion on their own, as well as the public's, interest. The constitutional position of Governor Altgeld—himself a member of the ABA—Cooley criticized as "unwarranted" and "revolutionary."[31]

American Legislature," 17 *ABA Rep* 245 @ 271 (1894); Charles C. Lancaster, 10 *ABA Rep* 36 (1877); George W. Biddle, "An Inquiry into the Proper Mode of Trial," 8 *ABA Rep* 201 @ 218-19 (1885); D. S. Troy, 10 *ABA Rep* 34-36 (1887); "Report of the Committee on Jurisprudence and Law Reform," 11 *ABA Rep* 301 @ 306 (1888). [Irving Browne], "Current Topics," 36 *Albany Law Journal* 161 (August 27, 1887): "A report in favor of a Federal Court of arbitration was the subject of an interesting and amusing discussion of two hours, exhibiting the jealousy of their prerogatives by the legal profession."

31. Thomas M. Cooley, "Address of the President," 17 *ABA Rep* 181 (1894) @ 225-233. The *New York Times* considered the speech important enough to print long extracts, and thereafter the *Times* published three editorials referring to it in the most complimentary terms. (*New York Times*, August 23, 1894, 4, 8; August 24, 4; August 26, 4). Altgeld replied that Cooley was simply "grateful" to Cleveland for his appointment to the Interstate Commerce Commission and that Cooley's "bright reputation" ought "not be clouded by utterances that are born of a grateful dotage . . .. In addressing the bar association he was in the position of a fashionable preacher who, if he wished to be popular with his audience, must cater to

Yet despite the relief of most Association members at the failure of the strike, the innovative use of the injunction that contributed to breaking it also disturbed members who believed that traditional legal procedures were as necessary to the preservation of the social order as was the suppression of labor violence. William Howard Taft noted that "many conservative, unprejudiced and patriotic citizens" feared the "unwise stretching of an equitable remedy to meet an emergency which should have been met in other ways." St. Louis attorney Charles Claflin Allen (1855-1927) criticized the use of the injunction as either a dangerous and unnecessary innovation, subversive of trial by jury, or as "a mere *pronunciamiento* of no force...tending to bring the judicial process of a court of equity into disrepute."[32]

---

its tastes. The American Bar Association is a small body of men, most of whom have corporations for clients. They are shrewd and able men who know where fat fees come from. A lawyer whose clients are poor could not afford to go to Saratoga and have a good time and attend a bar meeting. Judge Cooley's utterance there must be taken with some others recently made, and the question is, how much importance attaches to them simply because they came from Cooley?" John P. Altgeld, *Live Questions* (Chicago: George S. Bowen and Co., 1899), 418-420. Neither Altgeld nor any official of the Association mentioned his own membership in the ABA. Presumably, it was a mutual embarrassment. Altgeld was a member of the Association from 1889 until 1897. According to Clarence Darrow, Altgeld "didn't like law"; after a few years of undistinguished practice, it "became a sideline to his real estate and construction ventures." Harry Barnard, *Eagle Forgotten: The Life of John Peter Altgeld* (New York: Duell, Sloan and Pearce, 1938), 61.

32. Taft, "Recent Criticism of the Federal Judiciary," 18 *ABA Rep* 237 @ 271-72 (1895); Charles Claflin Allen, "Injunction and Organized Labor," 17 *ABA Rep* 299 @ 324 (1894). Allen replied to criticism of the speech at 17 *ABA Rep* 50 (1894); Paul, *Conservative Crisis and the Rule of Law*, 146-49.

During the spirited discussion that followed, other members voiced their fears of placing excessive power in the hands of a single judge, of giving the public the impression that courts cared more for capital than for labor, or of allowing soldiers to act "as sort of special police without the declaration of martial law." Even Taft, who fully supported federal action, regretted the public impression that federal courts existed "to foster corporate evils and to destroy all effort by labor to maintain itself."[33]

The general sentiment at the 1894 meeting was that the federal government's novel use of the injunction was both legal and necessary under the circumstances. Chicago attorney E. B. Sherman (1832-1910) argued that rather than degrade the judicial process, using injunctions during strikes would "teach the people of this country who think they are above the law, to beware of the lightning of justice." There was some concern that even discussing the question might lend comfort to the enemies of law and order.[34]

Still, by upholding the exercise of judicial power, ABA leaders were not necessarily defending an inflexible Constitution created by demigods and interpreted by nine men writing with the pen of inspiration—although such thinking has commonly been attributed to the late nineteenth-century bar. For instance, in his 1914 novel, *A Far Country*, the

---

33. Henry Budd, 17 *ABA Rep* 31-34 (1894); Waldo C. Morse, 17 *ABA Rep* 47 (1894); Richard Wayne Parker, "The Tyrannies of Free Government," 18 *ABA Rep* 295 @ 306 (1895); Taft, "Recent Criticism," 272.

34. E. B. Sherman, 17 *ABA Rep* 38-39 (1894); Edward F. Bullard, 17 *ABA Rep* 25-26 (1894); Judson Starr, 17 *ABA Rep* 15 (1894); William Wirt Howe, 17 *ABA Rep* 22-23 (1894); George Tucker Bispham, 17 *ABA Rep* 27-28 (1894); Alfred Hemenway, "The American Lawyer," 28 *ABA Rep* 390 @ 399-400 (1905).

American Winston Churchill had his lawyer-protagonist assert that he and his Harvard Law School class had been inculcated with the doctrine that lawyers

> were a priestly class set aside to guard from profanation that Ark of the Covenant, the Constitution of the United States. In short, I was taught law precisely as I had been taught religion—scriptural infallibility over again—a static law and a static theology—a set of concepts that were supposed to be equal to any problems civilization would have to meet until the millennium.[35]

Two important ABA addresses reflect precisely this view of the Constitution, and legal educators delivered them both: Edward J. Phelps of Yale (1879) and J. Randolph Tucker of Washington and Lee (1892). Phelps and Tucker were almost exact contemporaries, both had achieved professional success before the Civil War, and both were founders and later presidents of the American Bar Association. Both of their addresses were delivered in the antebellum oratorical style, and both envisioned a static Constitution guarded by a class of quasi-religious professionals. Tucker's introduction described the American bar as "that priestly tribe to whose hands are confided the support and defense of this Ark of the Covenant of our fathers." Phelps' peroration exhorted ABA members to "join hands in a fraternal and unbroken clasp, to

---

35. Winston Churchill, *A Far Country* (New York: The Macmillan Company, 1914), 133-34; see also the analysis of this novel in Maxwell Bloomfield, "Law and Lawyers in American Popular Culture," in Carl Smith, et al., *Law and American Literature* (New York: Alfred A. Knopf, 1983), 156.

maintain the grand and noble traditions of our inheritance, and to stand fast by the ark of our covenant."[36]

The speeches of Phelps and Tucker have lent themselves to scholarly quotation, no doubt in part, because their quaintness makes them ridiculous to modern ears.[37] Nevertheless, these speeches are unrepresentative of the contemporary ABA. While the legal elite always remained receptive to the notion that the future of the republic rested with lawyers, only rarely did the annual meeting serve as a forum for professions of faith in the unchangeable nature of the Constitution.

To the contrary, Charles F. Amidon (1856-1937), judge of the U.S. District Court for the District of North Dakota, ridiculed the words of Chief Justice Taney in the Dred Scott case that the Constitution "'Speaks not only in the same words, but with the same meaning and intent with which it spoke when it came from the hands of its framers.' The only objection to that fine phrase is that it is not true. The exact contrary would be nearer the truth."

Frank B. Kellogg (1856-1937) likewise urged ABA members not to worship antique ideals. "The Constitution," he said, "is not a commandment of divine origin, everlasting and unchangeable."[38]

---

36. J. Randolph Tucker, "British Institutions and American Constitutions," 15 *ABA Rep* 213 (1892); E. J. Phelps, "Chief Justice Marshall," 2 *ABA Rep* 173 @192 (1879). John F. Dillon, "Address of the President," 15 *ABA Rep*167 @ 210-211 (1892); Hampton L. Carson, "Great Dissenting Opinions," 17 *ABA Rep* 273 @ 298 (1894); Lindley M. Garrison, "Democracy and Law," 41 *ABA_Rep* 382 (1916). Garrison, who resigned as Secretary of War in 1916, was the last ABA speaker to use the "Ark of the Covenant" metaphor.
37. Twiss, 149-151, 159-161; Brockman, 280; Paul, 62-63, 76-77.
38. Charles F. Amidon, "The Nation and the Constitution," 31 *ABA Rep*

As early as 1885, Richard M. Venable (1839-1910), professor of Constitutional Law at the University of Maryland, flatly criticized the Constitution for its outmoded procedures. The electoral college, he said, had become an empty form, and the Founding Fathers' attempt to establish checks and balances involved "the same kind of absurdity as a man's attempting to lift himself by his boot-straps." Even the conservative theoretician George Sutherland (1862-1942), one of the future "Four Horsemen" of the New Deal Supreme Court, cautiously conceded the flexible nature of the Constitution. While to Sutherland the "principles of the Constitution" were not outgrown any more than the "Ten Commandments or the enduring morality of the Sermon on the Mount," the Constitution itself should not be considered a "dead wall in the path of progress. . . but a wide, free flowing stream within whose ample banks every needed and wholesome reform may be launched and carried."[39]

Considering the openness with which many ABA speakers announced their belief in the mutability of law and the Constitution, it is not surprising that they also acknowledged the judge to be an instrument of legal change. "It was long a favorite fiction that the judges did not make, but only de-

---

463 @ 467-68 (1907); Frank B. Kellogg, "New Nationalism," 37 *ABA Rep* 341 @ 369 (1912).

39. George Sutherland, "The Courts and the Constitution," 37 *ABA Rep* 371 @ 391, 371, 385 (1912); see also Richard M. Venable, "Partition of Powers Between the Federal and State Governments," 8 *ABA Rep* 235 @ 257, 256 (1885); Edward Quinton Keasbey, "New Jersey and the Great Corporations," 22 *ABA Rep* 379 @ 412-413 (1899); Le Baron B. Colt, "Law and Reasonableness," 26 *ABA Rep* 341 @ 361 (1903); J. M. Woolworth, "Jurisprudence Considered as a Branch of the Social Science," 11 *ABA Rep* 279 (1888); Roscoe Pound, "The Need of a Sociological Jurisprudence," 31 *ABA Rep* 911 @ 917 (1907).

clared the law," said New York corporation lawyer John F. Dillon (1831-1914) in 1886. "But [judicial lawmaking] is no longer anywhere denied." New Hampshire lawyer John Shirley argued that the fellow servant rule pronounced by Chief Justice Lemuel Shaw (1781-1861) of Massachusetts had been "established by a great and wise legislator as a species of protective tariff for the encouragement of infant railway industries." And in an ironic attack on judicial recall, Henry D. Estabrook (1854-1917), general solicitor for Western Union Telegraph, announced, "Give me the right to interpret a law by which I am to be bound, and I care not who makes it. Thus judges do make law. It is the most hypocritical of all legal fictions to say that they don't."[40]

---

40. John F. Dillon, "Law Reports and Law Reporting," 9 *ABA Rep* 257 @ 260 (1886). Dillon exaggerated when he said that judicial legislation was no longer *anywhere* denied. His fellow New Yorker and influential leader of the Association of the Bar of the City of New York, James C. Carter, did flatly deny it before the annual meeting of 1890. However, Carter's address was couched in such theoretical phrases that perhaps even this single strong exception might have been interpreted by listeners as appropriate to Carter's ethereal level of discourse. James C. Carter, "The Ideal and the Actual in the Law," 13 *ABA Rep* 217 @ 224, 231 (1890).

Carter's version of law as enshrined custom sometimes seems on the brink of evaporating in a self-generated mist. For instance, Carter said customary law "may justly be called Divine" because "it can have no other author than that of human nature itself"—even though imperfect examples of this divine-human customary law had to pass through various stages of development before it reached the "present enlightened age." James Coolidge Carter, *Law: Its Origin Growth and Function* (New York: G. P. Putnam, 1907), 231, 119. William P. LaPiana, *Logic and Experience: The Origin of Modern American Legal Education* (New York: Oxford University Press, 1994), 139-140.

See also U. M. Rose, "Title of Statutes," 5 *ABA Rep* 221 (1882); John M. Shirley, "The Future of Our Profession," 6 *ABA Rep* 195 @ 215, 211

To have asserted that law was static and that judges were simply engaged in a search for preexisting legal rules would not only have strained credulity, it would also have run contrary to a cardinal tenet of contemporary thinkers, belief in evolutionary naturalism. Speakers at pre-World War I meetings of the American Bar Association repeatedly drew parallels between biological and legal evolution. As early as 1879, James Broadhead, the first president, compared the development of common law to Darwinian struggle. In 1900, Richard Venable made legal evolution the theme of his address, and New Jersey Governor John W. Griggs employed evolutionary theory to defend the common law from what he considered undue legislative meddling.[41]

(1883); Henry D. Estabrook, "The American Judicial System: The Judges," 37 *ABA Rep* 393 @ 400 (1912); John W. Griggs, "Lawmaking," 20 *ABA Rep* 257 @ 268 (1897); Alfred Russell, "Avoidable Causes of Delay and Uncertainty in Our Courts," 14 *ABA Rep* 197 @ 211 (1891).

41. James M. Broadhead, "Address of the President," 2 *ABA Rep* 51 @ 70 (1897); Robert Green McCloskey, *American Conservatism in the Age of Enterprise, 1865-1910* (New York: Harper and Row, 1951), 26-31; Richard M. Venable, "Growth or Evolution of Law," 23 *ABA Rep* 278 @ 286 (1900); John W. Griggs, "Lawmaking," 20 *ABA Rep* 257 @ 267 (1897): "The contemplation of the history of the system of English law which we inherit is to the lawyer a cause of enthusiasm and a lesson in conservatism. To trace the growth of this system from the earliest beginnings, from the proto-plasmic cells, so to speak, of village and tribal customs among the primeval fens and forests of Saxony, or the bogs and crags of Jutland, on through centuries of progressive evolution upon English soil and under English skies until we see its mature development is well calculated to arouse the admiration and enthusiasm of the lawyer and statesman as well as of the mere student of history. Modern scholars like Sir Henry Maine, Professor Austin, Doctor Stubbs and Professor Maitland, have done for the history of law what Darwin and his successors have done in the domain of biology." Henry Estabrook took the comparison between natural scientists and legal theorists one step further

Though the materialism and naturalism of Darwinian theory had its roots in Enlightenment thought rather than in conservative tradition, its philosophical origins did not prevent evolution from running under conservative colors. First, evolution was slow. As ABA President Charles Manderson said in 1899, "Nature, in her evolutionary processes, moves with a deliberation only equaled by her precision. Her motto seems to be, 'make haste slowly!'"[42] Further, legal evolution promised continued progress with a minimum of conscious—that is to say, legislative—direction. Finally, and perhaps most importantly, the evolutionary paradigm firmly linked law to science, an attractive association in an era that had witnessed the rise of scientific professionalism. Since science seemed to have shaken, if not destroyed, the religious foundation on which law had previously been predicated, leaders of the American Bar Association rushed to abandon old gods for new, substituting a hazy, if optimistic, vision of evolutionary progress for the older moral imperatives.[43]

---

by asking if anyone of his hearers could "doubt that Lyell, Darwin, Spencer and Huxley were great lawyers in the domain of natural science?"—a curious professional conceit. Henry D. Estabrook, "The Lawyer, Hamilton," 24 *ABA Rep* 351 @ 352 (1901).

42. Charles Manderson, "Address of the President," 22 *ABA Rep* 219 @228 (1899).

43. George R. Peck, "Address of the President," 29 *ABA Rep* 297 @ 301-02, 320 (1906); Richard Venable, "Growth or Evolution of Law," 297ff.; Richard L. Hand, "Government by the People," 28 *ABA Rep* 407 (1905); Mark Norris, "Some Notions about Legal Education," 30 *ABA Rep* 71 (1906). Peck was unsure if "evolution" were progress: "[W]e shall go forward, maybe to better things. But anyway, we shall go forward." Henry Adams noted that "Unbroken Evolution under uniform conditions pleased everyone except curates and bishops; it was the very best substitute for religion; a safe, conservative, practical thoroughly Common-Law deity." *The Education of Henry Adams* (New York: Modern Library, 1918), 225.

There were difficulties to be sure. In the first place, elite lawyers had to lift their sights above "Nature, red in tooth and claw." They had to imagine evolutionary struggle as a matter for the boardroom and courtroom, not for battlefields or barricades. Further, the legal elite failed to appreciate the consequences of subscribing to a thesis that ultimately made man a pawn of impersonal forces, a theory that, in the words of William Jennings Bryan, had "a tendency to paralyze the conscience."[44] Finally, the legal elite seem to have embraced the unwarranted confidence that the profession was riding an evolutionary wave that would fall in agreeable directions.[45]

Certainly, the elite insisted that evolutionary progress was contingent on untrammeled exposition of the Constitution by the courts.[46] When, at the annual meeting of 1883, the

---

44. *The Commoner* 16:3 (March 1916), 18.

45. James O. Broadhead, "Address of the President," 2 *ABA Rep* 51 @ 69 (1879); Emory A. Storrs, 6 *ABA Rep* 37 (1883); William P. Wells, "The Dartmouth College Case and Private Corporations," 9 *ABA Rep* 229 @ 254 (1886); Frederick N. Judson, "Liberty of Contract under the Police Power," 14 *ABA Rep* 231 @ 258 (1891); Montague Crackanthorpe, "The Uses of Legal History," 19 *ABA Rep* 343 @ 356 (1896); Edmund Wetmore, "Address of the President," 24 *ABA Rep* 203 @ 236 (1901); Roscoe Pound, "The Need of a Sociological Jurisprudence," 31 *ABA Rep* 911 @ 925 (1907); Frank B. Kellogg, "New Nationalism," 37 *ABA Rep* 341 @ 346 (1912). Simeon Baldwin managed to connect evolution with higher law, arguing that "principles, not cases" were "the building stones of law, here and everywhere, now and always." Simeon E. Baldwin, "Teaching Law by Cases," 14 *Harvard Law Review* 258-60 (1900). William P. LaPiana, *Logic and Experience: The Origin of Modern American Legal Education* (New York: Oxford University Press, 1994), 140-142.

46. Morton Keller, *In Defense of Yesterday: James M. Beck and the Politics of Conservatism, 1861-1936* (New York: Coward-McCann, Inc.,1958), 45; E. J. Phelps, "Chief Justice Marshall," 2 *ABA Rep* 173 @ 183 (1879); William Howard Taft, "Recent Criticism of the Federal Judiciary," 18 *ABA Rep* 237

young Galveston attorney Robert G. Street (1843-1924) argued that courts should *not* have the power to declare acts of the legislature unconstitutional, the mordant Irving Browne was on hand to describe the verbal fireworks that followed. Street's "heresy," wrote Browne, "raised in horror the few remaining hairs on the heads of the reverend seniors of the association, and Mr. Street was accordingly offered up for reprobation for two bad hours."[47]

Support of judicial power by the legal elite was hardly disinterested. "Law is not simply the latest guess of a Supreme Court," said Henry Estabrook; "a good lawyer may sometimes prevail upon that tribunal to guess again."[48] But guesses of

---

@ 251 (1895); Moorfield Storey, "Address of the President," 19 *ABA Rep* 179 @ 251 (1896); James D. May to William Howard Taft, February 2, 1914, Taft Papers; Thomas M. Cooley, "Address of the President," 17 *ABA Rep* 181 @ 212 (1894).

47. Robert G. Street, "How Far Questions of Public Policy May Enter into Judicial Decisions," 6 *ABA Rep* 179 (1883); "Current Topics," 28 *Alb. Law J.* 161 (1883); see also 17 *American Law Review* 790-91 (1883); 6 *ABA Rep* 14 ff. (1883). (Nevertheless, in 1915, when Street was 72, he served on the ABA Committee to Oppose the Judicial Recall.) "Let us encourage rather than retard, the work of judicial evolution," C. C. Bonney replied to Street. "Let us acknowledge and honor, rather than decry and seek to remove that golden crown of constitutional government, JUDICIAL SUPREMACY." C. C. Bonney, 6 *ABA Rep* 18 (1883).

In 1901, Congressman Charles E. Littlefield of Maine, an anti-imperialist, attacked the Supreme Court's handling of the Insular Cases. Adolph Moses attempted a rebuttal and was called out of order by the president. When he tried to leave the hall, "his progress was barred by a dozen men who crowded around him. 'Let me shake your hand.' 'Good boy, Moses.' 'Littlefield's attack was a shame.' 'Why didn't you say more?' and similar expression were offered him. Men grasped him warmly by the hand and an enthusiastic group almost carried him from the theater." *Denver Post*, August 22, 1901, 2.

48. Henry D. Estabrook, "The Lawyer, Hamilton," 24 *ABA Rep* 351-352

courts, whether first or subsequent, would be of limited value if the influence and prestige of courts could not be preserved.

Even the perennial request of the Association that federal judges be paid higher salaries was an innocuous way for elite lawyers to assure the judiciary of their support. Even criticizing certain aspects of court procedure might, in the long run, bolster the judicial system.[49]

An early debate regarding the possible reform or elimination of the jury system was largely framed around how such a change might affect the authority of the courts. During the first two decades of the Association's history, members sharply criticized juries as an gratuitous concession to ignorance and irrationality.[50] Speakers also noted with concern that some chambers of commerce and manufacturer's associations had established boards of arbitration to keep commercial controversies from the delay and haphazard results of jury trials.[51] In 1891, the Association endorsed legislation or a

---

(1901); see also James Bryce, *The American Commonwealth* (New York: Macmillan Company, 1910), rev. ed., 1: 266; 14 *ABA Rep* 4 (1891); James O. Broadhead, 1 *National Bar Association Proceedings* 21 (1888).

49. Lawrence M. Friedman, "Law Reform in Historical Perspective," 13 *St. Louis University Law Journal* 351 @ 358 (1969): "To admit to some defects in one's own system and to search for one's own solutions may be tactically wise."

50. Attacks on the intelligence and integrity of jurymen are easy enough to find. Alfred Russell, "Avoidable Causes of Delay and Uncertainty in Our Courts," 14 *ABA Rep* 197 @ 208 (1891); John M. Shirley, "The Future of Our Profession," 6 *ABA Rep* 195 @ 216-222 (1883); Edward B. Sturges, 9 *ABA Rep* 415 (1886); 9 *ABA Rep* 412 (1886). The Committee on Delay and Uncertainty in the Law, 9 *ABA Rep* 338 (1886); L. C. Krauthoff, "Malice as an Ingredient of a Civil Cause of Action," 21 *ABA Rep* 335 @ 386 (1898); "Minority Report of the Committee on Judicial Administration and Remedial Procedure," 14 *ABA Rep* 299 (1891).

51. Charles C. Lancaster, 14 *ABA Rep* 40 (1891). George Mercer, 4 *ABA*

constitutional amendment that, in civil cases, would permit a verdict by a three-fourths majority of the jury. Two members predicted that the jury system would disappear altogether.[52]

But defenders of the jury system never entirely disappeared, and gradually sentiment within the Association shifted in its favor. By the turn of the century, ABA members, who had listened to attacks on courts for at least a decade, now began to believe that juries might help bolster respect for the judicial system.[53]

As late as 1903, even as courts came under increasing scrutiny from critics outside the legal profession, the Committee on Judicial Administration and Remedial Procedure reported that it had nothing of sufficient interest to bring before the Association. Three years later, however, the Association found it politic to admit that there were defects in the judicial system, the catalyst originating in a speech at the St. Paul meeting of 1906 by the 36-year-old Roscoe Pound of the University of

---

Rep 77 (1881); Alfred Russell, "Avoidable Causes," 206 (1891); Martin W. Cooke, President of the New York State Bar Association, "Presidential Address," 11 *NYSBA Proceedings* 38 @ 47 (1888).

52. 14 *ABA Rep* 38ff., 281ff. (1891); Charles C. Lancaster, 14 *ABA Rep* 40 (1891); Henry B. Brown, "Judicial Independence," 12 *ABA Rep* 265 @ 287 (1889), Samuel Haber, *The Quest for Authority and Honor in the American Professions, 1750-1900* (Chicago: University of Chicago Press, 1991), 220.

53. John F. Dillon, "American Institutions and Laws," 7 *ABA Rep* 203 @ 219 (1884); see also George W. Biddle, "An Inquiry into the Proper Mode of Trial," 8 *ABA Rep* 201 (1885). Biddle recommended a smaller jury to obtain a more intelligent panel, to increase individual responsibility, and to decrease the expense of trials; he also argued that courts convene during non-business hours. J. M. Woolworth, "Address of the President," 20 *ABA Rep* 253 (1897); Harvey N. Shepard, 28 *ABA Rep* 17 (1905). In the absence of an expected speaker in 1905, Shepard led a discussion on the topic of what could be done to improve the jury. No one suggested the jury be abolished.

Nebraska. In professional legend, Pound's speech became a "celebrated address." John H. Wigmore, writing thirty years later, claimed it had kindled "the white flame of Progress" in the Association. Pound's first biographer asserted that it was "the most significant address ever delivered before the American Bar Association before or since." Sylvester Smith, President of the Association in 1962-63, dated a new era of the organization from the speech. In 1964 the Association dedicated a plaque at the site of its delivery.[54]

In the speech, Pound argued that Americans were dissatisfied with the current administration of justice for three basic reasons: disharmony between the individualist spirit of the common law and the collectivist spirit of the age, lack of a philosophic basis for legal reforms, and the adversarial nature of Anglo-American law. Pound criticized the multiplicity of courts, their concurrent jurisdictions, and the time wasted on points of pure practice. He shrewdly noted that modern law had now to do some of the work once performed by morality; and he criticized the lack of popular interest in justice, the degradation of the legal profession, and the courtroom reporting of the yellow press.[55]

---

54. 26 ABA Rep 10-11 (1903); John H. Wigmore, "Roscoe Pound's St. Paul Address of 1906: The Spark that Kindled the White Flame of Progress," 20 *Journal of the American Judicature Society* 176-178 (1937); Paul L. Sayre, *The Life of Roscoe Pound* (Iowa City: State University of Iowa, 1948), 146; Sylvester C. Smith, Jr., "The President's Annual Address: Where Does the Organized Bar Go from Here?" 49 *ABAJ* 847 (1963); Wayne K. Hobson, *The American Legal Profession and the Organizational Society, 1890-1930* (New York: Garland Publishing, 1986), 273-74.

55. Roscoe Pound, "The Causes of Popular Dissatisfaction with the Administration of Justice," 29 *ABA Rep* 395-417 (1906).

At the conclusion of Pound's speech, Everett P. Wheeler (1840-1925), a New York admiralty lawyer and urban reformer, moved that unanimous consent be given for the printing of four thousand copies of the speech. An acrimonious debate then ensued during which James Dewitt Andrews (1856-1928) and M. A. Spoonts (1857-1912), claimed Pound's speech to be an assault on the court system. The matter was referred to the Committee on Judicial Administration and Remedial Procedure, and in the following year, the Association endorsed Pound's criticisms.[56]

Though the speech was later represented as a moment when younger, more progressive, leaders replaced the old guard, that interpretation has been overstated. President George Peck (1843-1923), a railroad general solicitor, had invited Pound to speak and knew in advance what he was going to say. After delivering his speech, Pound was congratulated by Association mainstays.[57] James D. Andrews, Pound's chief antagonist, was a Wall Street attorney but also something of a crank who overrated his own importance in the scheme of things, believing that an introduction to law that he had

---

56. 29 *ABA Rep* 12, 55-65 (1906); 31 *ABA Rep* 52, 505-512 (1907); Sunderland, 128-29; N.E.H. Hull, "Restatement and Reform: A New Perspective on the Origins of the American Law Institute," *Law and History Review*, 8 (Spring 1990), 55-58.

57. John H. Wigmore's article is the most extreme example of Pound worship; but see also Smith's, "Address," and to a lesser extent Max Radin, "The Achievements of the American Bar Association: A Sixty Year Record," 25 *ABAJ* 1010 (1939); Norbert Brockman, "The Politics of the American Bar Association," Ph.D. dissertation, Catholic University of American, 1963, 62-63. More restrained is Whitney North Seymour, "The First Century of the American Bar Association," 64 *ABAJ* 1038 @ 1041 (1978).

written was destined to become "an American Blackstone." Spoonts of Texas was a comparatively minor trial lawyer. At the time, Pound expressed irritation at their "legal illiteracy," but in later years, he admitted that the opposition of Andrews and Spoonts "impressed Dean Wigmore, who was not an active participant in the work of the Association, as amounting to very much more than it really did."[58]

The ABA leadership found Pound's speech more than acceptable. Pound had emphasized the evolutionary nature of legal development; he had endorsed the scientific study of the law and the necessity for bar associations; he had stressed that only lawyers could determine which defects of the legal system were remediable and how to correct them. Finally, Pound had expressed the desire that the courts would be "swift and certain agents of justice, whose decisions will be acquiesced in and respected by all."[59]

After Pound's address, the Association created a Committee to Suggest Remedies and Formulate Proposed Laws to

---

58. Roscoe Pound to Norbert Brockman, May 24, 1960, copy in possession of the author; James D. Andrews, 29 *ABA Rep* 56 (1906). For insight into the character of Andrews, see the discussion at 47 *ABA Rep* 82-94 (1922); James D. Andrews to Roscoe Pound, August 20, 1921, Pound Papers, Box 160, folder 2.; Henry D. Estabrook, "Report of the Committee on Judicial Administration and Remedial Procedure," 31 *ABA Rep* 505 @ 506 (1907). Estabrook was stingingly sarcastic while recapitulating the arguments of Andrews and Spoonts. Roscoe Pound to Edward A. Ross, November 2, 1906, in David Wigdor, *Roscoe Pound: Philosopher of Law* (Westport, Conn.: Greenwood Press, 1974), 127.

59. Pound, "Dissatisfaction with the Administration of Law," 29 *ABA Rep* 395 @ 417 (1906). For an excellent example of an attack on Progressivism combined with high praise for Pound and sociological jurisprudence, see Henry D. Estabrook, "The American Judicial System: The Judges," 37 *ABA Rep* 393-410 (1912).

Prevent Delay and Unnecessary Cost in Litigation, a committee to which both Pound and James Andrews were appointed. Under the leadership of Everett Wheeler, who took his responsibilities seriously, the committee became one of the most active in the Association. Nevertheless, even ABA historian Edson Sunderland (1874-1959) admitted that only "very slight results" were obtained from the committee's "persistent and continuous efforts."[60]

When the committee attempted to explain why none of the reforms it had sponsored had been enacted into law, it blamed the failure on the "indifference of Congress."[61] Of all branches of the government—including the bureaucracy—the leaders of the American Bar Association most distrusted the legislative branch. Even before the Association was organized, Simeon Baldwin predicted that the ABA would be "of great service . . . in publishing the failure of unsuccessful experiments in legislation." Baldwin's constitution directed Association presidents to review "noteworthy changes in statute law" at the annual meeting, and in practice, these recitations often included sneers at what the legal elite considered inane legislation.[62]

---

60. 31 *ABA Rep* 193 (1907); Everett P. Wheeler, *Sixty Years of American Life* (New York: E. P. Dutton & Company, 1917), 403-04; Sunderland, 130-134; Maynard E. Pirsig, "The Historical Role of the American Bar Association in Judicial Administration," 16 *William Mitchell Law Review* 1195 @ 1202 (1990).

61. 50 *ABA Rep* 407 (1925).

62. Simeon Baldwin to Charles Train, *et al.*, May 23, 1878, in Simeon Baldwin, "The Founding of the American Bar Association," 3 *ABAJ* 658 @ 665 (1917); Constitution, Art. VIII, 2 *ABA Rep* 22 (1879); see also *New York Times*, August 18, 1881, 4; George G. Wright, "Address of the President," 11 *ABA Rep* 169 @ 211-212 (1888).

In 1881, ABA President E. J. Phelps claimed that the country might "endure all its other dangers with less apprehension than the action its federal and state legislation inspires." At more heated moments Association called legislators "reckless politicians" who truckled for "the unthinking vote," "social agitators" who sought office for "self-advantage, not for the public weal," and "professional demagogues" who filled the land with "ill-considered and impractical theories" and who engaged in "gross, persistent, flagrant and sometimes corrupt dereliction."[63] ABA speakers who defended legislators usually did so apologetically.[64]

The legal elite had three major reasons for its antipathy toward legislators. First, professional orthodoxy avowed that

---

63. Edward J. Phelps, "Address of the President," 4 *ABA Rep*_141 @ 172 (1881); Moorfield Storey, "The American Legislature," 17 *ABA Rep* 245 @ 248-250 (1894); Frederick N. Judson, "Liberty of Contract under the Police Power," 14 *ABA Rep* 231 @ 232 (1891); Alton B. Parker, "Address of the President," 31 *ABA Rep* 339 @ 344 (1907); George Sutherland, "The Courts and the Constitution," 37 *ABA Rep* 371 @ 373 (1912); S. S. Gregory, "Address of the President," 37 *ABA Rep* 255 @ 284 (1912); Charles F. Manderson, "Address of the President," 23 *ABA Rep* 179 @ 213 (1900); Charles F. Libby, "Address of the President," 35 *ABA Rep*_331 @ 333 (1910). As usual, David Dudley Field took the opposite position: "It is a bad omen when there is fomented, as there is now, a general disrespect for legislatures." David Dudley Field, "Address of the President," 12 *ABA Rep* 149 @ 150 (1889).

64. Edmund Wetmore, "Address of the President," 24 *ABA Rep* 203 @ 239 (1901): "[I]ndignation at iniquity, or impatience with ignorance and stupidity, should not habitually divert our attention from what is good and admirable." See also Simon Sterne, "The Prevention of Defective and Slipshod Legislation," 7 *ABA Rep* 275 @ 301 (1884); George R. Peck, "Address of the President," 29 *ABA Rep* 297 @ 306, 308 (1906); Richard C. Dale, "Implied Limitations upon the Exercise of the Legislative Power," 24 *ABA Rep* 294 @ 308 (1901).

lawyers bore a responsibility for maintaining the social order, that true legal progress was the product of gradual development, and that this evolution was best directed into acceptable channels by the judiciary.[65]

Second, in the early years of the nation's history, the legal elite had been entrusted with the legislative affairs of the state—or at least so the guild mythology averred. It was argued that beginning in the Jacksonian era, this hegemony of elite lawyers had been eroded by professional politicians. Bar association members could no longer challenge politicians on their own turf because elite lawyers would be forced to grovel for the votes of the masses while abandoning the more lucrative worlds of industrial and financial capitalism.[66]

---

65. Alexander R. Lawton, "Address of the President," 6 *ABA Rep* 137 @ 175 (1883); Andrew Allison, "The Rise and Probable Decline of Public Corporations in America," 7 *ABA Rep* 241 @ 256 (1884); John W. Stevenson, "Address of the President," 8 *ABA Rep* 149 @ 150 (1885); Edward J. Phelps, "Address of the President," 4 *ABA Rep* 141 @ 171 (1881); John W. Griggs, "Lawmaking," 20 *ABA Rep* 257 @ 269 (1897); see also William A. Glasgow, "A Dangerous Tendency of Legislation," 26 *ABA Rep* 376 @ 382 (1903); Henry D. Estabrook, "The American Judicial System: The Judges," 37 *ABA Rep* 393 @ 405 (1912); Alton B. Parker, "Address of the President," 31 *ABA Rep* 339 @ 341 (1907). Only one direct attack was made on judicial legislation during this period, beyond that of Robert Street in 1883: Richard C. Dale (1853-1904), "Implied Limitations upon the Exercise of the Legislative Powers," 24 *ABA Rep* 294 (1901). Dale, a Philadelphia lawyer, was not a significant figure in either the profession or the Association.

66. Ethelbert Callahan,12 *ABA Rep* 381 (1889); Maxwell Bloomfield, *American Lawyers in a Changing Society, 1776-1876* (Cambridge: Harvard University Press, 1976), 149. Luke P. Poland, who helped establish the American Bar Association, held more political offices than most of the bar elite. James Fairbanks Colby wrote that the "interruptions in his political career were due to his conservative character, aristocratic bearing,

The dilemma of the legal elite, as Maxwell Bloomfield recognized, was that their professional antagonism toward legislatures was difficult to reconcile with their support for the legal order: "if legislatures were corrupt and the laws they passed unwise, why should citizens obey?"[67] To maintain their credibility as professionals, elite lawyers had to find some way of reintroducing themselves into American political life. It seemed unlikely they would run for office. The low pay of a state legislator would "affright the able lawyer," and unless the elite curried favor with special interests, they would lose the elections anyway.[68]

Some ABA members adopted a popular suggestion of the period, that state legislatures be restricted to meeting only every other year. The rationale behind the proposal, in the sarcastic words of Simon Sterne, was that since "legislatures do more harm than good when they meet, cut their years of meeting to one half, and presto! but half the mischief." Sterne called this logic "the merest refuge of imbecility." Many new state constitutions did mandate short, biennial sessions for their legislatures, but the quantity of legislation was not much reduced nor the quality increased.[69]

---

unwillingness to sacrifice his self-respect in order to win popularity and, more than all, to his complete lack of the small arts of the politician." (*Dictionary of American Biography*, 8: 34) The same could be said for Simeon Baldwin and many other ABA leaders of this period.

67. Bloomfield, 152.

68. Ethelbert Callahan, 12 *ABA Rep* 381 (1889); John W. Griggs, "Law-making," 20 *ABA Rep* 257 @ 272 (1897); Reuben C. Benton, "The Distinction between Legislative and Judicial Functions," 8 *ABA Rep* 261 @ 265 (1885); J. Randolph Tucker, "Address of the President," 16 *ABA Rep* 159 @ 203 (1893); see also "The American Bar Association—Tenth Annual Meeting," 21 *Am. L. Rev.* 619 (1887).

69. Francis Kernan, "Address of the President," 5 *ABA Rep* 167 @ 175

More perspicacious was the proposal that some sort of drafting bureau be created in each state to revise "slipshod" laws. Not original with the ABA or even with the post-Civil War bar, the idea had been advanced in legal periodicals since the 1830s.[70] The ABA formally endorsed such drafting bureaus as early as 1882 and maintained a sporadic interest in the subject until 1921 when the Special Committee on Drafting of Legislation was discharged at its own request because it thought the idea of expert drafting assistance for legislative bodies had been "generally recognized." The model statute adopted by the Association was cautious in that it recommended only "a joint standing committee for the revision of bills" rather than an independent commission. However, in a flight of fancy, C. C. Bonney (1831-1903) envisioned state senates "composed only of experienced professional men, assimilated in tenure and compensation to the judiciary in order that bills might be constructed clearly." These bodies, said Bonney, would substitute for the "hereditary governing class of other countries."[71]

Broad use of drafting bureaus might have increased the influence of lawyers who would have likely been appointed to them. These lawyers might then have passed off the correction of slipshod legislation as technical, non-political im-

---

(1882); Cortlandt Parker, "Address of the President," 7 *ABA Rep* 147 @ 149-150 (1884); William Allen Butler, "Address of the President," 9 *ABA Rep* 153 @ 155 (1886); Henry Hitchcock, "Address of the President," 13 *ABA Rep* 147 @ 214 (1890); see also Edward J. Phelps, "Address of the President," 4 *ABA Rep* 141 @ 171 (1881). Simon Sterne, "The Prevention of Defective and Slipshod Legislation," 7 *ABA Rep* 275 @ 296-98 (1884); Morton Keller, *Affairs of State*, 319-322.

70. Maxwell Bloomfield, *American Lawyers in a Changing Society*, 153.

71. 5 *ABA Rep* 13, 305 (1882); 46 *ABA Rep* 68 (1921); Sunderland, 75-76, 147-48; C. C. Bonney, 7 *ABA Rep* 57 (1884).

provements, even if the modifications resulted in substantive change. Of course, support of the drafting bureaus would depend on the tender mercies of the very legislative bodies whose irresponsibility the bureaus were supposed to check. Though progressives in some states were able to create legislative reference libraries staffed with experts who could help with the technical side of drafting legislation, the notion of drafting bureaus really anticipated the development of bureaucracies, which could exercise authority with minimal political risk.[72]

A third cause of antipathy between legislators and the legal elite was ideological. Obviously, the conservative elite was as much concerned with the substance of the legislation as it was with shoddy drafting or lack of deference to the judiciary. A cynic examining selected passages from ABA speeches might conclude that lawyers' concerns about legislative incompetence were mere pretext to mask partisan goals. But that conclusion would be wrong. The American Bar Association could never reach agreement about which sort of legislation was constructive and which destructive.

The closest that the Association ever came to a consensus was in its attack on government "paternalism."[73] U. M. Rose

---

72. Bloomfield, *American Lawyers in a Changing Society*, 153; John W. Griggs, "Lawmaking," 20 *ABA Rep* 257 @ 274-75 (1897); Ross, *A Muted Fury*, 80; Russel B. Nye, *Midwestern Progressive Politics: A Historical Study of Its Origins and Development, 1870-1950* (East Lansing: Michigan State College Press, 1951), 219.

73. J. Randolph Tucker, "British Institutions and American Constitutions," 15 *ABA Rep* 213 @ 231 (1892). Tucker's speech was devoted to an attack on "paternalism," and, according to the *American Law Review* (26 *Am. L. Rev.* 746 [1892]), it "called forth much applause." See also Charles Manderson, "Address of the President," 22 *ABA Rep* 219 @ 239 (1899).

tied together two fears of the legal elite when he pointed out that if government should "buy up all the railroads and telegraphs" the controlling power "would be placed in the hands of American politicians," and the nation would be covered "with officials like the locusts of Egypt."[74]

Such sentiments expressed before the American Bar Association are hardly surprising. More remarkable are the host of contradictory statements made in the same years and before the same audiences. For instance, Randolph Tucker who, in Irving Browne's words, had "tossed, gored, trampled on and rent the detestable doctrine" of paternalism had also announced four years earlier that the regulation of interstate commerce by Congress was a positive good.[75] William

---

(Because of the absence of Joseph Choate as Ambassador to Great Britain in 1899, Manderson delivered two consecutive presidential addresses.) The implication was that as man had reached a level of evolution requisite for his own self-government, paternalism was retrogressive. Henry Jackson, "Indemnity the Essence of Insurance," 10 *ABA Rep* 261 @ 280 (1887); James Woolworth, "The Development of the Law of Contracts," 19 *ABA Rep* 287 @ 317 (1896); William A. Glasgow, Jr., "A Dangerous Tendency of Legislation," 26 *ABA Rep* 376 @ 393 (1903); Henry St. George Tucker, "Address of the President," 28 *ABA Rep* 299 @ 379-81 (1905); Henry Estabrook, "The American Judicial System: The Judges," 37 *ABA Rep* 393 @ 404 (1912). "No free people will ever submit to any such doctrine," said Edgar H. Farrar, "It is the socialism of Marx and Engel [sic] pure and simple." Farrar, "Address of the President," 36 *ABA Rep* 229 @ 250 (1911); see also John W. Cary, "Limitations of the Legislative Power in Respect to Personal Rights and Private Property," 15 *ABA Rep* 245 @ 277-278 (1892).

74. U. M. Rose, "The Law of Trusts and Strikes," 16 *ABA Rep* 287 @ 308-09 (1893); see also J. Randolph Tucker, "British Institutions," 15 *ABA Rep* 213 @ 232-33, 243 (1892).

75. J. Randolph Tucker, "Congressional Power over Interstate Commerce," 11 *ABA Rep* 247 @ 276 (1888); 26 *American Law Review* 746 (1892). Of course the Interstate Commerce Act had been drafted by, and was

Glasgow, who insisted in one part of a speech that governmental aid to individuals only sapped their character, declared in another that there was "no cause for anxiety or fear that the constitutional liberty of the individual" would be impaired by the growth of the state police power. In 1885, while reviewing the growth of the federal involvement in agriculture, education, and health, Richard Venable thought it would be hard to find any part of the Constitution that would sustain such legislation; but, he continued, "I see no occasion for making ourselves unhappy over this state of things, more than I do for mourning over evolution."[76]

The paradox of these conflicting views is at least in part attributable to the belief of the legal elite that government regulation of certain private activities was necessary for social order. In his presidential address of 1888, George Wright praised legislation that provided for "the better protection of labor [and the] more efficient means for its certain payment." Such laws, he said, would protect the public from "that spirit of anarchy and violence which scouts all law ...places the individual above courts, juries, their verdicts and judgments, and thus endangers not only the public peace and welfare but the very existence of organized government."[77] Other paternalistic legislation escaped criticism because it attempted to aid the unfortunate, including legislation that promoted railway safety, food and drug laws, and provision for parks,

---

administered by, lawyers, not by special interests.

76. William A. Glasgow, Jr., "A Dangerous Tendency of Legislation," 26 *ABA Rep* 376 @ 383-384 (1903); Richard M. Venable, "Partition of Powers between the Federal and State Governments," 8 *ABA Rep* 235 @ 259 (1885).

77. George G. Wright, "Address of the President," 11 *ABA Rep* 169 @ 214 (1888).

water, sewers, fire codes, and public libraries.[78] In his presidential address of 1909, Frederick Lehmann dismissed the notion that laws "which look to shorter hours of arduous and dangerous labor, to the relief of women from the thrall of unwomanly drudgery, and to the care of children that they may develop into strong manhood and good womanhood" bore any relationship to "the bread and circuses of decadent Rome." Even a reactionary like Alexander Lawton believed that protecting Yellowstone Park and planting shade trees along highways in New York were "in the direction of a more cultivated state and a higher civilization."[79]

A few ABA speakers went further and advocated just those kinds of government action that others had called paternalistic. That Roscoe Pound, Eugene Wambaugh, and Charles Amidon would advocate more governmental regulation is not surprising—though the fact that they were invited to address the Association at all is worth consideration.[80] Nevertheless, even

---

78. Thomas J. Semmes, "Address of the President," 10 *ABA Rep* 157 @ 231 (1887); Eugene Wambaugh, "The Present Scope of Government," 20 *ABA Rep* 307 @ 322-23 (1897); John W. Stevenson, "Address of the President," 8 *ABA Rep* 149 @ 167,183 (1885); Cortlandt Parker, "Address of the President," 7 *ABA Rep* 147 (1884), passim.

79. Frederick W. Lehmann, "Address of the President," 34 *ABA Rep* 347 @ 371 (1909); see also Amos M. Thayer, "The Louisiana Purchase," 27 *ABA Rep* 312 @ 333 (1904). Alexander R. Lawton, "Address of the President," 6 *ABA Rep* 137 @ 170-71 (1883). Lawton criticized a Tennessee liability compensation law that provided damages for accidental death to the next-of-kin. "If the damages referred to are pecuniary," said Lawton, "the next of kin can scarcely suffer them by the death of a relative. They often have their condition much improved by 'his taking off.'" The best that can be said for such a crack is that Lawton had spent a good part of his life serving armies and railroads.

80. Roscoe Pound, "The Causes of Popular Dissatisfaction with the

the more forward-looking of ABA members were perhaps startled by an address delivered in 1893 by Supreme Court Justice Henry B. Brown (1836-1913). Brown not only advocated wage and hour legislation and health regulations for factories—legislation state courts had been striking down for a decade—but he went on to support government ownership of gas, electricity, telephones, rapid transit, telegraphs, express delivery, and ultimately canals and railways. He ruminated on the possibility of setting a million-dollar limit for any individual inheritance and, in conclusion, pronounced himself "by no means satisfied that the maxim that the country that is governed least is governed best, may not, in these days of monopolies and combinations, be subject to revision."[81]

Administration of Justice," 29 *ABA Rep* 395 @ 403; Pound, "The Need of a Sociological Jurisprudence," 31 *ABA Rep* 911 (1907); Eugene Wambaugh, "The Present Scope of Government," 20 *ABA Rep* 307 @ 321, 324 (1897); Charles F. Amidon, "The Nation and the Constitution," 31 *ABA Rep* 463 @ 474, 485 (1907).

81. Henry B. Brown, "The Distribution of Property," 16 *ABA Rep* 213 (1893); see also Arnold M. Paul, *Conservative Crisis and the Rule of Law*, 84-88. In his best-selling, 1956 biography of Louis Brandeis, Alpheus Thomas Mason (1899-1989) asserted that the bar elite were all laissez-faire conservatives: "Economic activity, they all held, is governed by natural laws of its own; so long as government does not interfere, these basic laws work inevitably for universal human betterment. To these partisans, all movements of dissent were stimulated by 'foreign agitators,' and had to be ruthlessly suppressed if American institutions were to endure." Mason continued with the startling assertion that this "dogma was very clearly stated in 1893, in an address before the American Bar Association, by Supreme Court Justice Henry Billings Brown." Mason then quoted a few carefully edited sentences, which even then did not support his argument. Other ABA speeches would have better served Mason's purpose, and it would be curious to know why he chose Brown's speech to buttress his thesis. Alpheus Thomas Mason, *Brandeis: A Free Man's Life* (New York: Viking Press, 1956), 101.

Brown's musings were certainly unrepresentative of most ABA leaders. But then so were orations that gloried in laissez-faire capitalism or the unchangeable nature of the American Constitution. The conservatism of the American Bar Association was as broad as it was deep. Between 1878 and 1914, its members never reached a consensus about how to solve the contemporary problems of unrestrained capital, predatory labor, and government paternalism. They were united only in believing that courts, not legislatures, ought to make these determinations.

Chapter **5**

Between Gentlemen's Club and Professional Association 1911-1928

In 1911, the American Bar Association began a campaign to oppose the recall of judges and judicial decisions, and in the same year, the Association undertook its first membership drive. These concurrent initiatives were not coincidental. If the ABA were to truly represent the American legal profession, it had to be more inclusive than a private club.[1]

Even so, the Association's first membership solicitation was discreet. In 1911, the Executive Committee asked the vice presidents and members of the local councils to submit names of the "most desirable" attorneys in their respective states to be invited to join the Association. The result was 1,100 new members, an increase of 27%.[2]

The following year the ABA created a Standing Committee on Increase in Membership, to which Lucien Hugh Alexander (1866-1926) was appointed chairman.[3] Alexander,

---

1. James Willard Hurst, *The Growth of American Law: The Lawmakers* (Boston: Little, Brown and Company, 1950), 287; Michael J. Powell, *From Patrician to Professional Elite: The Transformation of the New York City Bar Association* (New York: Russell Sage Foundation, 1988), 38.

2. George Whitelock, "Secretary's Report," 36 *ABA Rep* 66 (1911).

3. *National Cyclopaedia of American Biography*, 28: 269-270.

a Philadelphian who had studied at the right schools and belonged to the right clubs, also enjoyed giving orders and tabulating percentages. His committee consisted of all former ABA presidents who would lend their names to the effort, plus a half dozen or so active members. Alexander tried to draft vice-presidents and local council members as foot soldiers in his campaign, but because these offices had long been honorary, his overbearing recruitment letters were not always received with enthusiasm. ("Pardon our putting this point so personally direct—but this means YOU, the recipient of this copy of this letter.") Still, before retiring in 1921, Alexander boasted of having added over ten thousand new members to the Association.[4]

Alexander's principal strategy was to send individually typed form letters to the best prospects. The key to getting results, he believed, was finding individuals of sufficiently high status to sign them. These "process letters" proved a surprisingly effective tool. Many recipients really thought they had received a personal request from the man who had signed the letter, an illusion Alexander tried hard to preserve.

---

4. George Whitelock to William Howard Taft, November 16, 1917, Taft Papers; 38 *ABA Rep* 676 (1913); 2 *ABAJ* 489 (1916); Lucien H. Alexander to Charles H. Carey et al., May 27, 1913, Carey Papers; Nathan William MacChesney, 41 *ABA Rep* 631-32 (1916); F. Dumont Smith, 52 *ABA Rep* 76 (1927); Edson R. Sunderland, *History of the American Bar Association and its Work* (Chicago: American Bar Association, 1953), 97; Lucien Hugh Alexander to Vice Presidents of the American Bar Association, et al., June 24, 1913; Alexander to the Vice Presidents and Members of the Local Council for Oregon, May 27, 1913; Alexander to Charles Carey, September 5, 1914, Carey Papers; "Organization and Plan of the Membership Committee," 7 *ABAJ* 26-27 (1921). For the haphazard method of electing members at the annual meeting, see *Milwaukee Sentinel*, August 28, 1912, 2.

The Association was thus able to tap a pool of potential members who had been "restrained by a fine sense of delicacy from suggesting their own election" and who were flattered by the thought that some nationally recognized lawyer wanted to nominate them for membership.[5]

Obviously, this promotional technique was subject to the law of diminishing returns, and by the late twenties the membership committee had shifted to mass mailings directed at the "desirable rank and file." At one point Alexander even encouraged non-members to submit their own names for consideration. The Association also modified, then eliminated (1927), the requirement that members must have practiced law for five years before applying, and it eventually bypassed

---

5. Alexander to Carey, June 24, 1913; Alexander to Carey, September 5, 1914; Alexander to D. Webster Dougherty, May 31, 1913, Carey Papers. Alexander listed the preferred prospects as leaders of the bar, prominent judges, professors of law, bar examiners, district attorneys, prominent lawyer-legislators, lawyer-executive officials (mayors, governors, etc.), and rising members of the junior bar. In 1916, the Membership Committee received an appropriation of $3000. The next highest amount was a thousand dollars each for the Committee on Noteworthy Changes in Statute Law and the NCCUSL.

See Alton B. Parker Papers, Box 3, August 1913, Library of Congress, for numerous replies to his "process letter." There are also a few such replies in the Taft Papers, but since Alexander asked for them, most addressed to Taft have disappeared. Alexander to Taft, March 28, 1914, May 19, 1914, Taft Papers. Alexander advised Taft that it would "add very much to the force of the letters if, in the cases of Judges whom you know well, you were to add a few words, even if only two or three holographically." Alexander to Taft, March 21, 1914, Taft Papers; J. M. Dickinson, "Address of the President", 33 *ABA Rep* 341 @ 355 (1908). The "desirable rank and file of the bar" received a less expensive letter from the state membership chairman along with a printed version of a model letter from a member of the local or national elite.

the foot-dragging Local Councils by appointing district and state membership directors.[6]

Membership soared from 3690 in 1910 to 26,595 in 1928, with the largest percentage of increase occurring in 1911, 1913, and 1921, years in which new membership campaigns were launched. Other factors also contributed to membership growth, such as the generally healthy economy and the well-publicized fight of the Association against judicial recall. Then too, although the average yearly percentage of membership increase from 1911 to 1928 was 12%, that increase was less than 3% higher than growth during the previous decade when the Association had made no solicitations.[7] Further, although the percentage of American lawyers who were members of the American Bar Association rose from 3% in 1910 to 18% in

---

6. Lucien H. Alexander, "The Legal Profession and the War," 5 *ABAJ* 681 @ 689 (1919); Sunderland, 41, 97-98; Alton Parker Papers, Box 7; "Report of the Committee on Membership," 53 *ABA Rep* 94 @ 95 (1928); "Report of the Standing Committee on Membership," 50 *ABA Rep* 465 (1925). In all probability the membership declined slightly in 1919 both for economic reasons and because the Association had waived dues for members in military service during the war. "The Organized Lawyer and His Beneficiaries," 13 *ABAJ* 706-707 (1927).

7. During the thirteen years from 1929 to 1942, the Association had a net gain of only 2303 members, a growth rate of less than one percent a year. Obviously, the Depression and World War II were significant factors. Membership rose at a rate of 27% a year between 1911 and 1914, the years during which the Association was most actively engaged in the fight against judicial recall. The ABCNY grew at a similar rate immediately following a moment of courage when it supported five socialists who had been expelled from the New York Assembly in 1919. George Martin, *Causes and Conflicts* (Boston: Houghton Mifflin Company, 1970), 213.

1928, the percentage of doctors who joined the American Medical Association during the same period was 65%.[8]

Finally, there was a high turnover rate. Between 1921 and 1925, 15,604 new members joined the Association, but the net increase was only 8165 because some newly elected members never paid their dues. In 1928, the obvious solution of requiring dues before election was instituted, a practice perhaps indecorous for a social club but one that made perfect sense for a professional association.[9]

Abandoning selectivity troubled some older members. When requested to continue his honorary position on the Membership Committee in 1919, Simeon Baldwin, now in his late seventies, grumbled that "the original policy of the Association, which was to confine membership to leading men or those of high promise, was a sound one."[10] But most

---

8. Lucien Hugh Alexander, 39 *ABA Rep* 50-51 (1914); Richard L. Abel, *American Lawyers* (New York: Oxford University Press, 1989), 45, 290.

9. "Report of the Standing Committee on Membership," 50 *ABA Rep* 465 @ 466 (1925); "Report of the Committee on Membership," 53 *ABA Rep* 94 @ 95 (1928).

10. Some prospective members were still rejected by local officials. In one unusual recorded case, a Jewish lawyer was secretly barred for "doing a collection business" and engaging "in promotion schemes of somewhat doubtful character." Thomas Kemp to Charles Carey, September 26, 1912; Carey to Kemp, October 1, 1912, Carey Papers; see also Samuel P. Goldman, 41 *ABA Rep* 17 (1916). John H. Wigmore, "The Movement to Amend the Organization and Procedure of the Association," 1 *ABAJ* 564 @ 581, 590 (1915); Hampton Carson, 45 *ABA Rep* 78 (1920); "The Membership Situation," 2 *ABAJ* 488 @ 492 (1916); Hampton Carson to Simeon Baldwin, November 12, 1919; Baldwin to Carson, November 13, 1919, Baldwin Family Papers. Carson entreated Baldwin to reconsider since the absence of his name on the letterhead "would occasion much loss of prestige and perhaps misunderstanding." Baldwin scribbled at the bottom of the letter, "I surrender unconditionally." Carson to Baldwin, December

ABA leaders were more than willing to trade exclusivity for the possibility of greater political clout. That same impulse, typical of the Progressive era, was at work in contemporary state and local bar associations, and only the Association of the Bar of the City of New York restrained the natural impulse to increase organizational membership.[11]

Baldwin's irritation with the membership drives is more understandable in light of the greatest internal crisis that the Association faced during its first half-century. In 1911, the Association discovered it had inadvertently admitted an African American to membership, and the resulting discord bedeviled ABA leaders until 1914.

William H. Lewis (1868-1949), a leading black lawyer of Boston, had been educated at Amherst and Harvard Law School. In 1911, Booker T. Washington wangled Lewis's appointment as an assistant Attorney General, the highest appointive office held by an African American in the federal government to that date. Just before the Senate confirmed Lewis' nomination, someone noticed that he had been admitted to the American Bar Association earlier that year.[12]

2, 1919, Baldwin Papers.

11. Wigmore, "The Movement," 566-67, as well as the replies to his questionnaire; Adolph H. Grundman, "The Early History of the Colorado Bar Association: 1898-1938," 14 *Colorado Lawyer* 7 @ 8 (1985); Lawrence E. Sommers, "Lawyers and Progressive Reform: A Study of Attitudes and Activities in Illinois, 1890 to 1920," Ph.D. dissertation, Northwestern University, 1967, 100; Margaret F. Sommer, "The Ohio State Bar Association: The First Generation, 1880-1912," Ph.D. dissertation, Ohio State University, 1972, 63-67; George Martin, *Causes and Conflicts*, 201-02, 216-18; "The Association's 'Semi-Centennial Year,'" 13 *ABAJ* 512 (1927).

12. August Meier, *Negro Thought in America, 1880-1915* (Ann Arbor: University of Michigan Press, 1963), 113, 241; Stephen R. Fox, *The Guardian of Boston: William Monroe Trotter* (New York: Atheneum, 1970),

While it is doubtful that a black assistant attorney general could have become a member of the American Bar Association twenty years earlier, the second decade of the twentieth century was a nadir in the enforcement of Jim Crow laws. Upper-class acceptance of segregation mirrored a growing belief in eugenics and related anthropological claptrap about Aryan superiority. Centuries-old prejudice recently veneered with scientific authority meant that racial segregation could now be justified as a Progressive reform.[13]

18, 159-160; Louis R. Harlan, *Booker T. Washington: The Wizard of Tuskegee, 1901-1915* (New York: Oxford University Press, 1983), 348-49; "The Color Line at the Bar," *Nation* 94 (May 23, 1912), 509-510; "Fight for Negro Lawyer," *New York Times*, August 25, 1912, III, 5; Peter Shiver, Jr., "William Henry Lewis," *DAB*, Supplement 4, 492-94.

In 1893, when Simeon Baldwin and George Sharp organized the Section of Legal Education, they considered inviting representatives of black law schools to meet with them. Sharp confessed that he did not know whether their appearance at the occasion would "create friction" but thought it would be safer to omit them for the time being, leaving open the possibility of their later admission. George M. Sharp to Simeon Baldwin, February 25, 1893, Baldwin Papers; Moorfield Storey to Members of the American Bar Association, undated (1913), Carey Papers. Ironically, Lewis' nomination was opposed by a militant segment of the African American community, which disliked his opportunism. Among other things, Lewis had defended Theodore Roosevelt's course in the Brownsville affair. Evan J. Albright, "The Three Lives of an African American Pioneer: William Henry Lewis (1868-1949)," *Massachusetts Historical Review* 13 (2011), 145.

13. On the connection of racism, eugenics, and progressivism see Jack Temple Kirby, *Darkness at the Dawning: Race and Reform in the Progressive South* (New York: Lippincott, 1972); Mark H. Haller, *Eugenics: Hereditarian Attitudes in American Thought* (New Brunswick, NJ: Rutgers University Press, 1963); Steven Selden, *Inheriting Shame: The Story of Eugenics and Racism in America* (New York: Teachers College, Columbia University, 1999); and Constance Areson Clark, "Evolution for John Doe: Pictures, the Public, and the Scopes Trial Debate," *Journal of American History*

The first protests about Lewis's election came from recently recruited members of the rank and file, and their threats of resignation persuaded the Association's inner circle to halt the printing of the 1911 Report, which (as usual) contained a list of members.[14] In January 1912, the Executive Committee rescinded Lewis's election, an action that neither the Committee, nor for that matter, the Association, had the constitutional authority to take.

Attorney General George Wickersham (1858-1936) protested, writing to all ABA members and including a postcard on which they could express their opinion to ABA Secretary George Whitelock (1854-1920). Whitelock was not amused, calling Wickersham "discourteous and dogmatic" for questioning the good intentions of the Executive Committee. Unfortunately for Whitelock, almost as soon as he had declared that no other nonwhites had ever been admitted to the Association, two more black members were discovered, one of whom had served on the local entertainment committee in Boston the year before.[15]

(March 2001), 1275-1303. Even Darwin himself made injudicious remarks about the gorilla and the Negro occupying evolutionary positions between the baboon and the "civilized races of man." *The Descent of Man*, 2nd ed. (London: John Murray, 1874), 156.

14. *New York Times*, September 3, 1911, 7. H. H. Watkins of Anderson, South Carolina, called for Lewis' resignation out of consideration for the members of his race in the South. S. O. Pickens of Indianapolis condemned the election as "very indiscreet" and found Lewis blameworthy for having applied for membership in the first place. Alexander Troy of Montgomery, Alabama, said he felt "so deeply on the subject that I cannot trust myself to be quoted, except to say that the proposition before the American Bar Association looks to me like this: you keep your negro and lose a thousand members throughout the South."

15. *New York Times*, March 1,1912, 5; April 1, 1912, 12; "The Color Line at the Bar," *Nation* 94 (May 23, 1912), 510; George Whitelock to George

Wickersham and his supporters threatened to resign if the black members were not retained. One anonymous "lawyer of national standing" quoted in the *Nation*, confidently predicted that the ABA would have to face the issue squarely and that whatever action it took would probably split the association.[16]

But Association leaders finessed the issue, longtime treasurer Francis Rawle orchestrating a compromise at the 1912 meeting. Association leaders pleaded that there be no discussion, an obscure member took the chair—perhaps so that President S. S. Gregory (1849-1920) could avoid sullying his hands—opposition to the formula was ruled out of order, the resolution was gaveled through, and the session was adjourned with "the convention in an uproar." By terms of the compromise, the three black lawyers were allowed to retain their membership but with the clear implication that their election had been a mistake and that their presence was unwelcome.[17]

Wickersham, February 8, 1912, April 6, 1912, NAACP Administrative Files, Box C-192, Library of Congress; James Grafton Rogers, "The American Bar Association in Retrospect," in *Law: A Century of Progress* (New York: New York University, 1937), 179; Lucien H. Alexander to Moorfield Storey, January 24, 1914, Taft Papers; George Wickersham to George Sutherland, September 2, 1916, Sutherland Papers.

16. *New York Times*, August 25, 1912, III, 5; "The Color Line at the Bar," *Nation* 94 (May 23, 1912), 510.

17. James Grafton Rogers, American Bar Leaders (Chicago: American Bar Association, 1932), 124; J. M. Dickinson, 37 *ABA Rep* 12 (1912); 37 *ABA Rep* 13-16 (1912); *Milwaukee Journal*, August 27, 1912, 1; August 28, 1912, 1; Moorfield Storey to Members of the American Bar Association, undated (1913), Carey Papers.

"WHEREAS three persons of the colored race were elected to membership in this Association without knowledge upon the part of those electing them that they were of that race, and are now members of this

The Association's solution to the question of black membership received more public comment—most of it unfavorable—than any action the organization had ever taken. Although newspapers and popular journals generally had no problem with racial segregation in social clubs, they were surprised that ABA members considered their organization one. Adverse comments were also made about the "sneaking settlement" that closed the dispute. "The association did not even have the courage to do a mean thing manfully," said the *New York Sun.*[18]

Some Northern and Western members felt that the compromise had conceded too much to the "colorphobes" and

---

Association, Resolved, That as it never has been contemplated that members of the colored race should become members of this association, the several local councils are directed if at any time any of them shall recommend a person of the colored race for membership to accompany the recommendation with a statement of the fact that he is of such race."

The next day, one of the three African Americans, William R. Morris of Minnesota, resigned from the Association. Joseph Hansell Merrill, a Georgian who had openly opposed admission of Negroes, proposed a resolution praising Morris for his "dignified appreciation of the conditions as manifested by his telegram of resignation." 37 *ABA Rep* 29 (1912) At the annual banquet, the main speaker, a former congressman from Mississippi, attacked Attorney General Wickersham and told racist jokes that were "hailed with laughter and applause." *Milwaukee Sentinel,* August 30, 1914, 1.

18. A summary of newspaper comments is given in "Lawyers and the Color Line," *Literary Digest* 45 (September 7, 1912), 361; "A Select Jury," *Independent* 73 (September 5, 1912), 576-77; "The Bar Association and the Negro," *Outlook* 102 (September 7, 1912), 1.

"Will someone tell us," said the editor of the *Independent,* "why the American Banker's [sic] Association can give full privileges of membership to a Virginia negro. . . and without serious complaint, while objection is made to the admission of a colored lawyer to the American Bar Association?" The *New York Tribune* observed that if there was "one place where race prejudice should not exist, it [was] in an organization which purport[ed] to be representative of a learned profession."

resigned or declined to pay their dues—in a few cases, publicly. Other lawyers refused to join the Association because they did not want to endorse racial discrimination.[19]

Furthermore, the governing circle of the Association had not yet faced that perennial advocate of unpopular causes, Moorfield Storey, former president of the ABA and current president of the NAACP. Storey had planned to use his considerable influence within the Association to support the cause of a nondiscriminatory admissions policy, but he had been taken seriously ill in Europe and had been unable to attend the 1912 meeting. On his return to Massachusetts, he addressed a circular letter to ABA members, sharply criticizing the leadership for railroading through its resolution without discussion. Storey vowed to work for its repeal and continue "the contest for equal rights." Then, in curious deference to the organization he might have riven, Storey followed his broadside with a call for a truce during the 1913

---

19. Unfortunately, it is no longer possible to determine the number of resignations resulting from this incident. Page Morris to Taft, April 9, 1914; H. J. Jaquith to Taft, August 3, 1914; Sanford Dole to Taft, May 6, 1914, Taft Papers; Wood, Montague and Hunt to Carey, July 24, 1913, Carey Papers. For the resignation of Albert E. Pillsbury (1849-1930), former Attorney General of Massachusetts, see *New York Times*, July 16, 1913, 2, and Lucien H. Alexander to Moorfield Storey, January 24, 1914, Taft Papers. Alexander called Pillsbury's public letter to Treasurer Frederick Wadhams a "miserable and undignified screed" written "to make cheap political capital of the situation."

Morris Ernst (1888-1976), a founder of the National Lawyers' Guild, enjoyed twitting the ABA membership committee. Every year, he said, the Association would send him a letter soliciting his membership, and he would write back inquiring whether the organization accepted Negroes. Then he would receive the reply, "We're sorry, we didn't know you were a Negro." *New York Times*, December 23, 1936, 13.

meeting in Montreal because "distinguished Englishmen" had been invited as guests.[20]

The prospect of having to fend off a challenge from Storey annoyed Association leaders, especially because he had recommended that the question be put to the membership on a postcard vote. In ten overwrought pages of alternating denunciation and pleading, Lucien Hugh Alexander exhorted Storey to accede to the wisdom of the Executive Committee rather than involve the membership "in a race war of words." The Executive Committee scotched the proposed referendum but agreed to Storey's request for a place on the 1914 program, fearing that he would have his say in any case.[21]

Again the leadership struck a deal. This time the compromise was moved by Henry St. George Tucker of Virginia and defended by Storey, who said that he was unwilling "to begin a discussion which might become bitter and might perhaps disturb the pleasant relations that have hitherto existed between the members of this Association." The Tucker resolution was adopted almost unanimously, Storey grasped Tucker's hand, and the audience broke into applause. The session was then quickly adjourned to prevent discussion. In the halls, there were jokes at Storey's expense.[22]

---

20. Moorfield Storey to Members of the American Bar Association, undated (1913), Storey to Members of the American Bar Association, April 9, 1913, Carey Papers; Storey to Charles Francis Adams, August 12, 1912, in M. A. DeWolfe Howe, *Portrait of an Independent: Moorfield Storey* (Boston: Houghton Mifflin, 1932), 301, 273, 304.

21. Alexander to Storey, January 24, 1914; Storey to Taft, January 20, 1914; Whitelock to Taft, January 27, 1914, February 5, 1914; Taft to Whitelock, June 30, 1914, Taft Papers.

22. Henry St. George Tucker, 39 *ABA Rep* 64 (1914); Moorfield Storey, 39 *ABA Rep* 62 (1914); Washington Star, October 23, 1914, 5; Washington

The compromise of 1914 replaced that of 1912 but required that all applicants for membership state their race and sex. As William Howard Taft wrote to his niece, it simply substituted "one thing for the other so as not to carry on the face of the minutes a reflection on the negro race, although the sting is there just the same I should think." By typically attaching "more importance to the abstract than to the actual," Storey had both increased the power of the Executive Committee and helped prevent further public discussion about admitting African Americans until 1943.[23]

Nor could the problem of race made to disappear simply by requiring that the applicant state his race on the application. Applicants came in varieties other than black and white, and like racists in other times and places, the Executive Committee soon became enmeshed in an impossible tangle of racial line drawing. Even before the 1914 compromise, Alexander had written to Whitelock asking advice about the applications of

---

Post, October 23, 1914, 5; *New York Times*, October 23, 1914, 10; Taft to Mabel Boardman, October 27, 1914, Taft Papers. A *New York Times* editorial of October 26 (8) viewed the second compromise as even less courageous than the first.

23. 39 *ABA Rep* 64 (1914); Taft to Mabel Boardman, October 27, 1914, Taft Papers; Sidney Ģunn, "Moorfield Storey," *DAB*, 18: 97. In 1943, the Association adopted a resolution that declared "that membership in the American Bar Association is not dependent upon race, creed or color," and the Board of Governors—the lineal descendent of the Executive Committee—admitted a black municipal court judge to membership. However, it ignored the application of Francis Ellis Rivers, a Yale Phi Beta Kappa and an assistant attorney general for New York, who had publicly challenged discrimination in the Association. In May 1956, the question concerning race was removed from the application. Adoa Artis Aiyetoro, "Truth Matters: A Call for the American Bar Association to Acknowledge Its Past and Make Reparations to African Descendants," 18 *George Mason University Civil Rights Law Journal* 51 (2007)@ 75-79.

one William F. Crockett, a African American practicing in Hawaii, and William H. Heen (1883-1973), "certified to be part Hawaiian and part Chinese." Intensifying the dilemma, Heen was described as "a gentleman of ability and good standing" who resented "being classed with the African."[24]

In January 1922, the Executive Committee, by a close vote, left the door of membership open to "native members of the Filipino Bar." But later that year it received the application of Seid G. Back of Oregon, an American of Chinese parentage. Influential Executive Committee members endorsed Back's membership. Wadhams acknowledged that Back's admission would cost the Association some members and seemed inconsistent with "the Americanization campaign now in progress," but it was his understanding that the Association had only definitely barred Negroes. Furthermore, the Association had already elected a Japanese to honorary membership and two "Chinese-Hawaiians" to regular membership. "I am sure that if we bar this Chinese-American from our Association," said Treasurer Frederick Wadhams (1848-1926), "and all the above facts were known, the Association would be ridiculed for glaring inconsistency and would be

---

24. Whitelock to Taft, June 30, 1914; Taft to Whitelock, July 3, 1914, Taft Papers; *Honolulu Star Bulletin*, March 23, 1917, 4. Neither Crockett nor Heen were admitted. ABA President William Howard Taft also questioned Whitelock about the propriety of inviting the Haitian minister to the annual meeting. "He will not look any darker than a good many others from South America. A man who was Minister when I was in Washington was as black as the ace of spades, but I am quite sure they have made a change. The way to do such a thing is just to do it, if we decided to do it, and not ask anybody. It is a very different thing from inviting a man of color to become a member." Taft to Whitelock, October 12, 1914, Taft Papers.

severely criticized." Nevertheless, the Executive Committee denied Back admission.[25]

As Moorfield Storey was pressing the Association for the admission of African Americans, Lucien Alexander warned him that a "stand pat" attitude was necessary because the matter was "tied up very closely with the woman question." In the scientific literature of the period, presumed incapacities of blacks and women were frequently linked, and professional societies that could exclude them were often considered more prestigious. Thus, the American Medical Association refused to admit either blacks or women while some medical irregulars accepted both.[26]

---

25. "Minutes of Meeting of the Executive Committee of the American Bar Association, January 9-11, 1922," Carson Papers; Frederick Wadhams to Thomas Shelton, October 20, 1922, John W. Davis Papers, Series III, Box 14. Back believed himself to be the first person of Chinese descent to be admitted to the bar in the United States. Seid Back to L. H. Alexander, February 18, 1909, Alexander Papers.

There was more consistency to Back's rejection than Wadhams allowed. The Association's Japanese, "Chinese-Hawaiian," and the Filipino members lived far away, unable to participate in the social activities of the organization. During the Association's cruise to Great Britain in 1924, meetings of Harvard alumni, Delta Kappa Epsilon members, and other elite groups were announced on the ship's bulletin boards. Some jokester added the notice of a meeting for all lawyers from the Philippines, Puerto Rico, and Guam. "The Veracious Log of the London Fleet," 10 *ABAJ* 665 @ 666 (1924).

26. Lucien H. Alexander to Moorfield Storey, January 24, 1914, Taft Papers; Samuel Haber, *The Quest for Authority and Honor in the American Professions, 1750-1900* (Chicago: University of Chicago Press, 1991), 332. The American Medical Association could more easily hide its institutional prejudice than the American Bar Association because, as early as 1847, the AMA had organized by incorporating local units. Through much of the 20th century, the AMA allowed its constituent medical societies to enact segregationist and sexist admission standards, which the national

The possible admission of women to the American Bar Association had been broached as early as 1901, when two Colorado lawyers, Mary F. Lathrop (1865-1951) and Minnie K. Liebhardt (1863-1947), joined male colleagues in a discussion of women in the legal profession before the Section of Legal Education. At the annual meeting, a member then moved that women be admitted to the Association—a resolution referred to the General Council, which ruled it "inexpedient."[27]

In 1914, the year of the Storey compromise, three women also applied for admission. The leadership sidestepped the issue by postponing a decision until 1918, the year Congress passed the Nineteenth Amendment. Then, without fanfare or recorded dissent, two women, including Mary F. Lathrop, were admitted to membership.[28]

---

association then supported. State societies in the North could integrate, state societies in the South could segregate, and the AMA was free "to pursue its business untroubled by issues of race or gender." Robert B. Baker, "The American Medical Association and Race," *American Medical Association Journal of Ethics*, 16: 6 (June 2014), 479-488.

The textbook from which John Scopes taught evolution to his science class (*Hunter's Civic Biology*) described the "five races or varieties of man" as capped by "the highest type of all, the Caucasians, represented by the civilized white inhabitants of Europe and America." Paul Carter, *The Twenties in America* (Arlington Heights, Illinois: AHM Publishing, 1975), 95.

27. 24 *ABA Rep* 37-38, 470-77 (1901); 25 *ABA Rep* 5 (1902).

28. *Washington Star*, October 21, 1914, 5; *Washington Post*, October 21, 1914, 8; *New York Times*, October 24, 1914, 12; Thomas J. O'Donnell, 43 *ABA Rep* 29 (1918). The other woman lawyer admitted in 1918 was Mary B. Grossman, who practiced in Cleveland, the site of the 1918 convention. *Cleveland Plain Dealer*, August 30, 1918, 12. In 1915 the General Council voted 37 to 8 to admit Helen Hamilton of Grand Forks, South Dakota, but she was still rejected because five nay votes denied admission. *Deseret Evening News*, August 18, 1915, 5.

Once admitted, women were given more than their share of committee assignments and honorary positions. In 1921, Pearl McCall (1876-1977) of Idaho became the first women elected to the General Council, a position of real importance in the internal politics of the Association.[29] Punctilious—if not necessarily equal—treatment of women members also probably helped the ABA reduce the influence of the Women Lawyers Association (after 1923, the National Association of Women Lawyers), which had been trailing around ABA conventions. Female members of the ABA proved as socially conservative as their male peers, and Mary Lathrop even reported hints of restive feminism to the ABA leadership.[30]

The decision to admit women to the Association, like so many other questions of policy, was made behind closed doors by a small group of influential members. George Wickersham, who had good reason to know, complained bitterly of the "little group of mutual admirers" that ran the Association. After privately protesting a reduction in the size of a committee on which he served, Roscoe Pound resigned himself to having the leadership "put it through by means of

---

29. Mary Lathrop to John W. Davis, September 30, 1922, John W. Davis to W. Thomas Kemp, September 20, 1922, Davis Papers; "Women and the American Bar Association," 7 *ABAJ* 440 (1921); 13 *ABAJ* 528 (1927). By 1922, there were fifty women members of the ABA. When the question of a separate table at the banquet arose in that year, the women present voted against it unanimously. *San Francisco Examiner*, August 10, 1922, 14.

30. Rose Fall Bres to Margaret J. Carns, June 29, 1925, Carns Papers, Nebraska State Historical Society; Lathrop to Davis, September 30, 1922, Davis Papers; Charlotte E. Gauer, "National Association of Women Lawyers," 35 *Women Law. J.* 15 (1949).

the steamroller as they have done everything they have proposed in recent years."[31]

Some ABA leaders of this period were men of national prominence such as John W. Davis (1873-1955), James M. Beck (1861-1936), and most notably, William Howard Taft (1857-1930).[32] Others were men of only local reputation who had shouldered the mundane duties of the organization. Among the latter was Frederick E. Wadhams, who served officially as treasurer from 1909 until his death but was, like Francis Rawle before him, nearly an executive secretary.[33] The promotion of ordinary members to positions of leadership reduced the earlier,

---

31. George Wickersham to George Sutherland, September 2, 1916, Sutherland Papers; Wickersham to Taft, November 5, 1914, Taft Papers; Roscoe Pound to Everett Wheeler, July 25, 1919; see also W. A. Hayes to Wheeler, August 6, 1919, Wheeler Papers; *New York Times*, June 1, 1916, 9; John W. Davis to Frederick Wadhams, November 6, 1922, Davis Papers; Frank Kellogg to Taft, November 17, 1913, Taft Papers.

32. Between his loss of the presidential election in 1912 and his nomination to the Supreme Court by Warren Harding, William Howard Taft was especially influential in Association affairs; see for instance, 40 *ABA Rep* 45 (1915); 52 *ABA Rep* 122; *San Francisco Chronicle*, August 10, 1922, 3; Henry Lamm to Charles Nagel, July 13, 1915, Taft Papers; C. W. Thomas, "Impressions of the American Bar Association Meeting at Philadelphia," 4 *Oregon Law Review* 40 @ 42 (1924).

33. Wadhams—clubman, amateur musician, and vestryman of his church—was diligent, vain, excitable, and strongly opinionated. As soon as he died, the Executive Committee paid him the backhanded tribute of amending the constitution so as to restrict the secretary and treasurer to terms of only three successive years. *National Cyclopedia of American Biography* 24: 277; John Austin Matzko, "The Early Years of the American Bar Association, 1878-1928," PhD dissertation, University of Virginia, 1984, 249-51, 604-05.

patrician quality of the organization while stimulating a narrower, more formalistic traditionalism.[34]

Election to the presidency was now highly contested, and campaigns were sometimes organized years in advance.[35] The National Conference of Commissioners on Uniform State Laws, whose members were chosen from active members of the Association, played an important role in the politicking because the Conference met a week before the Association and in the same city. The work of the Conference was time-consuming and uncompensated, and at least part of its implied mission was to impede the growth of federal power. Therefore, the Conference had a tendency to attract some of the Association's wealthiest and most reactionary members. Its manipulation of Association affairs was considered deleterious even by Francis Rawle.[36]

---

34. James Grafton Rogers referred obliquely to this change during a luncheon talk on the Association's history. After commenting on the way in which the old leadership had reacted to the self-seeking of David Dudley Field during the medal fiasco, Rogers reflected that the Association had "grown out of the ability to enforce the system as a system. There are too many of us. Now through sheer inertia of the great mass, active men somehow gain, and along with the old methods, I think something of value and dignity has departed also." James Grafton Rogers, "Fifty Years of the American Bar Association," 53 *ABA Rep* 518 @ 529 (1928).

35. Two considerable collections of letters document ABA presidential campaigns of this period: The Hampton Carson Papers, Pennsylvania Historical Society, and the Nathan William MacChesney Papers, Hoover Presidential Library. MacChesney's losing campaign is more extensively documented than Carson's successful one.

36. Rogers, "The American Bar Association in Retrospect," 184; Francis Rawle to John W. Davis, June 18, 1923, Davis Papers; T. J. O'Donnell to Henry Upton Sims, February 27, 1919, Carson Papers; Thomas A. Bryson, *Walter George Smith* (Washington: Catholic University Press, 1977), 44.

Nevertheless, growth in ABA membership also meant growth in income. Total disbursements rose from $17,725 in 1911 to $193,882 in 1928. Increased appropriations encouraged committees to make more vigorous attempts to influence legislation, even though little of consequence was actually accomplished.[37] In the words of J. Willard Hurst, ABA leaders were "crude amateurs" at operating a political pressure group.[38] Committees frequently lacked clearly defined goals, and proposed legislation was often little more than the cause of a single individual or a small group. Even when committee proposals received approval from the Association, they were often incapable of weathering even the mildest political challenge.[39] In fact, during this era, ABA

---

37. Since appropriations for committees and sections were considered at the midwinter session of the Executive Committee, that meeting, usually held in the South, gained increased importance as committee chairmen waited to present their requests. 36 *ABA Rep* 81 (1911); 53 *ABA Rep* 302 (1928); H. H. Brown to John W. Davis, October 18, 1922, Davis Papers. One committeeman, perhaps more sensitive than most, wrote his chairman, "I enclose bill for my expenses to New York and return. It is some expensive trip these days and I doubt if it was worth the money either to the Association or myself. However, I enjoyed the meeting very much . . .. I hope we will be able to make a report that will look as if we were trying to do what we should." J. C. Slonecker to Everett R. Wheeler, May 6, 1919, Wheeler Papers.

38. James Willard Hurst, *The Growth of American Law*, 361; John H. Wigmore, "The Movement to Amend the Organization and Procedure of the Association," 1 *ABAJ* 564 @ 567 (1915).

39. Edson Sunderland, *History of the American Bar Association* has provided a summary, 102-169. For example, the Committee on Commercial Law finally abandoned its attempt to have a model insurance code adopted in the District of Columbia; and a long crusade for a federal court of patent appeals was torpedoed by some off-hand remarks made by President Taft. 50 *ABA Rep* 398 (1925); Sunderland, 151-52; Robert S. Taylor, 36 *ABA Rep*

committees often served as lightning rods into which politically sensitive issues could be discharged.[40]

The Association's inefficiency also encouraged sections and related organizations to exercise more independence. Neither the American Law Institute (1923), founded to prepare "restatements" of the common law, nor the American Judicature Society (1913), which advocated progressive organization of the legal profession, chose to affiliate with the American Bar Association. Twenty years earlier they likely would have become sections of the Association or at least affiliated bodies like the Association of American Law Schools (AALS). Instead, the AALS co-opted the ABA's Section of Legal Education.[41]

---

35 (1911); William Howard Taft, 36 *ABA_Rep* 55 (1911); "Report of the Committee on Patent, Trade-Mark and Copyright Law," 38 *ABA Rep* 515 (1913); R. S. Taylor to Taft, September 14, 1914, Taft Papers; 45 *ABA Rep* 51-52, 398-399 (1920).

40. See Joseph B. Davis to Taft, February 3, 1914, Charles A. Boston to Robert R. Reed, July 22, 1914, Taft Papers; C. C. Carlin to John W. Davis, April 10, 1923; Davis to Anna W. Hochfelder, September 6, 1923, Davis Papers.

41. Charles H. Kinnane, "Review of History of the American Bar Association by Edson R. Sunderland," 29 *Notre Dame Lawyer* 328 @ 330 (1954); Hobson, *The American Legal Profession and the Organizational Society, 1890-1930*, 415-18; N.E.H. Hull, "Restatement and Reform: A New Perspective on the Origins of the American Law Institute," *Law and History Review*, 8 (Spring 1990), 55-96; Robert Stevens, *Law School: Legal Education in America* (Chapel Hill: University of North Carolina Press, 1983), 114-115; Herbert Harley, "Organization of the Bar," *Annals of the American Academy*, 52 (March, 1914), 77-82. Harley called the organizational structure of the ABA "conspicuously inefficient" and suggested that the American Judicature Society, of which he was secretary, might "prove to be the logical response of the bar to the present insistent need for guidance." (81-82); Michal R. Belknap, *To Improve the Administration of Justice: A History of the American Judicature Society* (Washington: American Judicature Society, 1992).

Influential lawyers had long recognized the organizational weakness of the ABA and had credited the effectiveness of the American Medical Association to its reorganization as a representative body. ABA President J. M. Dickinson (1851-1928) claimed the AMA wielded a power to enforce ethical standards and pass legislation "incomparably greater than that exercised by it when its organization was somewhat similar to ours." John Wigmore (1863-1943), dean of Northwestern Law School, called the American Medical Association an example "of what it is possible for this Association to achieve, if it seeks with a will to do so." Henry Moore Bates (1869-1949), dean of the University of Michigan Law School, dismissed the ABA as "a husk." To Roscoe Pound he wrote, "Its journal is a joke, its principal activity is the annual meeting with its pompous banquet and days devoted mostly to guff. It is utterly failing to have the influence in law that the Medical Association is having in its field."[42]

In 1913, Wigmore received reluctant permission from the Executive Committee to consider a reorganization of the Association. The governing clique warned him, in the words of crusty William A. Ketcham (1846-1921), "to be damned careful." Wigmore drew up a questionnaire and sent it to ABA vice-presidents and the presidents of state bar associations, many of whom agreed that the American Bar Associa-

---

42. Harry S. Mecartney, 31 *ABA Rep* 108-109; see Mecartney, 45 *ABA Rep* 33 (1920); 33 *ABA Rep* 106 (1908); J. M. Dickinson, "Address of the President," 33 *ABA Rep* 341 @ 355-358 (1908); 35 *ABA Rep* 94 (1910); Sunderland, 84-85; H. A. Bronson, 35 *ABA Rep* 12 (1910); John H. Wigmore, "The Movement," 1 *ABAJ* 564 @ 565 (1915); Lucien Alexander to Moorfield Storey, January 24, 1914, Taft Papers; Bates to Pound, March 16, 1916, Pound Papers.

tion needed some type of representative government. Nevertheless, members of Wigmore's committee differed among themselves and were able to agree only on the banal recommendation that the Association allot four, rather than three, days to its annual meeting. The Executive Committee not only rejected this proposal but refused to print the majority and minority reports as had been customary. Wigmore then distributed a lengthy report to ABA members (printed with the financial support of the American Judicature Society) explaining the need for representative government in the Association. And he prefaced it with a criticism of the Executive Committee for using "gag rule" tactics to prevent "bona fide and moderate proposals from receiving any consideration on the floor of the meeting."[43]

The broadside had no direct effect, but ABA President Elihu Root (1845-1937), who had expressed appreciation for Wigmore's work, almost immediately organized delegates appointed by state and local bar associations into an affiliated organization. In 1917, it became the Conference of Bar Association Delegates; and in 1920, the Conference became a section of the Association.[44]

Root realized that the ABA could not raise admission standards or purge "unfit practitioners" from the profession without the cooperation of the local associations, but he also

---

43. Sunderland, 85-87; 38 *ABA Rep* 20 (1913); William R. Roalfe, *John Henry Wigmore: Scholar and Reformer* (Evanston: Northwestern University Press, 1977), 109-111; Wigmore, "The Movement," 564-69, 572.

44. Roalfe, 112; Sunderland, 87-91; "Conference of Bar Association Delegates," 41 *ABA Rep* 588 (1916). Root had Simeon Baldwin made chairman of the first Conference in order to lend weight to the proceeding. Thus the wheel came full circle: Root used Baldwin for a purpose similar to that for which Baldwin had used senior professional leaders in 1878.

understood that attempting a reorganization of the Association was, for the moment, impossible. In the short term, Root thought the ABA could establish informal ties with local bar associations. To this end, and with Executive Committee approval, Root presented the 1916 Conference with two proposed amendments to the ABA constitution. The first provided for referenda of ABA members on questions of pressing public importance. The second provided that the president of every state bar association already a member of the ABA would become an *ex officio* member of the politically important General Council, thus creating "a point of functional contact" between the national and state associations. One segment of the ABA leadership also hoped these measures would dilute the power of the Association's "elder statesmen" who, they believed, were not "fully in touch . . . with active heads of the local associations." Unremarkably, Frederick Wadhams opposed the latter amendment.[45]

Though both amendments were passed by the Association, their effect was negligible. Only one referendum was taken during this period—on the hardly controversial topic of raising the salaries of federal judges—and the provision to enroll state association presidents in the General Council was dropped in a 1919 revision of the constitution. Furthermore, a third amendment proposed by the Conference itself was

---

45. 3 *ABAJ* 580-629 (1917); Sunderland, 87-91; "Conference of Bar Association Delegates," 592-93, 605; Max Radin, "The Achievements of the American Bar Association: A Sixty Year Record," 26 *ABAJ* 227 @ 230 (1940); Philip J. Wickser, "Bar Associations," 399fn; Herbert Harley, 6 *ABAJ* 33 (1920): "The clique is necessary under the present style of constitutions and bylaws . . . but the clique government is standing in the way of the proper evolution of the power to make it responsible to the public, which is perhaps its ultimate purpose."

opposed by the Executive Committee and defeated by the Association, a provision that would have required applicants for membership in the ABA to first join their state bar associations. Some ABA members complained that such a requirement would reduce ABA membership because "first-class practitioners" might not want to join their more inclusive state organizations.[46]

While the old guard held tenaciously to its power, an increasing number of ABA leaders understood the need to coordinate state and national bar activities both to police the profession and to uphold a conservative political philosophy. In his presidential address of 1923, John W. Davis expressed both opposition to the regulatory state and support for a federal union between national and state bar associations. President R. E. L. Saner did virtually the same thing the following year, again comparing the strength of the American Medical Association with the weakness of the ABA.[47]

In 1923, an attempt was made to pass a constitutional amendment that would allow state bar associations—rather than ABA members who happened to be present at the annual meetings—to choose General Council members. Former president C. A. Severance (1862-1925) spoke in favor of the amendment, warning that if the Association was "to function with the utmost power" it would have to work with

---

46. Sunderland, 88; Wickser, 399-400fn.; 41 *ABA Rep* 11-18 (1916).

47. William H. Harbaugh, *Lawyer's Lawyer: The Life of John W. Davis* (New York: Oxford University Press, 1973), 195; *New York Times*, January 21, 1921, 16; Sunderland, 91-92; R. E. L. Saner, "Governmental Review," 49 *ABA Rep* 127 (1924) and "Memorandum of National Federalization of the Bar," 49 *ABA Rep* 152 (1924); John W. Davis, "Present Day Problems," 48 *ABA Rep* 193 @ 194 (1923).

state associations: "[T]here is a feeling that has grown up for years in favor of having a federated system just as the physicians have in their organization. . . . They can go to legislatures and get almost anything they ask for."[48]

The amendment did not pass, but the tide had begun to run against the old guard. A new representative constitution was finally approved in 1936, although diehard opposition continued to the bitter end. By that date, however, the Association was divided on ideological grounds, and both factions believed that a federative association would strengthen their respective positions.[49]

While the debate over representative government continued, the Association took further steps to bring its formal organization more in line with the growth in its membership and prestige. A revised constitution, written by Charles Thaddeus Terry (1867-1923) and promulgated by the Executive Committee, was passed after several days of repartee at the 1919 annual meeting. In theory, the new constitution gave the Association greater control over the affiliated bodies that waited on it for appropriations; in fact, its chief importance was to give the Executive Committee authority "to perform all functions which the Association itself might do" except to amend the constitution.[50]

---

48. *New York Times*, January 16, 1923, 3; C. A. Severance, 48 *ABA Rep* 79 (1923).
49. Sunderland, 92-96; Radin, 319-21; Brockman, "The Politics of the American Bar Association," 89-90, 255-57.
50. R. E. L. Saner, "Charles Thaddeus Terry," 9 *ABAJ* 331 (1923); Charles Thaddeus Terry, 44 *ABA Rep* 85 (1919); *Boston Globe*, September 5, 1919, 8; September 6, 1919, 14; Lucien H. Alexander to John W. Davis (on a copy of letter to Henry Upton Sims), September 10, 1920, Davis Papers. A copy of the constitution may be found at 44 *ABA Rep* 121-131 (1919).

In 1927, the Association incorporated in Illinois after previously establishing headquarters for its secretary and the *Journal* in rented office space at 209 South LaSalle Street, Chicago.[51] Following Wadham's death in 1927, the treasurer's office was moved to the same location. Before that the Association had had no permanent offices, except that as all four secretaries had lived in Baltimore, the ABA might be said to have been headquartered there. By 1925, the unpaid job of the secretary had become a nearly full-time responsibility; his office not only did the copy editing and proof reading of the *Report* but also arranged the details of the annual meeting and handled an increasing volume of correspondence. In 1927, the Executive Committee hired an executive secretary, Olive Graham Ricker (1885-1977), who went on to have a long and influential career at the Association.[52]

---

51. The Association had earlier investigated the possibility of incorporating under a federal charter as the American Historical Association had done some years earlier. Incorporation had been suggested as early as 1890, but the old guard believed it might destroy some of the "spontaneous and affectionate" life of the organization. Wadhams, in this case, was a hearty devotee of reform, since on several occasions he had had to borrow money on his own account to pay Association expenses. He also hoped some members could be induced to leave the ABA a legacy if the organization were incorporated. National incorporation received Association approval in 1923, but a House Judiciary Subcommittee refused a federal charter. Charles C. Lancaster, 13 *ABA Rep* 52-53 (1890); Hampton Carson to Frederick Wadhams, May 7, 1921; Wadhams to Carson, May 20, 1921, Carson Papers; 49 *ABA Rep* 313 (1924); *New York Times*, February 23, 1924, 12. Amasa M. Eaton, President of the Rhode Island State Bar Association, believed that incorporation "would give dignity and character, and would enable us to influence legislation and public opinion," Amasa M. Eaton in Wigmore, "The Movement," 578.

52. H. S. Mecartney, 31 *ABA Rep* 105-111 (1907); Mecartney, 37 *ABA Rep* 61

So long as the American Bar Association continued to consider itself more a gentleman's club than professional organization, publicity for ABA activities remained rudimentary. Nevertheless, a sentiment gradually developed that the Association ought to "popularize itself" in order to convince the laity that the Association was working for the public good. To that end, a Committee on Publicity was organized in 1912, and by the end of the decade its chairman was providing information about Association affairs to over thirteen hundred newspapers and journals around the country. The committee frankly operated on the belief that "the more times the American Bar Association could be mentioned with approbation in the papers . . . the more sanction would be given to it, and more weight would be given to its recommendation." While the committee was satisfied with the number of stories placed, the whole operation remained amateurish even by contemporary standards. There was no press bureau, even at annual meetings, and the Association employed no press agent until 1937. The Committee on Publicity saw its major responsibility as collecting, duplicating, and distributing speeches and committee reports before the annual meeting—as if all the newsworthy aspects of the event could be assembled before they occurred.[53]

(1912); cf. J. M. Dickinson, "Address of the President," 33 *ABA Rep* 341 @ 357 (1908); "Report of the Secretary," 50 *ABA Rep* 314-316 (1925) 51 *ABA Rep* 344 @ 357 (1926), 52 *ABA Rep* 212-214 (1927); "On a Business Basis," (editorial), 13 *ABAJ* 512-513 (1927); Maurice A. Langhorne, 53 *ABA Rep* 29-30 (1928). By contrast, in 1909, the American Library Association had a salaried executive officer and a headquarters office at the Chicago Public Library. (Wiegand, 126.) Rowland L. Young, "Olive G. Ricker, 1885-1977," 63 *ABAJ* 1464 (1977).

53. The Association did work through a press bureau in 1907 and presumably in other years as well. Chicago-Western Press Bureau to Alton B. Parker, August 17, 1907, Parker Papers; Roderick E. Rombauer, 40 *ABA Rep* 741 (1915); Charles A. Boston, 38 *ABA Rep* 33 (1913) and 44 *ABA Rep* 34 (1919);

During the same period the annual *Report* fell out of favor as an agent of ABA publicity. Though the secretary still labored over it and distributed it freely to libraries around the country, there was less inclination to believe that it was being read. In fact, Wadhams suggested that a special letter be addressed to the membership concerning the London trip of 1924 because he said, with pardonable hyperbole, "a great many of our members do not even know that there is such a thing as a *Report* issued every year."

During the first decade of the century the physical bulk of the *Report* grew until, in 1904, it included not only the proceedings and papers read before the Association and all the committee reports, but lists of members by state and alphabetically, a list of those present at the annual meeting, a list of new members, obituaries of deceased members, proceedings of affiliated bodies, a summary of the proceedings of state bar associations, a list of bar associations in the United States, and lists of all the speeches ever made before the ABA and some before ancillary groups as well. The 1906 *Report*, the largest ever published, had to be divided into two large volumes. At this point, though, affiliated organizations began to publish their own proceedings, and the Association pared down the *Report* as an economy measure.[54]

Mitchell D. Follansbee, 47 *ABA Rep* 60 (1922); Leo P. McNally to Arthur T. Vanderbilt, March 8,1937, Newton D. Baker Papers.

54. For instance, in 1913, the ABA stopped printing obituary notices; in 1925, it dropped the "Review of State and Federal Legislation"; and in 1927, it cut the list of all the speeches ever given before the Association. In 1909, the Secretary, John Hinkley, resigned because he said that the editing of the annual Report required forty or fifty nights of hard work every year. John Hinkley to Simeon Baldwin, August 4, 1909, Baldwin Papers; Wadhams to John W. Davis, November 22, 1923, Davis Papers; Wadhams to Taft, October 28, 1914, Taft Papers; Leo McNally to Arthur T. Vanderbilt, March

The possibility of publishing an ABA periodical had been discussed since the early years of the century. One reason for the growing interest was frankly imitative: other professional groups had journals. Another reason was the possibility of drawing back the affiliated organizations, such as the AALS, into a closer relationship with the parent body by publishing some of their proceedings. Finally, the growing number of announcements and advance programs could more conveniently be included in a journal than mailed separately.[55]

At the annual meeting of 1914, the Executive Committee gained authority to begin a new publication, and the first number of a quarterly *American Bar Association Journal* was published in January 1915. The debt-ridden and dilettante *Bulletin* of Simeon Baldwin's Comparative Law Bureau was incorporated into the new periodical, and Baldwin was made chairman of the Committee on Publications. For its first five years, the *Journal* was exceptionally dull, filled with long committee reports and other indigestible material. The Publications Committee was so stodgy and fearful of controversy that it even refused to print letters to the editor, though it was not above editing out criticisms of ABA policy from the stenographic record. The frustrated John Wigmore unsuccessfully tried to persuade Baldwin and the Executive Committee

---

8, 1937, Newton D. Baker Papers. 38 *ABA Rep* 11 (1913); 50 *ABA Rep* 477 (1925); 52 *ABA Rep* 112-113.

55. J. M. Dickinson, "Address of the President," 33 *ABA Rep* 341 @ 357 (1908); B. E. Barlow to Simeon Baldwin, January 26, 1915; Barlow to Taft, January 26, 1915, Taft Papers; 1 *ABAJ* 1 (1915); James O. Burrow, *AMA: Voice of American Medicine* (Baltimore: Johns Hopkins Press, 1963), 13: "The establishment of the [AMA] Journal [in 1883] did more to enhance the prestige of the Association than any other action the organization took in the nineteenth century."

to purchase the *American Law Review* and convert the Association's official organ into a law school-type journal.[56]

In 1920, a new publication committee gained control of the *Journal* and turned it into a relatively more popular monthly. The sponsor of the change, former President S. S. Gregory, became editor-in-chief and managed to bring out two issues before his death the same year. In the new format the *Journal* featured editorials, letters to the editor, and "articles of general interest." It republished speeches given to national and state bar associations and contained a review of Supreme Court decisions by its second and longtime editor, Edgar B. Tolman (1859-1947). It even included pictures and jokes—to the distaste of the stuffier members. Still, most members appreciated the changes, one declaring that since the passage of the Eighteenth Amendment, things had been "quite dry enough."[57]

Even the social life of the Association began to reflect the ABA's shift toward professionalism. For instance, in 1921, Wadhams had guarantee companies told "in a courteous manner" that they would be no longer permitted to provide free lunches and stenographic services to members during the annual meet-

---

56. On the problems of the Comparative Law Bureau see a letter and memorandum, "The Work of the Comparative Law Bureau," Axel Teisen to Robert P. Schick, September 6, 1916, Roscoe Pound to Schick, September 23, 1927, Pound Papers; Barlow to Taft, January 26, 1915; W. Thomas Kemp to Edgar A. Bancroft, June 17, 1920, Taft Papers; Henry Upton Sims to T. J. O'Donnell, February 17, 1919, Carson Papers; Roalfe, *Wigmore,* 110.

57. "Explaining Our Appearance," 6 *ABAJ* 34 (1920); 6 *ABAJ* 156, 118-124 (1920); 13 *ABAJ* 480 (1927). Some members of the Executive Committee insisted new periodical be titled *Journal Issued by the American Bar Association,* presumably to disassociate themselves from possible controversial expressions of personal opinion. However, the awkward title was soon quietly dropped.

ings—Wadhams fearing "something very unpleasant" would happen otherwise. The banquet speeches, first published in the 1915 *Journal*, become more formal and less frivolous than those delivered in earlier years. The great social event of the period, an official visit to Great Britain in 1924, was arranged with caution. Although the leadership was in virtual agreement that the trip should be made, General and Local Council members were polled to determine whether "a feeling of animosity" would be aroused among the rank and file who could not afford to go or who did not "instinctively feel any kinship with England."[58]

In many ways the American Bar Association did become more of a professional association between 1911 and 1928. A growing percentage of American lawyers—female as well as male—had been recruited by membership campaigns; a professional journal was being published by full-time employees at an organizational headquarters; and the Association's positions on various political issues had become newsworthy. Nevertheless, the Association's refusal to admit African Americans was professional only in the sense that racial discrimination might enhance an organization's professional status. Certainly, the ABA's ineffective committee system and its continued control by an inner circle of active members left no doubt that the Association retained many features of a social club long after its fiftieth anniversary.

---

58. Wadhams to W. Thomas Kemp, June 15, 1921, Carson Papers; Samuel Williston, "Salutations from Renowned Members of the Bar," 39 *ABAJ* 701 (1953); Reginald H. Smith to John W. Davis, May 21, 1923, Davis Papers; Wadhams to Pound, August 9, 1923; John W. Davis to Vice Presidents and Members of the General and Local Councils, May 10, 1923, Pound Papers; "Memorandum of Conference between Mr. Wadhams and Mr. Kemp in New York, June 4, 1923," Davis Papers.

Chapter **6**

Gatekeeping
Legal Education

During the fifty years that followed the founding of the American Bar Association, the relative professional status of law and medicine switched places. The early nineteenth century had been the age of the lawyer. Religious pluralism and the growth of republican institutions had elevated the bench and bar to a position at least equal to that of the clergy, confirming Tocqueville's judgment that in his day lawyers were the "American aristocracy." Medicine, on the other hand, was lightly regarded. As law school dean William Draper Lewis (1867-1949) told the Section of Legal Education in 1906, in the early nineteenth century, medicine had been "recognized as a profession, only to cast a shadow on the social position of those that followed it."[1] Yet by the turn of the twentieth century, doctors had clearly surpassed lawyers in status, and by the ABA's fiftieth anniversary in

---

1. William Draper Lewis, "Legal Education and the Failure of the Bar to Perform its Public Duties," 30 *ABA Rep* 41 (1906); Samuel Haber, *The Quest for Authority and Honor in the American Professions, 1750-1900* (Chicago: University of Chicago Press, 1991), 109-110; William R. Johnson, *Schooled Lawyers: A Study in the Clash of Professional Culture* (New York: New York University Press, 1978), 173; Paul Starr, *The Social Transformation of Medicine* (New York: Basic Books, Inc.,1982), 82-83.

1928, organized medicine could control entry to its profession with an authority lawyers could only envy.

Important to the rise of professional medicine were the clear advances that had been made in physiology and anesthesiology; and with popular acceptance of the germ theory of disease, both physicians and their patients gained new confidence in aggressive medical therapies. Medicine became both social and preventative as governments allied themselves with physicians to check and prevent illness. Even Tammany Hall declared public health to be above politics. Popular confidence in the medical profession likewise increased because of more reliable diagnoses, from advances made in alleviating suffering, and from the expectation that "the baffling and terrifying world of illness was finally becoming intelligible and comprehensible."[2]

During the Progressive Era, the medical profession even assumed some attributes of revealed religion. Medicine was science, and science, in the words of Robert Wiebe, was "the basic word that every school of thought claimed and worshipped." Modern doctors were "like religious men" descending on "cities and towns with a scientific gospel." The medical

---

2. Robert H. Wiebe, *The Search for Order: 1877-1920* (New York: Hill and Wang, 1967), 115-16; Samuel Haber, *The Quest for Authority and Honor in the American Professions, 1750-1900* (Chicago: University of Chicago Press, 1991), 202-204; Abraham Flexner, *Medical Education in the United States and Canada* (New York: Carnegie Foundation for the Advancement of Teaching, 1910), 26; Stephen J. Kunitz, "Professionalism and Social Control in the Progressive Era: The Case of the Flexner Report," *Social Problems* 22 (October, 1974), 16-27; Kenneth M. Ludmerer, *Learning to Heal: The Development of American Medical Education* (New York: Basic Books, 1985), 76-79; Donald Fleming, *William H. Welch and the Rise of Modern Medicine* (Boston: Little, Brown and Company, 1954), 11.

profession even expanded the notion of illness to include social problems previously considered to be in the sphere of religion and law: insanity, drug addiction, and, to a lesser extent, even criminality.[3]

In a 1913 *Atlantic* article, pioneering psychologist George M. Stratton (1865-1957) compared the medical with the legal profession to the latter's disadvantage. In Stratton's view, "the refinement, the intelligence, the silent mastery" of doctors represented the "scientific progress of the age." Lawyers, on the other hand, were like adepts of an outworn theology who would "apply and expound and defend against misconstruction a body of revealed truth.... When Huxley went forth in the name of Darwin to smite the embattled bishops, the fray was not so different... from that which now, as at all times, society must wage against its lawyers."[4]

Some elite lawyers responded that their profession was also scientific. Charles A. Boston, a New York corporation lawyer and Chairman of the ABA Publicity Committee, took special exception to Stratton's insinuation that law resembled "priestcraft." Henry D. Estabrook went so far as to suggest to

---

3. Wiebe, *Search for Order*, 115, 147; Fleming, *Welch*, 116; J. Willard Hurst, *The Growth of American Law: The Lawmakers* (Boston: Little Brown and Company, 1950), 261; Kunitz, "Professionalism and Social Control," 25; J. Richard Woodworth, "Some Influences on the Reform Schools of Law and Medicine," *Sociological Quarterly*, 14 (1973), 513; Rogers Hollingsworth, "Causes and Consequences of the American Medical System," *Reviews in American History* 11 (September, 1983), 327; James G. Burrow, *Organized Medicine in the Progressive Era: The Move Toward Monopoly* (Baltimore: Johns Hopkins University Press, 1977), 154.

4. G. M. Stratton, "Lawyer and Physician: A Contrast," *Atlantic*, 111 (January 1913), 48-51.

the ABA meeting of 1901 that "the legal mind [was] the scientific mind with an ethical kink in it."[5]

But most American Bar Association leaders were all too aware of invidious comparisons that could be drawn between the legal and medical professions during an age in which Karl Marx could call his notions "scientific socialism" and Mary Baker Eddy could call hers "Christian Science." By the second decade of the 20th century, the medical profession had become a model that the legal profession hoped to emulate. Slighting fundamental differences between medicine and law, bar association leaders argued that medicine's rise in status derived from the trust the laity placed in a professional association that could control medical education. As Harvard Law School Dean Roscoe Pound wrote in a 1913 letter to William Howard Taft, the legal profession was "far behind the medical profession in organization and training" and was so because it had "lost the confidence of the public."[6]

In the single decade between 1900 and 1910, the American Medical Association grew from 8,400 to over 70,000 members. Unlike the ABA's modestly successful attempt to expand its membership and coordinate its activities with

---

5. Wiebe, *Search for Order*, 117; Charles A. Boston, "The Lawyer's Conscience and Public Service," *Atlantic* 114 (September, 1914), 400-410; Henry D. Estabrook, "The Lawyer, Hamilton," 24 *ABA Rep* 351 @ 352 (1901).
6. "Report of the Committee on Legal Education and Admission to the Bar," 37 *ABA Rep* 596 @ 599 (1912); Preble Stolz, "Training for the Public Profession of the Law (1921): A Contemporary Review," in Herbert Packer and Thomas Ehrlich, *New Directions in Legal Education* (New York: McGraw-Hill Book Company, 1973), 230; Samuel Haber, *The Quest for Authority and Honor in the American Professions, 1750-1900* (Chicago: University of Chicago Press, 1991), 107; Pound to Taft, June 13, 1913, Taft Papers.

existing state and local associations, the medical profession could virtually ignore the state boundaries that were fundamental to the practice of American law. Jurisdictions might force all lawyers to become members of an "integrated bar association," but such a requirement might also press elite lawyers into unwilling association with the lower echelons of the profession. By contrast, orthodox medicine was firmly united in an effort to crush what doctors considered medical equivalents of the "ambulance chaser": the osteopath, the neuropath, and the chiropractor.[7]

Elite lawyers admired not only the systematic organization of the American Medical Association but also its ability to serve as a gatekeeper of the profession by supervising medical education. In remarks made to the Section of Legal Education in 1915, William Draper Lewis noted that lawyers would be unable to "weed out [the] unfit" from their profession unless they followed the lead of the medical profession. Medicine, he said, had gained "the greatest respect by making every man go through a medical college.…[W]e must have the same rule in regard to law students."[8]

---

7. Edson R. Sunderland, *History of the American Bar Association and its Work* (Chicago: American Bar Association, 1953), 96; *James G. Burrow, A. M. A.: Voice of American Medicine* (Baltimore: Johns Hopkins University Press, 1963), 49; Max G. Cohen, 33 *ABA Rep* 22 (1908); Lucien H. Alexander to Moorfield Storey, January 24, 1914, Taft Papers.

8. William Draper Lewis, 40 *ABA Rep* 724 (1915); David J. Brewer, "A Better Education the Great Need of the Profession," 18 *ABA Rep* 441 @ 451 (1895); Max Radin, "The Achievements of the American Bar Association: A Sixty Year Record," 25 *ABAJ* 1007 @ 1011 (1939); Everett C. Hughes, "Professions," in Kenneth S. Lynn, *The Professions in America* (Boston: Beacon Press, 1963), 7-8: "One way in which an occupation . . . can document its high status is by being able to take its pick of the young

As a group, neither the prominent lawyers whom Simeon Baldwin chose to sign the ABA call, nor those who attended the first meeting, exhibited unusual interest in strengthening legal education. Nevertheless, the Saratoga clique included many part-time law school teachers, and their dedication to legal education sometimes extended to the donation of their time. As an extreme example, Henry Hitchcock, not only served as dean of St. Louis Law School (Washington University School of Law) for seven years without pay, he also used his wife's inheritance to endow the school. Baldwin himself taught at Yale Law School from 1869 to 1912, and during some of the earlier years, he virtually *was* the Yale Law School.[9]

A Committee on Legal Education and Admission to the Bar was one of the original standing committees created in 1878, and at the following meeting its chairman, law school dean Carleton Hunt, presented an elaborate report recommending the "public maintenance" of law schools with faculties of no less than four "well-paid" teachers; a graded, highly theoretical, three-year course of study concluded by written examinations; and admission to the bar granted only after graduation. As modified the following year, the resolu-

---

people about to enter the labor market, and then to keep them in school a long time before admitting them to the charmed circle."

9. James Willard Hurst, *The Growth of American Law: The Lawmakers* (Boston: Little, Brown and Company, 1950), 361; "Henry Hitchcock," *DAB*, 9: 75-76; members of the "Saratoga clique" with law school affiliations included Simeon Baldwin (Yale); James O. Broadhead (St. Louis Law School [Washington University]); William Allen Butler (City College of New York Law School); George Hoadly (University of Cincinnati); Carleton Hunt (University of Louisiana [Tulane]); Edward J. Phelps (Yale); Thomas J. Semmes (University of Louisiana); George G. Wright (Iowa).

tions received the approval of ABA President-elect Edward J. Phelps. Phelps said the need to "to exterminate the rats" made it necessary to endorse "the most elevated standard it is reasonable to require of legal education, looking to a time when [it] will be both practicable and a requisite, as it is with regard to the medical profession."[10] Nevertheless, the Hunt resolutions, were too radical to be adopted in 1880, and the call for mandatory law school training before admission to the bar aroused a "storm of protest."[11]

While there was comparatively little interest in legal education during most of the 1880s, industrial growth in those same years led to an increased demand for legal services, which in turn encouraged ambitious young men (and even a very few women) to enter the profession. Some of these new entrants were recent immigrants or the children of immigrants, who were of significantly lower social status than that of the legal elite. Simultaneously, the earlier apprenticeship system of training lawyers became less viable. The invention of the typewriter and carbon paper had eliminated the need for clerks to "copy all the letters in a big, round hand."

---

10. Sunderland, *History of the ABA*, 72-73; 2 *ABA Rep* 209-236 (1879); Stevens, *Law School*, 92-93; Edward J. Phelps, 3 *ABA Rep* 31 (1880).

11. Max Radin, "The Achievements of the ABA," 26 *ABAJ* 19 @ 20 (1940); 3 *ABA Rep* 35-37 (1880). Part of the problem was that Hunt, as dean of a Louisiana law school, overestimated the importance of the civil law in legal education. (Irving Browne commented that Hunt's course of study "if properly pursued, with the indispensable attention to the living common law, would require nearer six than three years." [Irving Browne], "The American Bar Association," 20 *Albany Law Journal* 176 @ 177 (1879). Hunt to Simeon Baldwin, August 10 and October 30, 1881, Baldwin Family Papers; Carleton Hunt, 3 *ABA Rep* 15 (1880); "Carleton Hunt," *DAB*, IX, 382-83.

Further, many elite lawyers no longer viewed teaching apprentices to be a profitable use of their time; and remaining clerks learned less from observing courts in session because their erstwhile preceptors were making fewer appearances there. Elite lawyers spent more time counseling their clients how to *avoid* courts, and the technical skills most useful in office practice could be taught more systematically and effectively in a classroom.[12]

Although it is common to associate the advance of professionalism with a decline in apprenticeship and the rise of formal education, that connection is feeble. The new law schools were often profit-making ventures that required limited prior education for entry, and they offered courses of study that were often short and part-time.[13] Proprietary law schools were also less concerned than early nineteenth century practitioner-teachers had been with a student's antecedents and ethnic origin. (Admitting women and African Americans was a different matter, partly because their admission did not make good business sense at the time.)[14] What the gradual disappearance of the apprentice

---

12. William R. Johnson, *Schooled Lawyers: A Study in the Clash of Professional Cultures* (New York: New York University Press, 1978), xiii-xiv. The Remington Model 2 typewriter, the first with a key shift and two letters mounted on each type bar, was introduced in 1878, the year the ABA was founded. See Alfred Z. Reed, *Training for the Public Profession of the Law* (New York: The Carnegie Foundation for the Advancement of Teaching, 1921), 128, for a brief discussion of the profitability of the apprenticeship system to established lawyers during the early republic.
13. Richard L. Abel, *American Lawyers* (New York: Oxford University Press, 1989), 43-44.
14. Wayne Karl Hobson, *The American Legal Profession and the Organizational Society, 1890-1930* (New York: Garland Publishing, 1986), 118-19; Robert

system did do was transfer gatekeeping from elite practitioners to a heterogeneous group of law schools.

After the Committee on Legal Education awoke from its nine-year slumber in 1891, the Association passed a resolution calling for two years of legal education (though not necessarily in law school) as a prerequisite to bar admission. The Association also deprecated the "diploma privilege"—that is, automatic admission to the bar after completion of a law school course—although the ABA had weakly endorsed the practice only a decade before. Finally, the Association, specifically censured "needless multiplication" of law schools, especially those conducted for profit.[15]

While full-time instructors at elite law schools would undoubtedly have applauded the latter sentiment, a significant philosophical difference continued to separate ABA leaders from elite law school teachers. During the 1890s, legal educators who had been influenced by the methodology of Christopher C. Langdell (1826-1906) tended to find legal science either in Langdell's methodology or in his notion that the law library was the lawyers' laboratory. There was much science-

---

Stevens, *Law School: Legal Education in America from the 1850s to the 1980s* (Chapel Hill: University of North Carolina Press, 1983), 81-84.

15. 4 *ABA Rep* 28, 30 (1881). The resolutions were adopted unanimously, though Reed argues that the ABA "dodged the issue" of the diploma privilege on this occasion. The wording was indeed diplomatic. Reed, *Training for the Public Profession*, 265-66; Stevens, *Law School*, 94. The Committee on Legal Education was apologetic about requiring even two years of law school believing that the "sentiment of the profession and the public will not sustain, at least in some parts of the country, a longer course than two years, and even this is impracticable in some places." 15 *ABA Rep* 326 (1892). 14 *ABA Rep* 349-51 (1891); 15 *ABA Rep* 19-20 (1892); Sunderland, 73-74; James Barr Ames, "Chairman's Address," (Section of Legal Education) 27 *ABA Rep* 508 (1904).

talk in the reports of the Committee on Legal Education, but the Committee's idea of science was quite different from that of Langdell's disciples. Committee members, like Simeon Baldwin, were not primarily litigators, and they had been humanely educated. Therefore they had little sympathy for Langdell's case method of instruction, indeed, pronounced it "unscientific."[16] To them, lawyers were the natural leaders of society and therefore, law students should be broadly educated in the "science of government," "political and social science," and (even early on) "moral and political philosophy."[17]

---

16. Christopher Columbus Langdell, "Harvard Celebration Speeches," 3 *Law Quarterly Review* 123 @ 124 (1887); Stevens, *Law School*, 52-59; "Report of the Committee on Legal Education," 14 *ABA Rep* 301 @ 331-340 (1891); 15 *ABA Rep* 340-41 (1892); Moorfield Storey, 17 *ABA Rep* 379 (1894). William A. Keener (1856-1913), dean of Columbia Law School, presented a defense of the case method of instruction to the Section of Legal Education by flying it under conservative colors. Keener, "The Inductive Method in Legal Education," 17 *ABA Rep* 473-490 (1894). For some excellent commentary on the "science" of Langdell, see G. Edward White, "The American Law Institute and the Triumph of Modernist Jurisprudence," *Law and History Review* 15: 1 (Spring 1997), 1-6.

Simeon Baldwin managed to keep the case method out of Yale until he relinquished the deanship to Henry Wade Rogers in 1903. The mutual admiration of the two men allowed Rogers to ease in the Harvard system, and according to Samuel Williston, Baldwin "accepted his defeat ungrudgingly." Samuel Williston, *Life and Law: An Autobiography* (Boston: Little, Brown and Company, 1940), 232-33; Simeon Baldwin, "The Study of Elementary Law: The Proper Beginnings of a Legal Education," 13 *Yale Law Journal* 1-15 (1903).

17. "Report of the Committee on Legal Education," 15 *ABA Rep* 327 (1892), 20 *ABA Rep* 361, 365 (1897), 2 *ABA Rep* 27-28 (1879); William P. LaPiana, *Logic and Experience: The Origin of Modern American Legal Education* (New York: Oxford University Press, 1994), 136.

The breech between the elites of legal education and the elites of legal practice might have widened had not "over-crowding" from increasing numbers of non-Anglo-Saxon lawyers posed a challenge to both groups and obliged a closer, though persistently strained, relationship. In 1895, Justice David Brewer (1837-1910) warned the Association about a "growing multitude crowding in, . . . nibblers after crumbs which a dog ought to be ashamed to touch." Brewer thought it would be a blessing "if some Noachian deluge would engulf half of those who have a license to practice."[18] Twenty years later, John Wigmore, dean of Northwestern University Law School, repeated the charge that the bar was "over-crowded with incompetent, shiftless, ill-fitted lawyers who degrade the methods of the law and cheapen the quality of services by unlimited competition." Elihu Root, emphasizing a typically Progressive notion of efficiency, weighed the economic cost of "superfluous lawyers" in his presidential address of 1916. Such unnecessary practitioners, he said, were "mere pensioners and drags upon the community," who might more profitably be employed "on the farms of the country."[19]

---

18. David J. Brewer, "A Better Education the Great Need of the Profession," 18 *ABA Rep* 441 @ 452 (1895). "Overcrowding" may have been a matter of perception. A 1935 survey of the Wisconsin bar concluded that the volume of legal business after 1880 had grown much more rapidly than the increase of either lawyers or the general population, that there were fewer lawyers in proportion to the population in 1920 (1: 1145) than in 1880 (1: 948). Lloyd K. Garrison, "A Survey of the Wisconsin Bar," 10 *Wisconsin Law Review* 131 @ 133-149 (1934); Johnson, *Schooled Lawyers*, 170-71.

19. John H. Wigmore, 40 *ABA Rep* 736 (1915); Elihu Root, "Public Service by the Bar," 41 *ABA Rep* 355 @ 359 (1916). Wigmore also hoped the number of lawyers could somehow "be reduced by one half." Andrew A. Bruce, 40 *ABA Rep* 737 (1915); Herbert Harley, "Organization of the Bar,"

In 1897, the Committee on Legal Education and Admission to the Bar noted with apprehension that the number of law school students had increased by 175% in five years, whereas it had grown by only 17% during the previous twelve. Ignoring population growth, increased demand for legal services, and a growing preference for law school training over apprenticeship, the Committee concluded that a rise in higher educational standards for medical and other professional schools encouraged mediocre students to choose law as the professional career path of least resistance.[20] Influential ABA committeeman Edmund F. Trabue warned that if lawyers of "that class" got in control, "a premium would be put upon improper practices, and bad men at the Bar instead of the best men, and clients would find it possible to turn you away."[21] Most of his colleagues would have agreed, although their public arguments were usually pitched a bit higher. Thus, Simeon Baldwin, though finding the growing number of law students "alarming," told the Section of Legal Education in 1897 that his desire to limit bar admissions arose not from "guild feeling, the feeling that you want to keep things to yourself, but from the higher feeling that we want our country to have the best, that we want our profession to rank as high as the profession anywhere."[22]

Annals of the American Academy of Political and Social Science 52 (1914), 79-80. Harley suggested that the supply of lawyers be reduced by two-thirds.

20. "Report of the Committee on Legal Education and Admission to the Bar," 20 *ABA Rep* 362-64 (1897): "the result must inevitably be to elevate the other occupations and, relatively at least, degrade our own."

21. Edmund F. Trabue, 39 *ABA Rep* 809 (1914).

22. Simeon Baldwin, 20 *ABA Rep* 430 (1897); C. A. Severance, "The Constitution and Individualism," 47 *ABA Rep* 163 @ 178 (1922); Pierce Butler, "Some Opportunities and Duties of Lawyers," 48 *ABA Rep* 209 @ 214 (1923); Richard Abel, *American Lawyers*, 47: "It is always risky to

What the ABA leadership believed was necessary to "uphold the honor of the profession" was "not an increase of technical skill, but a great increase in cultural background and in the habit of scientific analysis" developed by traditional humanistic education in primary and secondary school and with theoretical studies in legal education. For instance, George Hoadly, a member of the Saratoga clique, argued in the Annual Address of 1888 that law students ought not to be admitted to practice without a knowledge of Latin and Roman law.[23] Henry Wade Rogers asserted in 1906 that lawyers ought to possess "some general culture" and an intellect "trained by previous study." Lucien Hugh Alexander found it "somewhat startling," considering the "overcrowded" profession, that the ABA had not already voted in favor of "a four year course of study, particularly when the medical profession has already blazed the way."

Herbert Harley (1871-1951), founder and secretary-editor of the American Judicature Society, went even farther,

---

impute motives, particularly bad motives, to individuals and especially dangerous to impute them to groups or organizations (whose members inevitably disagree). Yet the evidence is overwhelming that lawyers became increasingly anxious about their numbers and status as the twentieth century progressed."

23. Max Radin, "The Achievement of the ABA," 26 *ABAJ* 19 @ 23 (1940). In the Report of the Committee on Legal Education for 1891, the Committee asserted that "Admission to [law] school should not be restricted to the graduates of colleges, as has sometimes been proposed, but should be open to all who have a good English education." (14 *ABA Rep* 331).

George Hoadly, "Annual Address," 11 *ABA Rep* 219 @ 244 (1888); Gustave Koerner to Carleton Hunt, July 27, 1881, printed at 4 *ABA Rep* 296 (1881); Austin Abbott, 18 *ABA Rep* 15 (1895); "Report of the Committee on Legal Education and Admission to the Bar," 20 *ABA Rep* 372 (1897); Carroll, 33 *ABA Rep* 20 (1908), and for an opposing view James O. Crosby, 33 *ABA Rep* 21 (1908).

frankly equating intellectual training with virtue and rejoicing that in 1922 the ABA had finally realized "the tie between good education and good morals."[24] While the elite understood that the longer the period of study required, the more difficult it would be for men of an improper type to enter the profession, equating education with moral virtue was also widely endorsed by other professionals during the period. For instance, sociologist Edward Alsworth Ross (1866-1951) explained that society ought not to fear moral decline as religion disappeared because "while the priest is leaving...the school master is coming in."[25]

---

24. Henry Wade Rogers, 30 *ABA Rep*167 (1906); Elihu Root, "Address of the President, 41 *ABA Rep* 355 @ 361 (1916); Herbert Harley, "Group Organizations Among Lawyers," *Annals of the American Academy of Political and Social Science*, 101 (1922), 41; Harley, "Organization of the Bar," 80: "If it be true that wickedness is after all only stupidity, the lawyer obtained by intellectual selection can better be relied upon to maintain the honor of the profession than if the attempt were made to plot the moral curve of each applicant in advance." In the same year, an editorial in the *ABA Journal* claimed that while "Education may not convert the sinner, . . . it is one of the means of grace which enlightens his path lest he fall to destruction." "Legal Education," 8 *ABAJ* 160 (1922). Franklin Danaher, 3 *American Law School Review* 35 (1911); William Johnson, *Schooled Lawyers*, 155.

25. Edward Alsworth Ross, *Social Control: A Survey of the Foundations of Order* (New York: MacMillan Company, 1901), 175. A more modern (and more realistic) assessment of legal education notes that it "does nothing to alter self-interested motivation and indeed may strengthen it. Legal education fosters a cynicism about human nature in general, [and] destroys any belief in a transcendent body of law to which professionals owe a duty." Robert L. Nelson and David M. Trubek, "Arenas of Professionalism: The Professional Ideologies of Lawyers in Context," in Nelson, et al., *Lawyers' Ideals/Lawyers' Practices: Transformations in the American Legal Profession* (Ithaca: Cornell University Press, 1992), 183.

The collaboration of full-time law school professors and the gentlemen practitioners who served as part-time instructors was encouraged by the establishment of the Section of Legal Education in 1893. Before the new organization had an official name, George Sharp, its co-founder, called it the "Teachers' Association," and its first speakers included leaders from both segments of elite law school faculties. Organizers tried to avoid discussions about methods of instruction. Rather than rehash arguments for and against the case method, they hoped to address only subjects that could be "discussed without feeling." Within two years the Section had passed a resolution favoring the lengthening of law study to three years. This resolution was in turn approved by the ABA annual meeting of 1897, though with a good deal of parliamentary maneuvering and the deliberate omission of the words "in law school."[26]

From its inauguration, the Section of Legal Education was a great success. Attendance was high, both because of the eminence of the men who presented papers there and because there was opportunity for discussion, a luxury no longer possible at sessions of the Association itself. Though the ABA Committee on Legal Education virtually surrendered the field to the Section, the Section remained a "Teachers' Association" only briefly as other ABA members crowded in.[27]

---

26. George Sharp to Simeon Baldwin, April 27, 1893, Baldwin Family Papers; this does not mean that the merits of the case method of instruction were never discussed in the Section; see, for instance, William S. Curtis, "Examination in Law Schools," 26 *ABA Rep* 691 (1903); 20 *ABA Rep* 19-33 (1897); Stevens, *Law School*, 95.

27. Sunderland, *History of the ABA*, 31. The speakers for the first two years were Austin Abbott, Emlin McClain, Samuel Williston, Henry Wade Rogers, John F. Dillon, John D. Lawson, Simeon Baldwin, Woodrow

In 1899, law teachers, casting about for a more restrictive forum, had the Section issue a call for a joint meeting of the Section and of delegates from "reputable law schools." Two days before the scheduled meeting in August 1900, representatives of thirty-five law schools organized the Association of American Law Schools—the name being suggested by the Association of American Medical Colleges, founded in 1890.[28] Membership in the AALS was open only to law schools rather than to individuals—and only to law schools that complied with AALS requirements regarding admission, course of study, and adequacy of its library.

The Section criticized an AALS resolution that barred membership after 1905 to any school that did not offer a three-year curriculum. While George Sharp, now Secretary of the Section, successfully deflected criticism of the AALS, the episode marked the beginning of more than fifteen years of strained relations between the two organizations.[29]

Echoes of the squabble over the case method of instruction could occasionally be heard at annual meetings after 1900, but the focus of the legal education debate now shifted elsewhere. By the turn of the century most elite law schools had adopted the Harvard system, Simeon Baldwin's Yale being a conspicuous exception. It was now clear that the case method of instruction would become the university system because it discriminated against mediocre intellect. The

---

Wilson, John H. Wigmore, Edmund Wetmore, and William A. Keener. Hollis Bailey, "The Works and Aims of the Section of Legal Education," 37 *ABA Rep* 732 (1912); Roscoe Pound to Everette Wheeler, July 28, 1919, Wheeler Papers.

28. 22 *ABA Rep* 565 (1899); 23 *ABA Rep* 569-575 (1900).

29. 23 *ABA Rep* 449, 456 (1900); Emlin McClain, "Address of the President [of the AALS]," 25 *ABA Rep* 736 (1902).

textbook-lecture method would be relegated to proprietary schools. In 1889, Henry Wade Rogers had opposed the case method because it "was quite unsuited to the average student." But once "overcrowding" became a source of concern, this alleged unsuitability became an asset.[30]

Although before 1929 the ABA never enrolled more than 18% of American lawyers, membership grew dramatically during the first three decades of the century, and the original, more aristocratic, outlook of the organization was diluted. A rift opened between eastern, urban lawyers, more typical of the original ABA members, and newer men, more representative of popular sentiment in the nation's heartland. Whereas 65% percent of the 1878 committeemen had graduated from college, only 55% percent of the 1928 committeemen had done so.[31]

Many of the newer members were suspicious of the emphasis suddenly placed on "raising standards." Their own status had not been challenged by the country doctor. Their professional environment was still fashioned by the kind of informal controls that had prevailed in the early nineteenth century. Their business remained fairly stable, and they did not compete for clients or judgments with the immigrants whom the urban elite found so distasteful. "It was inevitable," admitted an editorial in the *ABA Journal*, "that some who achieved professional success without such educational advantages should feel that [raising educational standards for

---

30. Henry Wade Rogers, "The Law School of the University of Michigan," 1 *Green Bag* 189 @ 194 (1889); Johnson, *Schooled Lawyers*, 126-27.

31. John Austin Matzko, "The Early Years of the American Bar Association, 1878-1928," PhD dissertation, University of Virginia, 1984, 505-06.

bar admission] involved an unspoken reflection on their standing." For instance, a member from Oklahoma pointedly defended his apprenticeship training before a meeting of the Section of Legal Education, asserting that while his town had "quite a number of graduates from Harvard and Yale, [the] half dozen leading lawyers [had] obtained their legal education in a law office."[32]

To the annoyance of the urban elites, "the forces of prejudice and obscurantism" (as ABA historian Max Radin called the opposition) were able to bring to bear against them the potent weapon of democratic ideology. U. S. Attorney General Judson Harmon (1846-1927) told the Section of Legal Education that when he had tried to persuade an influential lawyer, a member of the Ohio legislature, to support a measure extending the required length of study before bar admission, his friend replied, "How long did you and I study for the bar?" Harmon guessed about thirteen months. Then, said his friend, "it was not fair to the rest of the boys, we having got in, to endeavor to shut the door on them."[33]

The Horatio Alger myth would have been difficult enough to counter, but the legal elite also had to deal with the "Lincoln Objection." As William Howard Taft once stated the argument in order to refute it, "Look at Abraham Lincoln. He never had any education of any sort. He educated himself, and note his greatness." The elite attempted various replies. One bar examiner dubiously argued that Lincoln was such a great man that in the contemporary environment it would have

---

32. "Legal Education," 8 *ABAJ* 160 (1922); see Auerbach, *Unequal Justice*, 97; Victor Kulp, 40 *ABA Rep* 729 (1915).

33. Max Radin, "The Achievements of the American Bar Association," 26 *ABAJ* 19 @ 26 (1940); 19 *ABA Rep* 448 (1896).

been "no trouble" for him to have gotten proper training before entering practice. Nicholas Murray Butler (1862-1947), speaking at the annual meeting of 1922, suggested that taxpayer-supported junior colleges were the answer to those who thought that required training would shut out the Abraham Lincolns. H. Claude Horack, a paid advisor to the ABA in the rating of law schools, shrugged off the argument by insisting that "if the bars are let down for the occasional Abraham Lincoln, there is let in a herd of untrained young men."[34]

Thus, despite widespread interest in both legal education and in reversing the perceived trend toward "overcrowding," the American Bar Association passed no important resolutions about legal education from 1892 until the approval of

---

34. William Howard Taft, "The Social Importance of Proper Standards for Admission to the Bar," 38 *ABA Rep* 924 (1913). As an example of Taft's complaint, see the remarks of J. N. Frierson, dean of the University of South Carolina Law School, *New York Times*, February 24, 1922, 12. Frierson charged that the proposed standards of the American Bar Association were "unjust and uncalled for," and he "pointed to Lincoln and other notable leaders who 'never saw the inside of a college.'"

Edwin C. Goddard, "The Bar Examination," 42 *ABA Rep* 533 @ 534 (1917); Elihu Root, 47 *ABA Rep* 490 (1922); Nicholas Murray Butler, "Preliminary Education for Lawyers," 47 *ABA Rep* 278 @ 279 (1922); "Opportunity for Poor Boys," 13 *ABAJ* 141 (1927); H. Claude Horack, "The Standards and Ideals of the American Bar Association," *National Education Association Addresses and Proceedings*, 66 (1928), 155. Horack implied the standard argument as well, that changed conditions had produced an environment in which Lincoln could have received a formal education: "There is hardly a young man in America today who is not within a few hours' auto ride of a college--and hardly a boy that does not have a collegiate flivver in which to make the trip . . . It would be rash to suggest to a group, familiar with present educational conditions, that a young man of ability and determination cannot make his own way in college." (156); Radin, "The Achievements of the ABA," 26 *ABAJ* 19 (1940).

eight rules for admission to the bar in 1918—and the formulation of those rules had been a project of the Section of Legal Education since 1906![35] The AALS, on the other hand, was requiring evermore rigorous standards. In 1900, students at member schools were required to have a high school diploma, take at least a two-year course, and have access to a library that contained both the federal and appropriate state reports. In 1907, the AALS required a three-year law school program; in 1912, it refused to accept members whose day and evening sessions were of equal length. In 1916, it demanded that its member schools have three "substantially" full-time faculty members.[36]

Nevertheless, the AALS was unable by itself to raise formal standards of legal education because it represented a steadily smaller proportion of the total law school population. Some member schools could not keep up with increased requirements and were dropped. Meanwhile, nonmember proprietary and part-time schools grew apace.[37] Concurrently the estrangement of the AALS and the ABA led to a break. During the first few years of its existence, feeble attempts were made to hold joint sessions of the AALS and the ABA's Section of Legal Education. Between 1906 and 1912, totally separate programs were organized, although the AALS met at the same time and in the same location as the ABA annual meeting. Then when ABA President William Howard Taft, scheduled "his" convention in October, rather than in August, 1914, Henry Bates, dean of the University of Michigan Law School, wrote him a huffy letter asking if the ABA meeting

---

35. Sunderland, *History of the ABA*, 140-143; 4 *ABAJ* 419, 423 (1918).
36. Sunderland, 47-49; Stevens, *Law School*, 96-97.
37. Stevens, 97-98.

had been deliberately planned to be inconvenient for academics in order to break the connection between the two organizations. The AALS scheduled its meeting for the Christmas holidays. Harry S. Richards (1868-1929), dean of the Wisconsin Law School, complained that the AALS had tried to live with the ABA for fifteen years, but they had given "us a poor place on the program, and then often after a fight, and paid no attention to us, so we took our things and moved out."[38]

Meanwhile, the American Medical Association was consolidating its influence over medical education. At a time when the ABA was still a small, voluntary association of individuals, the AMA, in 1901, reorganized into a body that represented state and local medical societies. In 1904 it established a Council on Medical Education to act in its behalf in matters regarding professional training. Two years later the Council initiated a survey of all medical schools in the country, which resulted in a ranking system.[39]

The Council proposed to Henry S. Pritchett (1857-1939), President of the Carnegie Foundation for the Advancement of Teaching, that the Foundation report on the status of medical education. Pritchett, who had been a leader in the successful fight to establish a national Bureau of Standards, had independently decided to investigate educational conditions in the three traditional professions of law, medicine, and theology—apparently in that order. But Pritchett said he

---

38. Sunderland, 48-49; Henry M. Bates to Taft, February 16, 1914; Taft to Bates, February 24, 1914, Taft Papers; Henry Wade Rogers, "Address of the President of the AALS," 30 *ABA Rep* 148 (1906); Richards quotation, 26 *AALS Proceedings* 30-31 (1926), quoted in Auerbach, *Unequal Justice*, 89; on Richards, see Johnson, *Schooled Lawyers*, 121ff.
39. Burrow, *Organized Medicine in the Progressive Era*, 32-42.

had found "no efforts being made by law to better the conditions in legal education and had met with some slight opposition in the efforts he was making," and being "agreeably surprised" by the work of the Council on Medical Education, he decided to study medical education first. Furthermore, he agreed that Carnegie Foundation report would present itself as an impartial study but "would be guided very largely by the Council's investigations."[40]

The Carnegie Foundation study became the famous Flexner Report of 1910, which "produced an immediate and profound sensation." Although Flexner's specific charges against certain medical schools ("disgraceful," "utterly wretched," "indescribably filthy") brought libel suits and death threats, the study was welcomed by the medical elite, who used Flexner's phrase "fewer and better doctors " as a "rallying cry of the profession." Flexner agreed with professional leaders that medical school should consist of a four-year course subsequent to at least two years of college, and he "considered a system of education substantially maintained by proprietary institutions wholly indefensible, particularly when such schools operated solely for profit." Furthermore, Flexner concurred with the medical elite that medical schools ought to be integrated with universities and their scientific departments.[41]

---

40. Quoted in Preble Stolz, "Training for the Public Profession," 230-31.
41. Abraham Flexner, *I Remember: The Autobiography of Abraham Flexner* (New York: Simon and Schuster, 1940), 130; Michael Schudson, "The Flexner Report and the Reed Report: Notes on the History of Professional Education in the United States," *Social Science Quarterly* 55 (1974), 351; Abraham Flexner, *Medical Education,* quoted in Burrow, *Organized Medicine,* 43; Magali Sarfatti Larson, *The Rise of Professionalism: A Sociological Analysis* (Berkeley: University of California Press, 1977), 163.

The immediate effects of the Flexner Report appeared dramatic. The number of medical schools dropped 47% in twenty years, from 160 in 1900 to 85 in 1920; the number of medical students fell proportionately, 45% during the same period. Nevertheless, the Carnegie Foundation study may have been more significant in professional myth than in reality.[42] Eleven medical schools collapsed in the single year between Flexner's investigation and the publication of the report. The earlier work of the Council of Medical Education, combined with the success of the medical profession in eliciting public support, were also factors in the elimination of some smaller proprietary schools. Perhaps even more significant was the increasing need for medical schools to provide expensive instructional facilities, such as laboratories and teaching hospitals. Such costs strained the budgets of proprietary schools or at least resulted in their being ineffective competitors with eleemosynary institutions endowed by philanthropists. "Nothing has perhaps done more to complete the discredit of commercialism," wrote Flexner, "than the fact that it has ceased to pay."[43] Whatever the cause for the decline in the number of medical schools, the legal elite were

---

42. Schudson, "The Flexner Report and the Reed Report," 350; Starr, 120.
43. Starr, 120; J. Richard Woodworth, "Some Influences on the Reform of Schools of Law and Medicine 1890 to 1930," *Sociological Quarterly*, 14 (1973), 503, 511. On the role of philanthropy in medical education, see Burrow, *Organized Medicine*, 11-12; Ellen Condliffe Lagemann, *Private Power for the Public Good: A History of the Carnegie Foundation for the Advancement of Teaching* (Middletown: Conn.: Wesleyan University Press, 1983), 72-73; Flexner, *Medical Education*, 11.

well aware of, and alarmed by, the trend represented in the following table:[44]

Year	Law Schools	Law Students	Medical Schools	Medical Students
1889-1890	61	4,486	133	15,404
1899-1900	102	12,408	160	25,171
1909-1910	124	19,498	131	21,526
1919-1920	146	24,503	85	13,798

Simply stated, while the number of medical schools and medical students had declined during the first two decades of the century, the number of law schools and law students had risen dramatically. In 1890, there were more than three medical students for every law student; in 1920, there were almost two law students for every medical student.

Furthermore, while the AMA had been squeezing commercial medical schools out of the marketplace, legal education was expanding fastest among the proprietary schools that catered to the urban lower-middle classes. Law schools run by a few moonlighting practitioners were often highly cost effective; and after the turn of the century, their numbers swelled to meet the demand. For example, Suffolk Law

44. Stolz, "Training for the Public Profession of the Law," 231. Slightly higher figures are given in Reed, *Training for the Public Profession of the Law*, 443.

School in Boston, founded by Gleason Archer Sr. (1880-1966) in 1906, had 460 students in 1915, 1512 in 1922, and 2018 in 1924. By 1928 Archer boasted that Suffolk had nearly 4,000 students and was the largest law school in the world. According to Richard Abel, "California law schools paid commissions to students and other solicitors for each new enrollee, and a faculty member from one school was hired as dean of another and paid for each student he lured away from his former employer."[45]

Unlike the medical profession, which went from strength to strength in promoting restrictive laws to state legislators, the legal profession found the same legislators unresponsive, even hostile, to the suggestion that they ought to raise educational standards for admission to the bar—especially because graduates of these part-time law schools had begun to appear in the legislatures. In 1920, one influential member of the Section of Legal Education said of state legislatures, "Let the doctors go there all they want to, but the moment lawyers start in and ask special privileges, the old antagonism rises up."[46]

---

45. Stevens, *Law School*, 75, 80, 102; Harry First, "Competition in the Legal Education Industry," 53 *New York University Law Review* 311 @ 348 (1978). Archer achieved the growth of Suffolk Law School "through aggressive promotion, including a weekly national radio broadcast, publication of books and speeches, the construction of a neon sign on the roof of the school building . . . and extensive advertising." Abel, 54.

46. Franklin M. Danaher, 6 *ABAJ* 78 (1920); Stevens, *Law School*, 98, 103; Max Radin, "The Achievements of the ABA." 25 *ABAJ* 1007 @ 1013 (1939). For the success of the medical profession in obtaining restrictive legislation, see Burrow, *Organized Medicine*, 52-70; Milton Friedman, *Capitalism and Freedom* (Chicago: University of Chicago Press, 1962), 151.

The Flexner Report, and its putative results, impressed leaders of both the ABA and the AALS. In February 1913 the ABA Committee on Legal Education and Admission to the Bar sent a "most anxious" request to the Carnegie Foundation for a study of legal education as "searching and far-reaching [as the Flexner Report] and one equally frank and fearless in its statement of the facts which the investigation may reveal."[47] To make the survey, Pritchett chose Alfred Zantzinger Reed (1875-1949), the son of a country doctor who had joined the Foundation staff shortly after receiving his PhD in politics from Columbia.

Flexner and Reed had much in common, but their differences were to prove at least as significant. Although Flexner's report had wit and bite and made good newspaper copy, Flexner had made his examination of medical schools in such haste—sixty-nine schools in twenty-two states in not more than seventy-eight working days—that his published report was justly criticized for ignoring the scientific standards he said he wanted to impose on medical schools. More importantly, Flexner began his task with "a feeling of inadequacy" and was therefore all the more willing to follow the lead of the professional elite.[48]

---

47. Schudson, "The Flexner Report and the Reed Report," 351; Committee of Legal Education and Admission to the Bar to Henry S. Pritchett, President of the Carnegie Foundation, February 7, 1913, printed in Alfred Z. Reed, *Training for the Public Profession of the Law*, xviii; Henry Wade Rogers, 38 *ABA Rep* 25 (1913).
48. Thomas Gordon Barnes, *Hastings College of the Law: The First Century* (San Francisco: Hastings College of the Law Press, 1978), 207; Burrow, *Organized Medicine*, 42, 181 (n. 31), 45-47; Schudson, "The Flexner Report and the Reed Report," 351.

Reed engaged in no such self-abasement. To him the legal profession was merely a "technical subdivision" of political science, his own specialty; therefore, he had no difficulty considering "himself qualified to inform the legal profession what it must do to reform itself."[49] And far from rushing his study to completion, Reed worked at such a deliberate pace that Pritchett was driven to exasperation. Granted that Reed's progress was impeded by the refusal of some law schools—remembering Flexner—to cooperate with him, the Reed survey still took seven years to complete as against Flexner's thirteen months.[50]

When the report was finally printed in 1921, the ABA elite found it both more and less than they had hoped for. Reed had produced a book of nearly five hundred pages, most of which was a history of American legal education that, even a century later, remains generally sound. But as one recent critic has put it, the "congeries of facts and many digressions robbed the manifesto of punch."[51] Reed's volume also lacked critiques of individual schools, which had made Flexner's work a popular as well as a professional success. Pritchett promised in the preface that the Carnegie Foundation would treat contemporary law schools in another book that would appear shortly;

---

49. Barnes, *Hastings College of the Law*, 208.

50. Stevens, *Law School*, 126 (n. 20); Howard J. Savage, *Fruit of an Impulse: Forty-Five Years of the Carnegie Foundation, 1905-1950* (New York: Harcourt, Brace, and Company, 1953), 150-51; Henry Wade Rogers, 42 *ABA Rep* 46 (1917); Lagemann, *Private Power*, 79.

51. Barnes, *Hastings College of the Law*, 210.

but true to form, Reed took another seven years to finish *Present-Day Law Schools in the United States and Canada.*[52]

More seriously for the legal elite, the Reed Report did not fully endorse the bar leaders' vision of legal education. In Reed's view, the public nature of the law necessitated that part-time legal education be made available to students financially unable to attend college and a full-time law school. Reed advocated a divided profession in which graduates of part-time schools would be ineligible to perform all the functions of a more broadly trained lawyer but would be capable of discharging more mundane tasks in such areas as probate, conveyancing, and criminal law. Reed thought that formal recognition of a "differentiated" bar would not only ratify the *de facto* division of the profession but would also help elevate requirements for the more selective part of the profession. Otherwise, he believed, state legislatures would resist raising standards at all.[53]

Reed argued that bar associations in general, and the American Bar Association in particular, might play a substantial role in the reform of American legal education if they patterned themselves after the more vigorous organizations of doctors. He recommended that bar associations shed their image as social clubs and form federated societies that would include a much greater percentage of lawyers and that would have an organic connection with elite law schools. Ironically, Reed argued that these reformed bar associations should

---

52. Reed, *Training for the Public Profession of the Law*, xviii; Alfred Z. Reed, *Present-Day Law Schools in the United States and Canada* (New York: The Carnegie Foundation for the Advancement of Teaching, 1928).
53. Stolz, "Training for the Public Profession of the Law," 243; Reed, *Training for the Public Profession of the Law*, 3, 59-60, 77-78, 416-20.

require "stiff educational qualifications for admission." But regarding the bar associations as they existed, Reed was frank. Many of them, he said, exerted "no influence," and he thought it "would be a hopeless task to attempt to catalogue . . . the associations that deserve to be taken seriously."[54]

While elite lawyers could hardly challenge Reed's criticism of bar associations, it was his proposal for a two-tiered profession that received sustained attack from the ABA elite. In all three of the fairly lengthy reviews of his book published in the *ABA Journal,* the reviewers announced their opposition to a "differentiated bar." Two of the reviews, one by John B. Sanborn Jr. (1883-1964) and the other by William Draper Lewis, were, in Reed's words, "fair and even generous in tone"; but the third and longest review by Harlan F. Stone (1872-1946), Dean of Columbia University Law School and future Supreme Court justice, was barely civil. Stone implied that Reed was unqualified to make the judgements he had made. Previously, "low grade" law schools had not tried "to justify their existence by an appeal to any profound political or social philosophy." Now Reed had given them one, "ready to hand... justifying and in fact commending their existence."[55]

---

54. Reed, 212-220: "The diffusion of professional responsibilities among national, state and local organs has made it no one's especial business to initiate a needed reform. . . . The associated lawyers, having no single recognized mouthpiece, would set up a discordant clamor if they really raised their voice. This is one of the reasons why, so often—let it be said without offense—they emit only a gentle buzz, made in large part of platitudinous generalities." (214)

55. John B. Sanborn, "Training for Public Profession of the Law," 7 *ABAJ* 615 (1921); Harlan F. Stone, "Legal Education and Democratic Principle," 7 *ABAJ* 639 (1922); William Draper Lewis, "American Bar Association's Position on Legal Education," 8 *ABAJ* 39 (1922); Alfred Z. Reed, "Criticism

At least part of the blame for the harsh professional criticism of the Reed Report rests with Reed himself and the ambiguousness with which he presented his views. Like a politician who promises more revenue from lower taxs, Reed had suggested that low entrance requirements would result in higher educational standards. The legal elite were more than skeptical. Reed protested that he had only intended to formulate "certain general principles" not a comprehensive program. Another failing of Reed's was that as a progressive, he was overly sanguine about his ability to guide the American Bar Association with logical argumentation buttressed by statistics, a notion he should have abandoned after completing the historical research. Even after his position had been flatly repudiated by the Root Committee (of which more below), Reed announced that its report showed an "entire sympathy" with his views.[56] Finally, whatever chance the "differentiated bar" had of acceptance by the profession was lost through Reed's delay in publishing his report. In short, events ran ahead of him.

No sooner had the AALS taken its marbles and gone home, snubbing the 1914 ABA meeting, than its leadership had second thoughts about self-exile. With few representatives of the AALS in attendance at ABA meetings, representatives of part-time law schools captured the Section of Legal

---

of Carnegie Foundation Bulletin," 8 *ABAJ* 114 (1922); cf. "Dean Stone's Rejoinder to Mr. Reed's Reply," 8 *ABAJ* 187 (1922); Harley, "Group Organizations Among Lawyers," 43; Charles E. Hughes, "Liberty and Law," 50 *ABA Rep* 183 @ 196 (1925); Pierce Butler, "Some Opportunities and Duties of Lawyers," 48 *ABA Rep* 209 @ 214 (1923).

The leadership of the AALS was just as opposed—if not more so—to the idea of the "differentiated bar." In 1921, Arthur Corbin devoted most of his presidential address before the AALS to rebutting the notion.

56. Reed, "Criticism," 114.

Education. As early as 1915, one AALS representative warned that this "inferior element" posed a "grave danger . . . to those interested in legal education." Privately, Roscoe Pound dismissed the Section as "a clearing house for cranks."[57] William Draper Lewis, an influential figure in both the ABA and the AALS, attempted a reconciliation of the two organizations in the interest of mutual gatekeeping goals.[58]

In 1915 AALS President Harry Richards discussed with admiration the effective "weeding out" of medical schools by the AMA, and he urged an "aggressive and sustained effort" to achieve the same results in law. To help law teachers overcome "the indifference or actual hostility" of much of the organized bar, Richards suggested that the ABA abolish the Section of Legal Education replace it with the AALS: "It may seem unnatural for the child of the Section . . . to demand the death of its parent, but the efficiency expert cannot allow himself the luxury of the softer emotions."[59]

More influential was the presidential address delivered to the AALS in the following year by Yale law professor Walter Wheeler Cook (1873-1943). Only half in jest, Cook said that "nearly all the poorly prepared students who were prevented from studying medicine because of the higher standards in that profession transferred their allegiance to the law." While Cook noted that the changes in medical education were wrought not by the Association of American Medical Colleges—the coun-

---

57. First, "Competition in the Legal Education Industry," 355; Reed, *Present-Day Law Schools*, 30-35; William R. Vance, *AALS Proceedings* 32 (1915); Roscoe Pound to Everette Wheeler, July 28, 1919, Wheeler Papers.

58. William Draper Lewis, *AALS Proceedings* 28 (1915).

59. Harry S. Richards, "Progress in Legal Education," *AALS Proceedings* 61-76 (1915).

terpart of the AALS—but by a Council on Medical Education, he also argued that this made little difference since both organizations were agents of medical school professors. Cook suggested that the ABA create a Council on Legal Education as an organization that would speak for both the Association and legal education professionals.[60]

At the next ABA meeting, Henry Wade Rogers, Cook's erstwhile colleague at Yale and Chairman of the Committee on Legal Education, pushed through—in the five minutes allotted to him on the convention floor—an authorization for a Council on Legal Education. (Accompanying legislation abolishing the Committee on Legal Education was not considered, and so for one confusing year, the ABA had a Committee, a Council, and Section of Legal Education.) The Council was promptly stocked with five leaders of the law school establishment: Rogers (as chairman), Roscoe Pound,

---

60. Walter Wheeler Cook, "A Plan for the Improvement of Legal Education and Standards of Admission to the Bar," *AALS Proceedings* 110 (1916). Cook was repeating the proposal of another Yale professor, Wesley Hohfeld (1879-1918), that the legal profession should try to establish a bar of two grades. Since Hohfeld had made his suggestion in an unpublished report to the Carnegie Foundation before 1916, Alfred Reed certainly knew about it. Yet nowhere did Reed give Hohfeld or Cook credit for the idea. Stolz, "Training for the Public Profession of the Law," 246-47.

Cook viewed the establishment of a Council on Legal Education as a matter for negotiation between the ABA, the Section of Legal Education, and the AALS; and he warned that to be effective, the Council could not be completely dominated by the AALS. Cook repeated his speech to the Section of Legal Education the following year as "The Improvement of Legal Education and of Standards for Admission to the Bar," 42 *ABA Rep* 547 (1917). He eliminated the reference to the "differentiated bar" but added an appeal for representation on the Council of Legal Education by non-law school men. (558-59.)

Harlan Stone, John Wigmore, and William R. Vance. In the following year, 1918, the Council reported a proposal to abolish the Section in favor of the AALS as well as a recommendation that would have required every applicant for admission to the bar to be a graduate of a three-year law school course (four years, in the case of night schools). Neither one of these explosive proposals was brought to a vote, although in the case of the latter, Rogers reserved the "right to press it next year or the year after, as we may choose." Obviously (in the words of Preble Stolz), elite legal educators "thought they were riding high and were in control of what the A.B.A. was likely to do with respect to legal education."[61]

They were wrong. In 1919 the Executive Committee, eyeing the Council with justifiable suspicion, refused to appropriate funds for its activities and later wrote it out of existence in the constitutional revision. From the Council's own report, it is clear that the part-time schools had succeeded in swaying an Executive Committee already concerned that ABA creations might scratch their own itches in the name of the Association. The Council fought back with a petition from the deans of thirty–three AALS-member law schools members and even a resolution passed by the leadership of the Section. Yet despite Rogers' reference to the strength of the medical profession and his warning that abolishing the Council would "estrange the leading law schools and law-school men of the country from the American Bar Association," the schoolmen and their supporters were voted down. The Council survived but was made

---

61. 42 *ABA Rep* 90-92, 95 (1917); 42 *ABA Rep* 76-77 (1918); Stolz, 236-37.

subject to the authority of the Section, which it had earlier planned to eliminate.[62]

The next meeting of the AALS was a gloomy affair with Harlan Stone, the president, and Professor Joseph Beale of Harvard reflecting "profound disenchantment" with the ABA. Draper Lewis, on the other hand, proposed that AALS members attend the next Section meeting in force and push through a resolution calling for a special committee to study legal education. The AALS then called for a special session at the next ABA convention, appointed a committee to "secure a large attendance," and appealed to their member law schools to pay the expenses.[63]

As had historically been the case in the American Bar Association, big names counted. Lewis was able to win assent of the venerable Elihu Root to become a candidate for the chairmanship of the Section, "a candidate so eminent that his election could not be denied." Once this business had been put through, Root became the chairman of the Special Committee as well and wisely invited five non-law school men to join Lewis and himself as members. In the spring of 1921, the Root Committee heard representatives of elite law

---

62. 44 *ABA Rep* 34, 124, 256 (1919); Stolz, 237; "Report of the Council on Legal Education," 44 *ABA Rep* 264 @ 267-68 (1919); 14 *Illinois Law Review* 205-07 (1919). At the same time, the Executive Committee also curbed the Red-baiting activities of the Committee to Oppose Judicial Recall and Allied Measures; see the comments of George T. Page, ABA President, 4 *American Law School Review* 458-59 (1919). The procedure by which the revised constitution was pushed through—by one-half vote—remains dubious.

63. *AALS Proceedings* 38-41, 91, 107-08 (1919); cf. First, "Competition," 355-56; Stolz, "Training for the Public Profession of the Law," 237-38; cf. Edward T. Lee, 46 *ABA Rep* 666-67 (1921).

schools, bar examination boards, and even a few carefully chosen night schools. It obtained advance copies of Alfred Reed's long awaited report and invited him to appear, in part to disarm resistance that might rally around his "differentiated bar."[64]

The resolutions that Root presented to the Section and then to the ABA meeting in 1921 were a compromise, but a compromise heavily favoring elite law schools. The Committee reported that "every candidate for admission to the Bar" should "give evidence of graduation from a law school" of the proper type and that two years of college ought to be required before admission to law school. Implied (but not explicitly stated) was that part-time law schools would be legitimatized only if they lengthened their courses to four years. Finally, a revived Council on Legal Education was directed to publish lists of law schools complying with the established standards and was instructed to urge adoption of these requirements to state authorities as minimum legal qualifications for admission to the bar. Chief Justice Taft was shrewdly importuned to second the Committee resolutions before the Section, and Root blandly announced to the annual meeting that the proposals were not really new, only clarifications of "expressions" previously approved by the ABA "in perhaps less positive form."[65]

Opponents of the report operated at a distinct disadvantage. When such prominent men as Taft and Root stood

---

64. Stolz, 238-39; George E. Price, 46 *ABA Rep* 673 (1921). Root said his Committee agreed with Reed and had even based its recommendations on his report. For his own reasons, Reed assented to this legal fiction. Elihu Root, 46 *ABA Rep* 38 (1921).
65. 46 *ABA Rep* 38, 661-62 (1921); Stolz, 239.

for such propositions, "who can withstand them?" asked Edward T. Lee (1861-1943) rhetorically. Lee, dean of John Marshall Law School and one of the most articulate foes of the AALS, then answered, "No one, unless he is clothed with truth." Reading from a pamphlet he had written, "Is there a Greek horse at the A.B.A. Gate?" Lee exposed the "scheme" of Draper Lewis, ridiculing the notion that potential lawyers could easily get a college education and arguing that the imposition of a college requirement would discriminate against urban residents and those of foreign extraction—the former because state universities were so "frequently situated in remote towns." He mocked the conservative's hatred of unionism by imagining a union leader's retort to the ABA: "You have applied in your profession by more clever means than we can adopt, the principle that we apply...with the strong arm." Lee even attacked a shibboleth of the legal elite, that law must follow the lead of medicine in raising academic standards. A rural doctor, said Lee, must be ready for the most serious emergency, but the country lawyer did not have to act on a moment's notice nor did he have to deal with complex problems.[66]

George E. Price (1848-1938), a member of the Root Committee from West Virginia, replied that the college requirement would not "shut out many . . . American youths," and he doubted that the ABA would "want to let down the tests

---

66. Edward T. Lee, 46 *ABA Rep* 42-43, 665-672 (1921); Lee, the son of Irish immigrants, had worked his way through both Harvard and Columbian (George Washington) law schools. William Wleklinski, *A Centennial History of John Marshall Law School* (1999), 24, https://www.jmls.edu/welcome/centennial-history/files/centennial.pdf (accessed September 24, 2018).

simply to let in uneducated foreigners." A young man, said Price, needed "to be segregated at least for two years under a different atmosphere in a college...where the proper principles are inculcated, and where the spirit of the American government is taught."[67] "Times have changed," added Chicago corporation lawyer Nathan William MacChesney (1878-1954). In earlier days "members of the Bar were looked up to as the intellectual and moral and political leaders of the times. The real question at issue is whether we are to maintain our comparative standing in the United States, or whether we are to take second place." The resolutions of the Root Committee were approved on a rising vote.[68]

A further recommendation of the Root Committee was to call for a conference on legal education in the name of the American Bar Association to which state and local bar association representatives would be invited. About 150 delegates appeared at the two-day session held in Washington on February 22 and 23, 1922. Since lawyers lacked the integrated professional associations of medicine, the legal elite contrived the Special Conference as the next best thing, "a publicity device...to energize the local bars and thus state governments" to adopt ABA educational standards as their own.[69] Predictably, the program was loaded with big names whose responsibility was to declare the official position that

---

67. George E. Price, 46 *ABA Rep* 672-677 (1921). Price presumably intended the last word of the final quotation to be "taught," rather than as printed, "thought." The *Reports* have very few typographical errors, and Price may said "thought."

68. 46 *ABA Rep* 44-47 (1921).

69. *New York Times*, February 25, 1922, 12; 47 *ABA Rep* 482-591 (1922); Stolz, "Training for the Public Profession of the Law," 241.

delegates were expected to ratify. Attorney General Harry Daugherty (1860-1941)—who later barely escaped preceding John Mitchell into prison from that office—vaguely endorsed "any effort that might tend to enhance the standards of the bar." Chief Justice Taft stressed "overcrowding." Root and former Attorney General George Wickersham made thinly veiled references to ethnic fears.[70]

The Conference did not go altogether as planned. Two delegates turned the tables on the organizers by suggesting that there was not much moral benefit from attending college when so many universities had become centers of "radicalism and socialism." The conference modified ABA standards by endorsing "equivalent training" as a substitute for two years of college. Nevertheless, when it appeared that the college requirement might be eliminated altogether, Root made a short but dramatic speech, and the proposals of the elite sailed through.[71]

As Jerold Auerbach has correctly noted, "the fight for higher standards was mostly sound and fury" if measured only by state statutes passed in the aftermath. Four years after the

---

70. *New York Times*, February 25, 1922, 12; 47 *ABA Rep* 490-92, 563 (1922). The ABA leadership also brought in the influential Carnegie Foundation advisor, Dr. William H. Welch, to explain how the medical profession had raised educational standards. 47 *ABA Rep* 529 (1922).

71. Thomas Patterson, 47 *ABA Rep* 567 (1922); cf. Adolph H. Grundman, "The Early History of the Colorado Bar Association: 1898-1938," 14 *Colorado Lawyer* 7 @ 13-14 (1985).

Elihu Root, 47 *ABA Rep* 583-84 (1922): "All that the opposition here comes to is simply to stop, to stop! to do nothing! How much better, instead of beating over the prejudices and memories of a past that is gone, it is to take dear old Edward Everett Hale's maxim, 'Look forward, not back; look upward, not down, and lend a hand.'"

Washington Conference, not a single state had adopted the ABA-AALS standards of two years of college and a law degree before admission to the bar.[72] Yet 1921-22 also marked a turning point for the elite position. While enrollment at non-AALS schools continued to climb for another half dozen years, the alliance of practitioners and teachers began to produce, almost immediately, the kind of results elite professionals had intended. As early as 1923, Roscoe Pound assured Harlan Stone that part-time schools were "on the run.... We [have] only to stand by our guns a little longer to see everything we have been struggling for...realized." At least in the field of legal education, the American Bar Association now commanded what ABA President Walter George Smith called a "position of recognized power and prestige."[73]

One indication of this power was demonstrated after the first list of ABA-approved schools was issued in 1923. Marquette Law School, which had agreed to require two years of college work by 1925, appeared neither in the category of law schools that had accepted ABA standards nor in the category of those which had announced their intention to do so. The reason given by John Sanborn, Secretary of the Council, was that Marquette's night school did not require two years of college, and the Council had decided to classify any school that had both day and night divisions according to the standards of the lower one. The upshot was that Mar-

---

72. Auerbach, *Unequal Justice*, 118.

73. Pound to Stone, January 2, 1923, Pound Papers, quoted in Auerbach, *Unequal Justice*, 119; Walter George Smith, "Civil Liberty in America," 43 *ABA Rep* 209 @ 219 (1918); Stevens, *Law School*, 172.

quette discontinued its evening division.[74] When the University of Mississippi was threatened with probation in 1926, Governor Bilbo approved a special appropriation to buy books and put up a new classroom building. The following year Denver Law School announced that it would hire three full-time faculty members in order to receive the ABA's "A" rating, although the dean was unhappy about capitulating to outside pressure and remained unconvinced that having a full-time faculty would improve the quality of the school.[75] Another indication of the Association's influence was the coast-to-coast coverage and editorializing that the adoption of the legal education standards received in the press.[76] Finally, there was the reaction of spokesmen for the part-time schools, who fought the requirements and their proponents with increased ferocity and heightened rhetoric—an unlikely development if the Association's actions had been of little effect.

In 1927, the Section of Legal Education, meeting by prearrangement with a "selected group of men" at a different time than usual, discussed the hiring of H. Claude Horack, secretary (and shortly, president) of the AALS, as a paid advisor to the ABA in the matter of ranking law schools. At

---

74. Johnson, *Schooled Lawyers,* 160-61; First, "Competition," 358-59. Predictably, the classification system itself was borrowed from the American Medical Association. Starr, 118.

75. Michael de L. Landon, *The Honor and Dignity of the Profession: A History of the Mississippi State Bar, 1906-1976* (Jackson: University Press of Mississippi, 1979), 63; Adolph H. Grundman, "The Early History of the Colorado Bar Association: 1898-1938," 14 *Colorado Lawyer* 7 @ 14 (1985).

76. "Comments of the Press," 8 *ABAJ* 156-57 (1922); "Admission to the Bar," *New York Times,* February 25, 1922. Of course, not all editorials were favorable to the position of the elite.

the same meeting William Draper Lewis was elected Chairman of the Section. The Secretary-Treasurer remarked on the unusual harmony of the meeting; the Section, he said, had met "as a happy family," and the resolutions offered "seemed to meet with no opposition."[77]

But Gleason Archer was furious. The dean of Suffolk Law School wrote an open letter to ABA members charging that developments in the Section were "only one phase of the struggle, now a quarter of a century old, in which the university law schools are seeking to duplicate in the legal profession what the university medical schools have already accomplished." Archer especially vented his anger at the Section meetings of 1928 and 1929. During the latter he noted that the ABA had provided the Section with $15,000 so that H. Claude Horack could act as a "field agent to capture the various states of the Union for the college monopoly."[78] At the 1929 meeting Edward Lee called the law school men "educational racketeers" who were using the "American Bar Association as an annex to the Association of American Law Schools,...boring from within our Association in the interest of their own." For good measure, one James Brennan of

---

77. Silas Strawn to Roscoe Pound, August 15, 1927; Gleason Archer to Members of the American Bar Association, September, 1927; Pound to Strawn, October 8, 1927; Strawn to Archer, October 11, 1927; Pound to Strawn, October 25, 1927, Pound Papers, Box 1. Also filed in the same box are resolutions presented to the ABA in 1927, including a much watered-down proposal calling for state supported collegiate training, passed at the annual meeting.

78. Gleason Archer to Members of the American Bar Association, September, 1927, Pound Papers; Charles F. Carusi, dean of the National Union Law School, to the *New York Times*, December 14, 1926, 26; 54 *ABA Rep* 732-38 (1929).

Massachusetts charged the ABA with "attempting to divide our schools into groups, using may I say, the blacklist—one of the most damnable and dangerous things in American life—the blacklist and the boycott."[79] The elite let them talk; the leadership knew when the questions were put to a vote, supporters of the part-time schools would lose.[80]

The question is, why did they lose? What had changed between 1919, when the Executive Committee scuttled the Council on Legal Education, and 1928, when the ABA began marching in virtual lockstep with the AALS? The answer is difficult to document statistically but seems to be congruent with Robert Stevens' assertion that "xenophobia, economic concerns, and professional vanity, coupled with genuine concern for the public interest" proved stronger than democratic ideology. Of the xenophobia there is no question. In 1922, Elihu Root might discuss, with euphemistic indirection, the "scores and hundreds" coming to the bar with no "conception of the moral qualities that underlie our free American institutions"; but at the end of the decade, prominent Philadelphia attorney (and amateur musicologist), Henry Drinker (1880-1965), spoke openly of the danger to the profession posed by "Russian Jew boys."[81] During the same decade the

---

79. Lee quoted in Stevens, *Law School*, 175-76; James Brennan, 54 *ABA Rep* 640 (1929).

80. 53 *ABA Rep* 620ff. (1928). There is a note of condescension in Lewis' ostentatiously fair-minded approach towards his opponents. In 1930 Archer and Lee finally got a resolution to the floor proposing that one-half of each law school faculty be composed of practicing lawyers. They were "defeated handsomely." The ABA then passed a resolution attacking proprietary law schools. Stevens, *Law School*, 176.

81. Stevens, 176; Elihu Root, 47 *ABA Rep* 491 (1922); Henry Drinker, 54 *ABA Rep* 622-23 (1929). Of special interest are the views of Julius Henry

Supreme Court upheld the legality of trade associations and their price and policy restrictions. Even middle levels of the bar "in small towns and cities began to see an important economic dimension to the complaints of unethical practice."[82] Finally, there was the example of organized medicine, now unquestionably first in prestige and political power among the professions. Only those, such as Archer, Lee, and to a lesser extent, Reed, who had a personal (and often financial) interest in alternate visions of the legal profession cared to question the medical model that elite lawyers had chosen to emulate. "'Science' and the orthodoxy of the case method had given them a solid base for their pride," Robert Stevens has written, "and anyone who did not follow the new religious creed was robbing them of their solidity and standing."[83]

Cohen, who "shared and relied upon many of the concerns of his contemporaries over the commercialization of legal practice." Samuel J. Levine, "Rediscovering Julius Henry Cohen and the Origins of the Business/Profession Dichotomy: A Study in the Discourse of Early Twentieth Century Legal Professionalism," *American Journal of Legal History* 47: 1 (January 2005), 1 @ 3.

82. Johnson, *Schooled Lawyers*, 157.

83. Stevens, *Law School*, 101.

Chapter 7

Gatekeeping

Bar Examinations and the Canon of Ethics

Besides attempting to raise educational requirements for prospective lawyers, the early American Bar Association endorsed two other potential gatekeeping devices: bar examinations and professional discipline based on prescribed rules of conduct. In the short run, neither of these mechanisms proved useful to the legal elite, and bar examinations may actually have benefitted more gate crashers than gate keepers. Still, as in the case of legal education, organized medicine once again served as the model in the ABA's attempt to better control legal practice.

By 1898, all states had licensing requirements for physicians, although only half required an examination as well as a medical school diploma.[1] Nevertheless, as states began to appreciate the scientific basis of orthodox medicine, more of

---

1. In *Dent v. West Virginia* (1888), Justice Stephen Field, though long a champion of individual rights, wrote for a unanimous court that states could exclude an individual from a profession based on "an authority competent to judge"—that is, the profession itself. "What is striking about this reestablishment of the professions in the eighties is how readily it was accepted by much of the public." Samuel Haber, *The Quest for Authority and Honor in the American Professions, 1750-1900* (Chicago: University of Chicago Press, 1991), 202.

them established boards of medical examiners. Abraham Flexner (1866-1959), who had helped spark a reform of medical education, was frank about the purpose of licensure examinations, calling them "the lever with which the entire field may be lifted; for the power to examine is the power to destroy." In 1915, the American Medical Association organized a National Board of Medical Examiners, and shortly thereafter, its examinations achieved sufficient acceptance to warrant a degree of reciprocity with qualifying boards in England and Scotland.[2]

Bar examination boards developed more slowly, the first being established by New Hampshire in 1878. By 1890, only four of forty-nine jurisdictions had bar examination boards. Somewhat prematurely, the ABA called a conference of state law examiners in 1898, when only twelve states had them. For a half dozen years their representatives held sessions in conjunction with the ABA's Section of Legal Education. On three occasions (1900, 1904, and 1914) law examiners unsuccessfully attempted to organize an independent professional association, but a permanent National Conference of Bar Examiners was not established until 1931.[3]

In 1922, Herbert Harley, the head of the American Judicature Society, hailed creation of state bar examination boards as a "great step forward," claiming that the bar "without

---

2. Abraham Flexner, *Medical Education in the United States and Canada* (New York: Carnegie Foundation for the Advancement of Teaching, 1910), 167-173; John Hubbard, *Measuring Medical Education* (Philadelphia: Lea & Febiger, 1971), 4-8.

3. Alfred Z. Reed, *Training for the Public Profession of the Law* (New York: Carnegie Foundation for the Advancement of Teaching, 1921), 102-103; Sunderland, *History of the American Bar Association*, 55-58.

realizing the fact, had gained possession of the gateway to the profession."[4] In fact, the usefulness of bar examinations in professional gatekeeping was limited by the hostility between bar examiners and law school teachers. Unlike medicine, where the elite perceived educational requirements and licensure examinations as complementary tools, in the legal profession they were often viewed as antagonistic.

Understandably, bar examiners opposed the "diploma privilege," whereby graduates of law schools that had been approved by a state legislature were admitted to practice without further examination. Elite law schools often paid lip service to opposing diploma privilege, in part because legislatures rarely distinguished between "good" and "bad" law schools. But once elite schools received diploma privilege, they did not renounce it; nor were they overly solicitous in lobbying state legislators about the matter.[5]

More importantly, bar examiners and legal educators differed on how best to restrict entry to the profession. Bar examiners insisted that bar examinations would accomplish the purpose that most schoolmen believed could only be achieved through higher education.[6] Perhaps I. Maurice Wormser (1887-1955), a professor of law at Fordham University—but also a lawyer who had been admitted to the

---

4. Herbert Harley, "Group Organizations Among Lawyers," *Annals* 101 (1922), 40.

5. John Wigmore, 30 *ABA Rep* 18 (1906); William R. Johnson, *Schooled Lawyers: A Study in the Clash of Professional Cultures* (New York: New York University Press, 1978), 145-48; George Martin, *Causes and Conflicts* (Boston: Houghton Mifflin, 1970), 134-38; "Admissions to the Bar," 11 *Albany Law Journal*, 360-61 (1875).

6. Reed, *Training for the Public Profession of the Law*, 263-70.

bar before receiving his law degree—submitted the baldest statement of the bar examiner's credo to the Section of Legal Education: "Better bar examination questions mean raised standards of admission to the Bar," said Wormser, "better lawyers [mean] a better brand of social and individual justice....[and] a nearer approach to a millennium of sweetness and light."[7]

Most legal educators remained unenthusiastic about bar examinations because they might help students attending lower-tier law schools. "Make your examinations as stiff as you please," wrote a *New York Times* editor sympathetic to these part-time schools, "but test the candidate's ability and knowledge fairly without requiring him to go through an expensive and apparently a magical process."[8] The democratic ring of the argument vexed the legal elite, who found it difficult to frame a convincing reply for lay consumption.

The elite believed, as had Langdell, that bar examinations could not be "at once rigorous and just. They must admit the undeserving or reject the deserving; and in the long run they will be sure to do the former."[9] If only bar examinations, rather than a law school diploma, were required of applicants, nothing prevented law school students from taking the exam, entering practice, and leaving law school. Bar examinations

---

7. I. Maurice Wormser, "The Results of a Comparative Study of the Examination Questions Framed by State Boards of Examiners," 39 *ABA Rep* 864 @ 873 (1914); George W. Bacon, "Professor I. Maurice Wormser, In Memoriam," 24 *Fordham Law Review* xxxiii (1955-56).

8. "Admission to the Bar," *New York Times*, February 25, 1922, 12; Orlando Potter, 15 *ABA Rep* 14 (1892); Edward T. Lee, 46 *ABA Rep* 670 (1921).

9. Annual Reports of the President and Treasurer of Harvard College, 1876-77, quoted in Reed, *Training for the Public Profession of the Law*, 269.

might also discriminate against graduates of elite schools, who might have better theoretical training but less familiarity with the minutiae of local practice. In other words, bar examinations might admit precisely those aspirants whom the upper strata of the profession hoped to exclude. For instance, in July 1925, 99% of the graduates of Boston's Suffolk Law School—a school established to provide legal education for immigrants and working class students—passed the Massachusetts bar examination compared with only 62% of the graduates of Harvard.[10] At the Washington Conference on Legal Education, Elihu Root protested that bar examinations could not measure "moral quality" and complained that non-traditional students were "acute, subtle, adroit, skillful. They had crammed for their examinations. They could trot around any simple-minded American boy from the country three times a day."[11]

A few year earlier ABA committeeman Edmund F. Trabue had suggested that bar examiners might be able to test an applicant's moral character, perhaps more like a background check that was attempted by the New York City and Philadelphia bars during the 1920s. The Pennsylvania Association did reduce the proportion of immigrants

---

10. Suffolk graduates were accused of cheating and were required to retake the examination; 99 percent passed the second exam as well. Richard L. Abel, *American Lawyers* (New York: Oxford University Press, 1989), 67; William Keysor, 30 *ABA Rep* 24 (1906); Reed, *Training for the Public Profession of the Law*, 255; Max Radin, "The Achievements of the ABA," 26 *ABAJ* 19 (1940).

11. Elihu Root, 47 *ABA Rep* 492 (1922); Walter George Smith, "Address of the Chairman [of the Section of Legal Education]," 38 *ABA Rep* 761 (1913); Walter George Smith, 40 *ABA Rep* 719 (1915); Andrew A. Bruce, 40 *ABA Rep* 714 (1915).

admitted to the state bar from 76% to 60% of total admissions; but compared with Jim Crow laws in the South, this attempt at discrimination was hardly an effective barrier to ambitious men of inferior social origins.[12]

Even if the American Bar Association could have agreed on a character test, it would still have had to convince the American public of its legitimacy. As one newspaper put it, educational requirements were "the trend of modern thought," but naked bias (except that directed against blacks) was unacceptable to most Americans even during the xenophobic 1920s.[13] Thus, bar examiners and law teachers remained at odds, the former capturing the Section of Legal

---

12. E. F. Trabue, 39 *ABA Rep* 810 (1914); Jerold S. Auerbach, *Unequal Justice: Lawyers and Social Change in Modern America* (New York: Oxford University Press, 1976), 121-29. (I have used Auerbach's discussion to reach diametrically opposite conclusions from his.) Clarence A. Lightner, "A More Complete Inquiry into the Moral Character of Applicants for Admission to the Bar," 38 *ABA Rep* 779 (1913); Charles A. Boston, 38 *ABA Rep* 748-49 (1913); Walter George Smith, 40 *ABA Rep* 719 (1915). Smith used the euphemism, "representatives of the most ancient race of which we have knowledge."

Certainly some Jewish applicants were unjustly excluded. George Wickersham related the case of a Jewish applicant who had appeared before him in New York. Investigation had revealed that no one of his name had been employed at a business to which he gave reference. The applicant frankly admitted having worked at the business under an assumed name and country of origin because the company refused to hire Jews. "That applicant, gentlemen," said Wickersham, "could not understand why he should be rejected by us." In the 21st century, the state would probably file suit against the employer and reconstitute the bar examination board. 39 *ABA Rep* 818 (1913).

13. *Newark (NJ) News*, quoted at 8 *ABAJ* 156 (1922).

Education, the latter, the AALS, while immigrants and their children rushed through the breech.

Another possible means of professional gatekeeping was enforcement of a code of ethics, especially one aimed at specific practices of lower caste lawyers. A code of ethics was indeed approved by the Association in 1908, and by 1924 it had been adopted by almost all the state and local bar associations and then remained in effect for another sixty years.[14]

The ABA once again looked to organized medicine as a model. The American Medical Association had adopted a code of ethics in 1847, partly as a public relations tool, partly as a guide to intramural etiquette for practitioners who were making their way in a hostile professional environment. As early as 1880, the president of the New York State Bar Association pointed to the rules of the state medical society as the basis for "substantial gain in that profession."[15] After the turn of the century, organized medicine pushed past voluntary controls by writing parts of its code into various state laws. In 1903, the AMA also renamed its code the "Principles of Medical Ethics," presumably in an attempt to elevate the tone of its pronouncements.[16]

In 1887, the Alabama State Bar Association adopted rules of professional conduct written by future governor and

---

14. James M. Altman, "Considering the A.B.A.'s 1908 Canons of Ethics," 2008 *Journal of the Professional Lawyer* 235 (2008), 236.

15. Samuel Hand, "Bar Association and the Profession," 3 *New York State Bar Association Proceedings* 67 @ 80 (1880).

16. James G. Burrow, *Organized Medicine in the Progressive Era: The Move Toward Monopoly* (Baltimore: Johns Hopkins University Press, 1977), 64. Despite the quasi-religious name, some constituent medical societies still tried to have the "principles" enacted into legal codes.

federal judge Thomas Goode Jones (1844-1914), which he had partially based on the *Essay on Professional Ethics,* first published in 1854 by George Sharswood (1810-1883), professor of law at the University of Pennsylvania and eventually Chief Justice of the Pennsylvania Supreme Court.[17] As had been the case with early medical rules, the Alabama code was more code of etiquette than code of ethics. For instance, it advised attorneys to be punctual, to refrain from displays of temper, and to provide free services to families of deceased lawyers. Ethics proper was not entirely ignored, but when the code ventured into such topics as the lawyer's sometimes conflicting duties to his client and to the state, it lapsed (in the words of one modern commentator) into "bombastic ambiguity."[18] Sharswood viewed the lawyer in a traditional nineteenth-century fashion as an independent, small-town litigator, not as the subordinate adviser to a corporation or, at a lower social level, as an ombudsman for the ethnic poor.

During the next twenty years, codes similar to that of Alabama were adopted by the bars of ten other states—all nonindustrial, primarily rural, and mostly Southern.[19]

---

17. Altman, 275-76. "With the exception of the Louisiana State Bar Association, each of the other eleven state bar associations that adopted a code of ethics between 1887 and 1907 acknowledged reliance upon the Alabama Code."

18. Jethro K. Lieberman, *Crisis at the Bar: Lawyers' Unethical Ethics and What to Do About It* (New York: W. W. Norton & Co.,1978), 54-56; Burton J. Hendrick, "How Should a Lawyer Behave?" *World's Work,* 33 (January 1917), 330; Walter B. Jones, "Canons of Professional Ethics: Their Genesis and History," 7 *Notre Dame Lawyer* 483 (1932).

19. The states were Georgia (1889), Virginia (1889), Michigan (1897), Colorado (1898), North Carolina (1900), Wisconsin (1901), West

Apparently these homogeneous and traditionally-minded bars found Jones and Sharswood reasonably congruent with reality. Though Sharswood's mid-century *Ethics* could only with difficulty be stretched to cover the moral dilemmas of the turn-of-century urban bar, the widening social and financial spectrum of the profession in major cities stimulated elite urban lawyers to promulgate codes as well.

This movement to establish ethical standards was usually described by contemporaries as an attempt to counter the growing commercialization of the legal profession—"commercialization" being an elastic term of reprobation whose meaning depended on speaker and context. Most often commercialization referred to the activities of "shysters" and "ambulance chasers" from the lower strata of the profession—often Irish Catholics or Russian Jews.[20] Such lawyers, said one speaker at the 1904 ABA convention, were "shysters-at-law," unsurpassed in their "resourcefulness of evil and varied

---

Virginia (1902), Maryland (1902), Kentucky (1903), Missouri (1906). 31 *ABA Rep* 676 (1907).

20. Wayne Karl Hobson, *The American Legal Profession and the Organizational Society, 1890-1930* (New York: Garland Publishing, 1986), 298-99; Maxwell Bloomfield, "Law and Lawyers in American Popular Culture," in Carl Smith, et al., *Law and American Literature* (New York: Alfred A. Knopf, 1983), 164. Previously "pettifogger" had been the preferred pejorative term, but pettifogger had "Anglo-Saxon connotations."

In Arthur Train's story, "The Shyster," a popular (though Train argues, an inaccurate) description of such a lawyer is "a down-at-the-heels, unshaved and generally disreputable-looking police-court lawyer—preferably with a red nose—who murders the English language and makes his living by preying upon the ignorant and helpless." Arthur Train, "The Shyster," in *By Advice of Counsel* (New York: Scribner's, 1925), 9-10.

and ingenious rascality," men who had "brought a great and noble calling into disrepute."[21]

No doubt, as Richard Hofstadter has argued, much of the professional interest in raising ethical standards was an attempt by richer lawyers to improve the reputation of the profession at the expense of their less prosperous colleagues.[22] Still, the motives of elite were complex, with xenophobia and professional self-interest mingling with high-minded concern for public welfare.[23] As James Altman has written, having achieved financial means to live like gentleman, "what these men apparently cared about far more than money was status or 'honor'—respect in the eyes of others—and self-esteem."[24]

---

21. Lucius H. Perkins, "The State Board—A Landmark in Lawyer Making," 27 *ABA Rep* 789 @ 790 (1904). "We owe it to ourselves, to the profession and to the State," asserted the president of the New York State Bar Association in 1888, to discipline those who "have brought the legal profession into disrepute and who are dragging or holding it down from the lofty position which it should enjoy in public esteem." Martin W. Cooke, "Bar Associations—What They May Undertake," 11 *Proceedings of the New York State Bar Association* 38 @ 45 (1888).

22. Richard Hofstadter, *The Age of Reform* (New York: Alfred A. Knopf, 1955), 157.

23. A study of the most recent edition of the ABA's ethical code (1983), now called the Model Rules, comes to the same conclusion: "In short, if one looks closely enough at the process in which the Model Rules were developed, no single grand theory, critical or functionalist, comes close to accounting for it. Detailed study of the making of a professional code may thus be a useful corrective to the soaring theories scholars have so far brought to the subject." Theodore Schneyer, "Professionalism as Politics: The Making of a Modern Legal Ethics Code," in Robert L. Nelson, et al., eds., *Lawyers' Ideals/Lawyers' Practices: Transformations in the American Legal Profession* (Ithaca: Cornell University Press, 1992), 143.

24. Altman, 336.

Jerold Auerbach has romanticized the nineteenth-century ambulance chaser as a counselor of "the urban poor, new immigrants and blue-collar workers."[25] The actual individuals were often less benevolent. At best, they might send "cappers" and "runners" after possible clients, pay policemen and hospital employees for information about accident victims, hound widows for powers-of-attorney before the funeral, scrutinize scandalous episodes in the lives of the wealthy, and examine property titles for flaws that might serve as an excuse for litigation. At worst, they dabbled in blackmail, fraud, and perjury. Richard Rovere created endearing rascals from New York's William Howe and Abraham Hummel, but these corrupters of justice are, like Billy the Kid, best appreciated from some chronological distance.[26]

Many elite lawyers also recognized "commercialization" in the behavior of some corporation lawyers. In 1913, a writer for the *Yale Law Journal* suggested that the lawyer's professional position had been usurped by the corporation, an "artificial creature of his own genius, for whom he is now simply a clerk on a salary." While other professional commentators argued that this subordination of the lawyer to the corporation was only a response to technological change, even they were uneasy at the growing tendency of the elite to follow big fees "rather than to pursue the law as a science."[27]

---

25. Auerbach, *Unequal Justice*, 42.

26. Richard Rovere, *Howe & Hummel* (New York: Farrar, Straus, 1947); Kenneth De Ville, "New York City Attorneys and Ambulance Chasing in the 1920s," *Historian* 59 (1997), 291-310; Burton J. Hendrick, "How Should a Lawyer Behave?" 333.

27. Richard Hofstadter, *The Age of Reform*, 158; see the sources that Hofstadter cites on 160, and those cited by his student Joseph Katz, "The

Occasionally, even technological improvements themselves were blamed for the lawyer's loss of professionalism. Walter George Smith, Chairman of the Section of Legal Education and future ABA president, spoke of a lesson subconsciously impressed on elite lawyers by the "modern law office, with its stenographers and typewriters and all the equipment of a counting house.... [L]ittle by little the commercial spirit pervades his entire activities."[28]

Some of the elite noted the similarity between the methods of the corporation attorney and his shyster colleague. "We have in our ranks the ambulance chaser," said ABA committeeman Andrew A. Bruce at a meeting of the Section of Legal Education. "We have lawyers of great talent and attainment, but who are merely hired men . . . employed on a

---

Legal Profession, 1890-1915," M.A. thesis, Columbia University, 1954, 29-39. Frank Gaylord Cook, "Lawyers and the Trust," *North American*, 183 (1906), 114; Alfred Russell, "Avoidable Causes of Delay and Uncertainty in Our Courts," 14 *ABA Rep* 197 @ 198, 202 (1891); Clarence H. Miller, 30 *ABA Rep* 12 (1906); George W. Bristol, "The Passing of the Legal Profession," 22 *Yale Law Journal* 590 (1913); William B. Hornblower, "Has the Profession of the Law Been Commercialized?" *Forum*, 18 (February, 1895), 684.

Laments over the commercialization of the bar remain a staple of professional discourse. For instance, in 1988, Sol Linowitz, addressing the Cornell Law School, grumbled about how much the profession had changed since he had graduated from law school fifty years before. Then, he said, the law had been "an esteemed and honored calling.... Over the years, however, something seriously disturbing has been happening to the legal profession. We have become a business, dominated by 'bottom line' perspectives"; quoted in Richard W. Moll, *The Lure of the Law* (New York: Viking, 1990), 216-17. "Access to Justice or the Bottom Line? The Growing Commercialization of the Practice of Law," U. S. Chamber of Commerce, October 26, 2011, e-bottom-line-the-growing-commercialization-of-the-practice-of-law (accessed August 2, 2018).

28. Walter George Smith, "Address of the Chairman," 38 *ABA Rep* 761 (1913); Haber, *Quest for Authority*, 223.

salary by great corporations....we need to reassert our position as the members of a profession."[29]

Yet, despite extensive discussion of "commercialization" in both popular and legal periodicals, the American Bar Association might not have adopted a code of ethics during the first decade of the twentieth century had it not been for an address delivered on June 28, 1905, at Harvard University by President Theodore Roosevelt. Roosevelt, whose experience in New York politics had not fostered a reverential view of lawyers, used the occasion to arraign upper-class members of the bar who made it "their special task to work out bold and ingenious schemes by which their wealthy clients, individual or corporate, can evade the laws which are made to regulate in the interest of the public the use of great wealth." Such a lawyer, said Roosevelt, was "doing all that in him lies to encourage the growth in this country of a spirit of dumb anger against all laws and of disbelief in their efficacy."[30]

Roosevelt's speech struck a nerve.[31] At the ABA annual meeting two months later, millionaire lawyer and former ABA Executive Committee member Alfred Hemenway flatly denied the truth of the President's charges. Although Hemenway thought ambulance chasers were a serious problem, his vision of the legal elite was serene: "We are not

---

29. Andrew A. Bruce, 40 *ABA Rep* 737 (1915); "Why I Gave Up My Practice," *Independent*, 60 (June 28, 1906), 1536; William F. Bundy, 32 *Illinois State Bar Association Report* 84 (1908); Hobson, 300-01; and for a slightly different comparison, Thomas Walsh, 33 *ABA Rep* 70 (1908).

30. Theodore Roosevelt, "Address at Harvard University, June 28, 1905," in *Presidential Addresses and State Papers* (New York: The Review of Reviews Company, 1910), 4: 419-20.

31. Lieberman, *Crisis at the Bar*, 58.

degenerates. Today is better than yesterday....As to the legal profession, its learning is broader and deeper than ever before, its ethics more exacting." ABA President Henry St. George Tucker took a more judicious tack. While claiming that elite lawyers stood "forth in priestly robes, as ministers at the altar of justice" and were representatives of "the most ennobling and powerful for good of all the secular professions," Tucker acknowledged that Roosevelt's "serious charge...must give us pause."[32]

The 1905 convention approved an Executive Committee resolution to establish a committee that would investigate adoption of a code of legal ethics. In the following year, the committee, chaired by Tucker, pronounced the drafting of such a code of as "of very great importance." While the report referred vaguely to the types of "commercialization" that could be attributed to the legal elite, it dealt specifically with the sins of those at the other end of the profession, whose "itching fingers are not. . . stayed in their eager quest for lucre," who never having grasped "the soul and spirit of law and justice...debase our high calling in the eyes of the public."[33]

A larger committee was then approved to draft the code, and those appointed to it were almost uniformly prominent: corporation lawyers such as Jacob M. Dickinson, George R.

---

32. Alfred Hemenway, "The American Lawyer," 28 *ABA Rep* 390 @ 398-99 (1905); Elihu Root, *Addresses on Government and Citizenship* (Cambridge: Harvard University Press, 1916), 66-68; Henry St. George Tucker, "Address of the President," 28 *ABA Rep* 299 @ 384, 389 (1905); Altman, 246.

33. "Report of the Committee on the Code of Professional Ethics," 29 *ABA Rep* 600-02 (1906); Sunderland, *History of the ABA*, 110-111. Evidence strongly suggests that Tucker wrote this report "without significant input from the other four original committee members." Altman, 249.

Peck, Thomas H. Hubbard, and Francis Lynde Stetson; appellate judges Alton Parker, Thomas Goode Jones, and Justice David Brewer; and law teachers Ezra Thayer and Henry St. George Tucker. Compared with the usual dawdling of ABA committees, this one worked expeditiously. Almost every member attended a three-day committee meeting in Washington. A draft code was submitted to ABA members, and a thousand letters of criticism were tabulated by that enthusiast of statistics, Lucien Hugh Alexander, before the suggestions were incorporated into later versions.[34]

Oliver Wendell Holmes, expressing "skepticism as to the advantages of abstract exhortation," urged that the code at least be made "short and pungent...omitting all moral platitudes."[35] He may not have been pleased with the final draft, presented to the annual meeting of 1908, for it was at least, in part, based on Sharswood's *Essay*. (In fact, Sharswood's *Essay* was reprinted as Volume 32 of the *ABA Reports* at the expense of Committee member Thomas H. Hubbard, president of the International Banking Corporation.[36]) As in the case of the medical profession, the ABA rules were given an elevated title: "The Canons of Legal Ethics." The word "canons," which had been associated with ecclesiastical law, suggested quasi-religious sanction. "The public and press expect that we shall formally promulgate some

---

34. 33 *ABA Rep* 56-57, 573 (1908); Sunderland, 110. For biographies of committee members and a thoughtful analysis of their disagreement about the lawyer's "duty to do justice," see Susan D. Carle, "Lawyers' Duty to Do Justice: A New Look at the History of the 1908 Canons," *Law & Social Inquiry: Journal of the American Bar Foundation*, 24: 1 (Winter 1999), 1-44.
35. Oliver Wendell Holmes to Lucien Hugh Alexander, December 12, 1907, Alexander Papers.
36. 32 *ABA Rep* 5 (1907).

decalogue," said one member. "The time is opportune if we wish to maintain the traditional honor and dignity of our profession."[37]

The Association approved without change 31 of the 32 canons drawn up by the Committee. Only Canon 13, which dealt with contingent fees, aroused long and bitter discussion.[38] Sharswood had argued strongly against the propriety of fees being paid to an attorney only if he won the case, and Sharswood's opinion was shared by the most influential ABA members at the end of the nineteenth century. For instance, in 1879, Calvin Child referred to contingent fees as "self-evident" evils; three years later, Gustave Koerner pronounced them "gambling contracts"; and in 1891, Alfred Russell blamed such "mercantile usages" for bringing down "the profession from its high place as a chief agency in our Christian civilization and [making] it a trade."[39]

The contingent fee was, of course, a device frequently employed by the lower strata of the bar and was viewed with

---

37. Max Radin, "The Achievements of the ABA," 26 *ABAJ* 135 (1940); Elmer B. Rogers, 33 *ABA Rep* 58 (1908).

38. 33 *ABA Rep* 59, 85-86, 575-85 (1908); Max Radin, "The Achievement of the ABA," 26 *ABAJ* 135 @ 138 (1940). Sunderland calls it "a very spirited debate," 111; Lindsay Gordon Robertson, "'Hazardous Philanthropy': Conflict over the Use of Contingent Fee Contracts in Civil Litigation, 1881-1919," M. A. Thesis, University of Virginia, 1986.

39. Calvin C. Child, "Shifting Uses from the Standpoint of the Nineteenth Century," 2 *ABA Rep* 71 @ 90 (1879); Gustave Koerner, "The Doctrine of Punitive Damages, and its Effect on the Ethics of the Profession," 5 *ABA Rep* 211 @ 220 (1882); Alfred Russell, "Annual Address: Avoidable Causes of Delay and Uncertainty in Our Courts," 14 *ABA Rep* 197 @ 202 (1891); see 26 *Alb. Law J.* 141 (1882); "Report of the Committee on Legal Education," 20 *ABA Rep* 378 (1897).

repugnance by many of the elite for that reason alone. In a letter to Lucien Alexander, Philadelphia Common Pleas Judge William H. Staake (1846-1924) complained that contingent fees allowed men "of mediocre ability [to] acquire wealth—if not reputation—while the learned, conscientious practitioner, who would not accept a case upon a contingent fee is delayed, hindered and debarred from practicing his profession."[40]

Yet even some within the ABA leadership circle believed contingent fees had a legitimate place in legal practice. With the dramatic increase in industrial accidents during the 19th century, the contingent fee was often, in the words of Simeon Baldwin, "the only protection for persons having meritorious causes of action to command the aid of competent counsel."[41] Another factor that prevented forthright condemnation of the contingent fee was its very ubiquity. A committee of the Massachusetts Bar Association studying the same question a few years later announced that contingent fees were "too usual in the practice of the Bar in this country to justify us in assuming a superior virtue about them."[42] Future Montana senator Thomas Walsh (1859-1933), warned his colleagues that if the ABA canons were to imply that accepting a contingent fee was "discreditable," business would be thrown "into the hands of the very lawyers whose reprehensible practices

---

40. William H. Staake to Lucien H. Alexander, March 29, 1908, Alexander Papers; Charles Biddle to Alexander, May 24, 1907, Alexander Papers.

41. Simeon Baldwin, 9 *ABA Rep* 498 (1886); "Report of the Committee on Delay and Uncertainty in the Law," 9 *ABA Rep* 355 (1886).

42. "Report of the Sub-Committee on Code of Ethics of the Massachusetts Bar Association," (1910) in Alexander Papers; Roscoe Pound to Edward A. Harriman, September 14, 1927, Box 1, Pound Papers; Lawrence M. Friedman, *A History of American Law* (New York: Simon & Schuster, 1985), 482.

have brought contingent fees into so much disrepute."[43] At the ABA meeting, cosmetic changes made Canon 13 read: "Contingent fees, when sanctioned by law, should be under the supervision of the court, in order that clients may be protected from unjust charges."[44]

In one respect, the Canons of Legal Ethics went beyond the strictures of Sharswood and normal professional practice before the turn of the century. Although Sharswood had strongly endorsed the view that business should seek the lawyer and not the other way around, his *Essay* did not mention, much less condemn, legal advertising. Moreover, the Alabama code of ethics, on which the ABA canons were patterned, sanctioned "tendering professional services to the general public" through newspapers and circulars. It only condemned the "special solicitation of particular individuals."[45] But both advertising and the idea of professionalism had changed between 1887 and 1908. The ABA canon specified that lawyers should not advertise beyond distribu-

---

43. 33 *ABA Rep* 61 (1908); Thomas Walsh, 33 *ABA Rep* 61-75 (1908), quote at 69. Rome Brown, the immediate past president of the Minnesota State Bar Association, grumbled that "the poor plaintiff in a personal injury case needs today...more protection against her lawyer than against the defendant." 33 *ABA Rep* 76 (1908).

44. Canon 13 originally read: "Contingent fees may be contracted for, but they lead to many abuses and should be under the supervision of the court." 33 *ABA Rep* 80 (1908). In 1918 the ABA voted to recommend state laws that would subject all contingent fee contracts to summary review by a court. Virtually nothing was accomplished. 5 *ABAJ* 62, 70, 74; Robertson, "Hazardous Philanthropy," 24-26.

45. George Sharswood, *An Essay on Professional Ethics* (Philadelphia: T. & J. W. Johnson & Co.,1854), reprinted as 32 *ABA Rep* (1907); Liebermann, *Crisis at the Bar*, 55.

tion of business cards, the language seemingly taken from the rules of the American Medical Association.[46]

Undoubtedly ABA acceptance of the advertising canon reflected the xenophobia and economic jealousy of the elite.[47] Most ABA members, as established practitioners, had no need to advertise for clients as immigrants and younger lawyers might feel constrained to do.[48] Yet the canon also took aim at the advertising practices of some elite lawyers when it censured "furnishing or inspiring newspaper comments concerning causes in which the lawyer has been or is engaged...the importance of the lawyer's position and all other self-laudation."[49]

Furthermore, unlike the persistent support given to the contingent fee, little theoretical justification was advanced in defense of legal advertising. Nor, for that matter, was there much rationalization for its exclusion. "Indeed, it is strange,"

---

46. Hendrick, "How Should a Lawyer Behave?" 333.

47. "Report of the Committee on Jurisprudence and Law Reform," 11 *ABA Rep* 308-09 (1888); 20 *ABA Rep* 379 (1897); Auerbach, *Unequal Justice*, 40-52; Lieberman, *Crisis at the Bar*, 59-61.

48. Altman, 326.

49. Speaking to the Association in 1925, U. S. Attorney General John G. Sargent criticized the self-advertisement of large firms: "How often we read, under glaring headlines, that the prominent law firm of Blank, Blank and Blank has been retained to bring suit against Rich and Prosperous in behalf of Much Wronged and Abused on account of a nefarious scheme carried out by the defendant, then detailing the plaintiff's grievances with a particularity showing the story could have been obtained only from Blank, Blank and Blank. . . . Blank, Blank and Blank think it will bring them more good business to have the public informed they have this important employment." "The Lawyer and His Practice," 50 *ABA Rep* 304 @ 311 (1925); Quinton Johnstone and Dan Hopson, Jr., *Lawyers and Their Work* (Indianapolis: Bobbs-Merrill Company, Inc., 1967), 121-130.

wrote Herbert Harley (an exception to the rule), "that so many lawyers themselves cannot explain why advertising is tabu among lawyers."[50] Likely the campaign of the medical profession against medical advertising had spilled over into the legal profession. The middle class now presumed that quacks advertised and professionals did not.[51]

Appropriately, therefore, the greatest hullabaloo over professional ethics in the early American Bar Association was occasioned not by the activities of obscure ambulance chasers but by the antics of a federal district judge, Kenesaw Mountain Landis (1866-1944), whose person and legal positions were both guaranteed to irritate elite lawyers. Landis was a high school dropout who had attended a YMCA law school in Cincinnati for one year and Union College of Law in Chicago for another. He was also Progressive who had no difficulty ignoring the law in the interest of what he conceived to be justice. For instance, he relished fining Standard Oil of Indiana the unheard of sum of $29 million. (The Circuit Court of Appeals revoked the penalty and reprimanded the judge.) He might set a petty thief free or fine him one cent, but as an ardent prohibitionist, he sent bootleggers to jail for maximum terms. Finally, and most infuriatingly, Landis was a "grand-stand judge" who thrived on publicity and enjoyed making a scene for reporters. Of Landis, sportswriter Heywood Broun (1888-1939) wrote, "His career typifies the

---

50. Harley, "Group Organizations Among Lawyers," 39.

51. Paul Starr, *The Social Transformation of American Medicine* (New York: Basic Books, 1982), 127-134.

heights to which dramatic talent may carry a man in America if only he has the foresight not to go on the stage."[52]

After the notorious "Black Sox" scandal of 1919, Landis was invited by team owners to become the first baseball "commissioner" (a title Landis chose himself) at a salary of $50,000—$42,500 more than his judicial salary. Landis accepted, but anxious to retain his public forum, he refused to resign his judgeship. Despite criticism from Congress, Attorney General Palmer ruled that Landis's decision violated no law. The new baseball commissioner might have weathered the storm of criticism had it not been for his native injudiciousness. In February 1921, Landis paroled a bank teller who had pleaded guilty to embezzling $96,000 from his employer, blaming the bank for paying the man only $90 a month. Impeachment proceedings commenced in the House of Representatives.[53]

At the annual meeting of 1921, former ABA president Hampton Carson (1852-1929), a leader of the Philadelphia bar, introduced a resolution pronouncing the Association's "unqualified condemnation" of Landis for "accepting private emolument while holding the position of federal judge," taking money from "allied clubs of baseball players" and thus dragging "the ermine in the mire."[54] "Stormy debate ensued,

---

52. Henry F. Pringle, "A Grand-Stand Judge," in *Big Frogs* (New York: Macy-Masius, 1928), 73-91; "Kenesaw Mountain Landis," *Current Biography, 1943* (New York: H. W. Wilson Co., 1944), 372-76; "Kenesaw Mountain Landis," *DAB*, Supplement Three, 437-439; Norman L. Rosenberg, "Landis, Kenesaw Mountain," *American National Biography*.

53. "Kenesaw Mountain Landis," *DAB*, Supplement Three, 437-439; "The Landis Case," 7 *ABAJ* 87-89 (1921).

54. Hampton Carson, 46 *ABA Rep* 61-62 (1921).

interrupted by applause as speakers in all parts of the convention hall arose to support or denounce the resolution." Eventually Landis was censured by voice vote, the only individual so reprimanded during the first fifty years of the Association's history.[55]

Though the story was front-page news across the country, the censure had little direct effect on Landis.[56] Congress shelved its investigations, and the commissioner-judge continued to hold both jobs. Washington attorney Edward Harriman grimly assured the American Academy of Political and Social Sciences that the inaction of Congress was due to the greater sympathy of the American people for "the standards of judicial conduct endorsed by the National Baseball Association than with those endorsed by the American Bar Association." Harriman even found a melancholy precedent "in Roman history as to the effect of a popular belief that amusements are more important than laws."[57]

On February 18, 1922, however, Landis resigned as district judge to devote his full attention to baseball. The same year the Association appointed a blue-ribbon Committee on Judicial Ethics to draft a code of conduct for judges, believing "it would be much fairer and better if the Association, instead of picking out individual cases for condemnation, should express its opinion of what the members of the American Bar Association

---

55. 46 *ABA Rep* 62-67 (1921); some of the debate was omitted from the *Report*; *New York Times*, September 2, 1921, 1.

56. Cf. 7 *ABAJ* 440 (1921) for some examples; "The Double Judge," (editorial), *New York Times*, September 3, 1921, 8. The Chicago papers were especially strong in Landis's defense.

57. E. A. Harriman, "The Need for Standards of Ethics for Judges," *Annals*, 101 (May, 1922), 30-32.

expect from those who sit upon the Bench." These expectations were adopted by the Association in 1924.[58]

It was one thing to write codes; it was another to enforce them. After a brief attempt to bring about uniformity between the ABA's Canons and the codes of various states—thus approximating the centralized power of the American Medical Association—the endeavor was abandoned. "There is no national Bar," announced the ethics committee of the Massachusetts association when it specified its departures from the ABA model; "every state bar is independent of every other."[59] A contemporary French observer, who respected the Association, nevertheless noted that the ABA could hardly go much further in implementing its ethical code than to simply answer a few questions about it in the *Journal*.[60] Of necessity, the practical work of enforcing the standards had to be left to local associations, especially those in New York. During this period, the Association of the Bar of the City of New York and its less exclusive sister organization, the New York County Lawyers' Association, together contributed up to $25,000 a year to prosecute delinquent lawyers.[61]

---

58. 28 *ABAJ* 136 (1922); Charles A. Boston, 49 *ABA Rep* 70 (1924); 49 *ABA Rep* 67-71, 761-69 (1924).

59. "Report of the Committee on Code of Ethics of the Massachusetts Bar Association, 1910," in Alexander Papers; Lawrence Edmund Sommers, "Lawyers and Progressive Reform: A Study of Attitudes and Activities in Illinois 1890 to 1920," Ph.D. dissertation, Northwestern University, 1967, 99; Michael de L. Landon, *The Honor and Dignity of the Profession: A History of the Mississippi State Bar, 1906-1976* (Jackson: University Press of Mississippi, 1979), 24.

60. Germaine Madier, *L'association du Barreau Américain* (Paris: M. Giard, 1922), 44-45.

61. Harley, "Group Organization Among Lawyers," 35.

Even when state and local associations followed the lead of the ABA in adopting a modified version of Jones and Sharswood, they discovered that those canons that were not dated when adopted by the ABA in 1908 became so as a result of changing economic conditions. In 1922, the Chairman of the ABA Committee on Professional Ethics and Grievances frankly admitted that the "ever increasing complexities of modern business, the rapid changes in its methods, and the relations of lawyers thereto, are constantly raising questions concerning proper professional conduct that were not contemplated—or even dreamed of—when the canons were prepared."[62] Likewise, Charles A. Boston, who more than any other member of the American Bar Association had promoted the idea of adopting codes of legal ethics, conceded that few of the questions submitted to the ethics committee of the New York County Association, of which he was chairman, could "be answered by any provision of the canons."[63]

Furthermore, bar associations became increasingly aware of an inadvertent consequence of prohibiting advertising: encroachment on legal business by non-lawyers. Accountants, real estate brokers, and trust and title companies not only advertised but set competitive fees for their services unencumbered by bar association strictures. Lawyers at every professional level could be irritated by a placard in a trust company window that asked, "Have you drawn your will?" Julius Henry Cohen, chairman of the New York State Bar Association's Committee on Unlawful Practice of the Law,

---

62. Thomas Francis Howe, "The Proposed Amendment to the Bylaws," 8 *ABAJ* 436 (1922).

63. Max Radin, "The Achievements of the ABA," 26 *ABAJ* 135 @ 136 (1940); Howe, "The Proposed Amendment," 436.

urged the ABA to fight the growing competition, warning that "if we do not set our teeth firmly against this effort of laymen throughout the country to commercialize what is the practice of law we shall find that we have handicapped ourselves by our own standards."[64]

Perhaps the most surprising and, in the end, most telling comment on the effectiveness of the ABA's Canons of Legal Ethics is that until 1922 the American Bar Association had no means of enforcing the code's standards on its own members. The Committee on Professional Ethics and Grievances (and its predecessors) could only collect information and make recommendations to the Association. The Association had no procedure to expel a member. In the words of one ethics committee chairman, this deficiency "led to much embarrassment and the necessity of constant explanation."[65] Another chairman called an unnamed ABA vice-president "one of the worst offenders against the spirit of a certain canon." The chairman could do nothing, of course, but worried that "if it should become generally known...the moral sanction of the Code of Ethics" would be totally destroyed.[66]

---

64. Julius Henry Cohen, 52 *ABA Rep* 107 (1927); Cohen, *The Law: Business or Profession?* (New York: G. A. Jennings, 1924), 336; James Willard Hurst, *The Growth of American Law: The Lawmakers* (Boston: Little, Brown and Co, 1950), 323-25; William D. Thompson to John W. Davis, May 29, 1923, Series III, Box 15, Davis Papers.

65. Howe, "The Proposed Amendment," 436; Francis J. Swayze, 42 *ABA Rep* 56 (1917); "Report of the Committee on Grievances," [1904], Tucker Papers.

66. Henry W. Jessup to Thomas McClellan, April, 1918, McClellan Papers; McClellan to George Weber, February 23, 1918.

In 1922, the Association finally gave the ethics committee authority to bring charges, hold hearings, and (subject to the approval of the Executive Committee) expel members. In 1928, for the first time, disciplinary proceedings against offending members were published by the Association, and the lawyer employed by the ABA to handle such affairs was authorized to "bring the matter to the attention of local authorities who have the power to disbar."[67]

The ABA canons certainly did have some practical effect. For instance, in 1928, a group of Reno divorce lawyers held a closed-door session to decide how best to answer an ABA request for copies of an advertising brochure that they had produced.[68] Like the pope, the Association had no legions, but its disapproval carried some weight even when rigorous enforcement of its rules would have required considerable time and expense—not to mention the possibility of publicly airing the unseemly conduct of professional brethren several cuts above the archetypal ambulance chaser. One member of the ABA Committee on Professional Ethics found it difficult to get information about violations "because of a fraternal feeling which exists among members of the profession."[69]

Herbert Harley wrote, "The work thus far done has helped, but after all it is more like bailing the boat than stopping the leak."[70] In fact, despite the limited success of the

---

67. Thomas Francis Howe, 53 *ABA Rep* 118, 477 (1928); H. Claude Horack, "The Standards and Ideals of the American Bar Association," *National Education Association Addresses and Proceedings*, 66 (1928), 152-53.
68. "Reno Lawyers in Quandary," *New York Times*, January 22, 1928, 28.
69. Joseph Katz, "The Legal Profession," 37; James D. Shearer, 42 *ABA Rep* 80 (1917).
70. Harley, "Group Organizations Among Lawyers," 36.

ABA in establishing standards of legal education, all the gatekeeping activities of the American Bar Association during its first fifty years had an element of boat bailing about them. By the 1920s, elite doctors had tightened their grip on the medical profession while elite lawyers were forced to rely on market forces only slightly inhibited by state law and professional suggestion.[71]

---

71. By contrast, during the Depression, when "the Council on Medical Education and Hospitals wrote a letter to the various medical schools saying [that they] were admitting more students than could be given the proper kind of training...every school reduced the number it was admitting." Milton Friedman, *Capitalism and Freedom* (Chicago: University of Chicago Press, 1962), 150.

Chapter **8**

"An Attitude of Opposition" 1911-1919

During the second decade of the twentieth century, while the American Bar Association recruited new members and considered ways of raising the standards of legal education, it also abandoned its "noiseless, unobtrusive way" for a career in political advocacy. Thirty-five years old, the Association was now recognized as a spokesman for the legal profession, and it was prepared to draw on that reputation. Concurrently, the Association also abandoned the safe, deliberate reform it had endorsed during the Gilded Age and drifted toward the sort of stand-pat conservatism with which it was to be associated during the New Deal years.

Before 1913, some ABA leaders were still strong defenders of progressivism. In an address given shortly before his election as president of the Association in 1912, "trust buster" Frank Kellogg endorsed antitrust actions, workman's compensation, and the federal regulation of hours and conditions of labor. Progressive change, Kellogg declared, was not the "work of demagogues" but had sprung from the people and could never "be checked or stopped."[1] Likewise,

---

1. Frank B. Kellogg, "New Nationalism," 37 *ABA Rep* 341 (1912).

S. S. Gregory, the outgoing president, expressed confidence in democratic trends, and advised members not to share "the dark forebodings of some of those elderly gentlemen, and their satellites, located at the lower end of Manhattan Island, who occasionally...emit a few hoarse and dolorous prognostications, bewailing the prevalent 'spirit of unrest' and declaring the outlook for the future to be most gloomy and portentous."[2]

But other speakers at the same convention did express disillusionment. Henry D. Estabrook, corporate solicitor for Western Union, attacked the "crass misrepresentation of current muckrakers" with regard to the judiciary, and asked what "awful cataclysm" had led American citizens to disparage the work of the Founding Fathers.[3] In a speech to the Association of American Law Schools, former President Taft asserted that lawyers were "not opposed to progress, real progress" but that radical proposals were goading them "into an attitude of opposition."[4]

Lesser men expressed their frustration in shriller tones. In his presidential address to the National Conference of Commissioners on Uniform State Laws of 1913, Charles Thaddeus Terry (1867-1923) advised his colleagues to set their "faces, inflexibly and sternly...against the onrushing horde of those

---

2. S. S. Gregory, "Address of the President," 37 *ABA Rep* 255 @ 287 (1912).

3. Henry D. Estabrook, "The American Judicial System: The Judges," 37 *ABA Rep* 393 @ 397 (1912). Estabrook provides an excellent example of the ambivalence of the ABA leadership towards progressivism. Later in this speech, Estabrook bestowed high praise on Roscoe Pound, who was more colleague than muckraker. (399).

4. William Howard Taft, "The Social Importance of Proper Standards for Admission to the Bar," 38 *ABA Rep* 924 @ 935 (1913).

who would overthrow our system of government and reverse the precepts of our fathers." Likewise, at the ABA banquet of 1914, former Texas Senator Joseph W. Bailey (1862-1929), an influential southern conservative, charged his audience to stand against all "forces of disorder" and warned of "a spirit of restlessness and discontent" abroad in the land, "a spirit of leveling destruction." Those who advocated liberty, said Bailey, had been stigmatized as reactionary, a word that now meant only "a man who believes in the constitution of his country." The speech was noteworthy for two reasons. First, Bailey had helped pass the Hepburn Act in 1906 and had initiated legislation that resulted in the adoption of the Sixteenth Amendment. Second, it had been customary for banquet speakers to make jokes, not calls for action.[5]

The reasons for this comparatively sudden discomposure of ABA leaders probably included weariness with the earnest remedies of the recent past.[6] More importantly, during the second decade of the century, the legal elite discovered that the political culture of the United States, which they had

---

5. Charles Thaddeus Terry, "President's Address [NCCUSL]," 38 *ABA Rep* 993 @ 1015 (1913); Joseph W. Bailey, 1 *ABAJ* 552-54 (1915); Nancy Beck Young, "Bailey, Joseph W.," *American National Biography*; George E. Mowry, *The Era of Theodore Roosevelt* (New York: Harper & Row, 1958), 204, 263. Bailey, a tenacious but unsystematic conservative, supported the institution of an income tax but opposed women's suffrage, national prohibition, and the Ku Klux Klan.

6. "I live in a state where we have had two decades of reform," said Colorado Bar Association president T. J. O'Donnell to the ABA convention of 1916, "and I have been for all reforms, one reform one year and another reform another year, until they were all tried out. And now I think I am against them all." T. J. O'Donnell, 41 *ABA Rep* 617 (1916); cf. George Sutherland, "Private Rights and Government Control," 42 *ABA Rep* 197 @ 200 (1917).

vaguely trusted would evolve in acceptable directions, seemed headed down alien paths. Only a few years before, in 1908, William Howard Taft had inherited the progressive mantle from Theodore Roosevelt and had promoted the sort of deliberate, judicially minded change that gladdened the hearts of elite lawyers. Then Roosevelt had attacked Taft as a reactionary. Of the fifteen million votes cast in the 1912 Presidential election, Roosevelt, Wilson, and Eugene Debs had received over eleven million. A leftward shift in national sentiment seemed undeniable. Neither Taft nor the leaders of the American Bar Association now seemed within the political mainstream. Appropriately, the ABA elected Taft its president in the year following his defeat in the national election.

Before 1912, progressivism had been too weak to threaten the legal status quo. Despite Roosevelt's extraordinary energy, his achievements were modest, in part, because conservatives in Congress remained too entrenched to permit passage of much of his proposed legislation. The situation was somewhat reversed during the Taft Administration, with its larger proportion of progressives in Congress but less energy in the White House. Suddenly, with the inauguration of Woodrow Wilson, Congress and the President found themselves in closer agreement, and a number of progressive measures became law within a few months: the Underwood Tariff, with its income tax provision; the Federal Reserve Act; the Federal Trade Commission law; and the Clayton Anti-Trust Act. These were followed in 1915 and 1916 by the Adamson Act, the LaFollette Seaman's Act, the establishment of the U. S. Shipping Board, a system of federal farm loan banks, and the Keating-Owen child labor bill. Though paltry by New Deal standards, this spate of legislation shook the legal elite.

Peter Meldrim (1848-1943), ABA President in 1915, spoke grimly of certain unnamed legislation enacted "under the guise of police power or public policy" that had encouraged "the Demos...to destroy the limitations of the Constitution." The next president, Elihu Root, warned his audience not to forget that "every increase of governmental power to control the conduct of life [was] to some extent a surrender of individual freedom." Walter George Smith, president in 1918, expressed alarm that "Socialistic theories [had] warped the former attitude of large bodies of voters," who now believed that competition ought to "give place to governmental regulation."[7]

In 1916, Former Secretary of War Lindley M. Garrison (1864-1932) devoted his entire address to an attack on progressivism. Garrison charged that "real efficiency and real public welfare" could be achieved only by keeping the government "within its proper confines and bounds." Garrison envisioned the coming era as one ripe for "the demagogue and the charlatan" who would "urge on the people from one excess to another in the abuse of power," sweeping over any opponent who had only "cold reason and right to support him."[8]

---

7. Peter Meldrim, "Address of the President," 40 *ABA Rep* 313 @ 327 (1915); Elihu Root, "Public Service by the Bar," 41 *ABA Rep* 355 @ 372; Walter George Smith, "Civil Liberty in America," 43 *ABA Rep* 209 @ 217-18 (1918); William A. Robinson, "A Constitutional Retrospect," 11 *ABAJ* 32 (1925). Robinson notes the changes that the legal elite discovered in the political culture after 1912.

8. Lindley M. Garrison, "Democracy and Law," 41 *ABA Rep* 375 @ 388-392. Garrison had resigned his cabinet post in the Wilson Administration because of his advanced preparedness views and his support for conscription and a federally-controlled military reserve.

The 1916 convention was held just as the Adamson eight-hour law for railroad workers was being rammed through Congress by the Wilson Administration in order to head off a threatened rail strike. At the banquet on September 1, the audience was startled when ex-president Frederick Lehmann, a Solicitor General under Taft, noted for his sense of humor, suddenly raised his voice and began to denounce Congress for submitting to the "dictation" of union leaders. Lehmann was unable to finish the sentence. Members sprang to their feet. Chairs were overturned and glasses crashed to the floor. The audience (including ladies in the gallery waving handkerchiefs) howled its approval for three minutes with a "roar of cheers and calls of 'let's hear more of it.'" But the Adamson Act passed Congress the next day and, when challenged in the Supreme Court, it was narrowly approved.[9]

That Court decision in *Wilson* v. *New* (1917) followed a trend. Most state courts had already approved a wide range of reform legislation.[10] Nevertheless, progressives complained about occasional rulings that nullified progressive laws, objecting that the courts had become a hotbed of reaction and were frustrating the will of the people. These critics condemned the uncertainty implicit in closely divided decisions, argued that judges were unsuited by training and temperament to render decisions in the light of social needs, and attacked the legitimacy and historic basis of

---

9. *Chicago Daily Tribune*, September 2, 1916, 1; Albro Martin, *Enterprise Denied: Origins of the Decline of American Railroads, 1897-1917* (New York: Columbia University Press, 1971); Harbaugh, *Lawyer's Lawyer*, 109-13.
10. Melvin I. Urofsky, "State Courts and Protective Legislation: A Reevaluation," *Journal of American History*, 72 (1985), 63-91.

judicial review. They argued that what they viewed as injustice could be remedied by the popular recall of judges or of their decisions.[11]

The notion of judicial recall was exceedingly unpopular at bar association meetings. If a judge could be recalled or his opinion overturned by popular vote, then the legal profession had no special expertise that could be defended against the laity. Even most progressive lawyers opposed recall, disposed to endure a few reactionary decisions in order to maintain the independence of their own judicial engineers.[12]

Unfortunately for the profession, judicial recall was championed by the buoyant and still popular Theodore Roosevelt. As President, Roosevelt had attacked an Illinois District Court judge, an action for which he might have been censured by the American Bar Association in 1907 had not the Association been unwilling to take a public (and partisan) stand.[13]

---

11. Alfred H. Kelly and Winfred A. Harbison, *The American Constitution: Its Origin and Development,* 5th ed. (New York: W. W. Norton & Company, 1976), 593-95; Barbara C. Steidle, "Conservative Progressives: A Study of the Attitudes and Role of Bar and Bench, 1905-1912," PhD dissertation, Rutgers University, 1969, 314-15.

12. Stephen Botein, "'What We Shall Meet Afterwards in Heaven': Judgeship as a Symbol for Modern American Lawyers," in Gerald L. Geison, ed., *Professions and Professional Ideologies in America* (Chapel Hill: University of North Carolina Press, 1983), 62.

13. Roosevelt to Charles B. Morrison, March 22, 1906, in Elting E. Morison, ed., *The Letters of Theodore Roosevelt* (Cambridge: Harvard University Press, 1951), 5: 189-90; *Congressional Record,* 59 Cong., 1st sess., 5500, 9531. Edward J. White, "The Judiciary and Public Sentiment," 24 *Missouri Bar Association Proceedings* 157 (1906); Theodore Roosevelt, "Sixth Annual Message" (December 1906), in Hermann Hagedorn, ed., *The Works of Theodore Roosevelt* (New York: Charles Scribner's Sons, 1926), "National

As an ex-President, Roosevelt felt even less compunction about airing his views, especially as the rift widened between conservative and progressive wings of the Republican Party. In September 1910, he made two speeches explicitly criticizing the judiciary. In the first, before a joint session of the Colorado legislature, Roosevelt referred to Supreme Court justices who had composed the majority in the *Knight* and *Lochner* cases as "perfectly honest, but...absolutely fossilized of mind." Two days later at Osawatomie, Kansas, he implied that courts were the most serious obstacle to progressive reform.[14]

In response to extensive criticism, Roosevelt backed down a bit, claiming his remarks had been taken out of context. Indeed, Roosevelt's commitment to judicial recall remained ambivalent at least until the New York Court of Appeals announced its decision in *Ives* v. *South Buffalo Railway Co.* on March 24, 1911. Not only did *Ives* rule the state employers' liability act unconstitutional under the Fourteenth Amendment but, by a quirk of federal law, the case could not be appealed to the U.S. Supreme Court, where it might well have been overturned. The *Ives* decision was denounced by progressives both because the principle of workman's compensation had been widely endorsed elsewhere and also perhaps because critics found it politically

---

Edition," 17: 408-11; 31 *ABA Rep* 84-85, 98-99, 105 (1907); "Lawyers Won't Censure Roosevelt," *New York Times*, August 29, 1907, 6.

14. Steidle, "Conservative Progressives," 326-27; Roosevelt, "Criticism of the Courts," *Outlook*, 96 (September 24, 1910), 149-53.

less risky to castigate courts other than the Supreme Court of the United States.[15]

Conservative alarm intensified when, during the same year, a judicial recall provision was incorporated in the proposed constitution of Arizona Territory. In an impassioned speech to the Senate—a speech differing widely from his usual "calm, analytical" style—Elihu Root opposed admitting Arizona to statehood. Root asserted that judicial recall struck "at the very heart of our system of government" and was "not progress [but] degeneracy." Even so, he concluded that the "most arrogant majority" could never override justice because God and "the eternal laws" stood behind it.[16] When the resolution admitting Arizona passed the Senate, President Taft vetoed it in less dramatic, but nonetheless determined, language.[17]

---

15. Roosevelt to Henry Cabot Lodge, September 12, 1910, *Letters*, 7: 123; Steidle, 331, 315fn.; Roosevelt to Charles Dwight Willard, April 28, 1911, *Letters*, 7: 245; Roosevelt, "Arizona and the Recall of the Judiciary," *Outlook* 98 (June 24, 1911), 378-79; *Ives* v. *South Buffalo Railway Co.*, 201 NY 271, 94 N.E. 431 (1911). Ironically, in 1914, Congress enacted a law that permitted appeals from state to federal courts on all questions arising under the Constitution and federal laws. Thus, one of the most successful of progressive reforms of the court system actually enhanced the power of federal courts. Ross, *A Muted Fury*, 80.

16. Philip C. Jessup, *Elihu Root* (New York: Dodd, Mead & Company, 1937), 2: 243; Root, "The Arizona Constitution and the Recall of Judges: Address in the Senate of the United States, August 7, 1911," in *Addresses on Government and Citizenship* (Cambridge: Harvard University Press, 1916), 387-404.

17. James Richardson, ed., *A Compilation of the Messages and Papers of the Presidents* (Washington: GPO, 1922), XI, 7636-44. Congress required removal of the judicial recall provision from the Arizona constitution. Arizona agreed to the change and was admitted as the forty-eighth state.

Growing popular interest in judicial recall produced a flurry of law journal articles and bar association discussions. With few exceptions, speeches at state bar associations flayed the proposal, and one law journal even criticized some stiff remarks earlier directed at the courts by William Howard Taft.[18] Taft's veto of the Arizona resolution occurred only two weeks before the ABA annual meeting. In his presidential address, Edgar H. Farrar took aim at the "virus" of judicial recall, a "new social poison" that established "the hydraheaded Demos on the throne of justice."[19] Farrar, though a prominent Gold Democrat and a corporation lawyer, was no reactionary. Neither was retired Associate Justice Henry B. Brown, who in addressing the Association in 1893 had suggested advanced labor legislation, government ownership of utilities, and a million-dollar limit on inheritances. Speaking to the ABA in 1911, Brown referred to recall in general as "a somewhat expensive and clumsy devise" that might nonetheless "turn out to be of great service in disposing of unpopular officials." But,

---

Then after admission, voters restored judicial recall through the amendment process, an eventuality foreseen by Taft in his veto message. In the election of 1912, Arizona gave Taft fewer votes than Socialist candidate Eugene Debs.

18. 72 *Central Law Journal* 453-54 (1911); for a bibliography of articles and speeches, see Steidle, 332-39. During the 1908 presidential campaign, Taft "assailed the shortcomings of the judicial system with a vigor unsurpassed by any radical or progressive," and during his presidency he "worked sedulously for procedural reform." Ross, *A Muted Fury*, 78.

19. Edgar H. Farrar, "Address of the President," 36 *ABA Rep* 229 @ 231-32 (1911); Hampton Carson, "The Relation of the Judiciary to Unconstitutional Legislation," 30 *Missouri Bar Association Proceedings* 75 (1912). Carson attacked judicial recall as "Demos run mad,...the insane fury of a mob wrecking the Temple of Freedom."

of course, he continued, it was hardly necessary to tell such an audience that recall was "inapplicable to the judiciary and utterly subversive of its independence. ... the last recourse of political folly."[20]

At the instigation of the Executive Committee and charter member Francis Rawle, Secretary George Whitelock—who had unsuccessfully led the attempt to censure Roosevelt in 1907—moved that a committee of six ex-presidents of the Association be appointed to formulate an official ABA position on judicial recall. The committee returned with a resolution that denounced it as "destructive of our system of government" and recommended an ABA committee be appointed to expose the doctrine. ABA members were warned that if they wanted "to save the country from the dangers" that threatened it, they would have to do so "not as modest lawyers but as energetic publicists."[21]

Only one obscure lawyer openly opposed the resolution, protesting the extreme language that implied the government would "crumble and fall" if judges were recalled. Alton Parker later reported that no more than three of more than six hundred members present voted against the resolution. Frank Kellogg, a moderate progressive,

---

20. Rogers, *American Bar Leaders*, 163; Henry B. Brown, "The Distribution of Property," 16 *ABA Rep* 213 (1893); Brown, "The New Federal Judicial Code," 36 *ABA Rep* 339 @ 357-58 (1911).

21. George Whitelock, 36 *ABA Rep* 8 (1911); Rogers, *American Bar Leaders*, 124; 36 *ABA Rep* 51 (1911); Charles M. Woodruff, 36 *ABA Rep* 52 (1911).

was appointed chairman of the Committee to Oppose the Judicial Recall.[22]

With considerably less fanfare, the Association also approved a draft bill extending the jurisdiction of the Supreme Court to cover appeals from decisions of state courts in which state legislation had been struck down under the federal Constitution. The bill's unstated purpose was to prevent reactionary state judges from embarrassing their professional brethren as they had done in *Ives.* (Despite the sponsorship of Senator Root and the approval of all three political parties, the bill moved through Congress "with tallow legs," not becoming law until December 1914.)[23]

Within a few months of the Association meeting, Theodore Roosevelt decided to challenge his protégé Taft for the Republican presidential nomination of 1912, and the issue of judicial recall proved to be the sharpest ideological division in the bitter struggle between the two former friends.[24] Roosevelt was sensitive to the criticism he had

---

22. J. Aspinwall Hodge, 36 *ABA Rep* 59-60 (1911); Alton Parker, "Annual Address," 19 *South Carolina Bar Association Transactions* 102 (1912), quoted in Steidle, 342.

23. 36 *ABA Rep* 48 (1911); Kelly and Harbison, *The American Constitution,* 597-99; Everett Wheeler to the *New York Times,* September 1, 1912, 10; Root to Taft, June 4, 1914, Root Papers, Box 166.

24. Roosevelt may have chosen this unusual issue out of some combination of genuine conviction, "naïve opportunism," and the need to confirm his progressive credentials at a time when many progressive Republicans had shifted their support to Robert La Follette. William G. Ross, *A Muted Fury: Populists, Progressives, and Labor Unions Confront the Courts, 1890-1937* (Princeton, NJ: Princeton University Press, 1994), 138-140.

received after his earlier denunciation of the courts, and he also seemed uncomfortable with the radical allies he had made in the process. Gradually he felt his way to a different, though not necessarily less advanced, position: judges themselves need not be recalled if their decisions could be.

Roosevelt published his views in *The Outlook* at the beginning of the new year and then again shortly before declaring his intention to run for President. On February 12, 1912, before the Ohio Constitutional Convention in Columbus, Roosevelt boldly advocated the recall of judicial decisions. Some of his political enemies whispered that he had gone mad. Henry Cabot Lodge admitted that his friend's action had made him "miserably unhappy," and Taft was "horrified to his very marrow."[25]

A month later, Roosevelt charged that an association to combat judicial recall, organized by Joseph Choate and other eminent New York lawyers, had as its real purpose the sustaining of "special interests against the cause of justice and against the interest of the people as a whole." Finally, in an article for *The Outlook* written before—but published after—the ABA's annual meeting of 1912, the ex-President attacked bar associations in general and the American Bar

---

25. "Judges and Progress," *Outlook* 100 (January 6, 1912), 40-48; William Henry Harbaugh, *Power and Responsibility: The Life and Times of Theodore Roosevelt* (New York: Farrar, Straus and Cudahy, 1961), 420-22; Roosevelt to Lodge, March 1, 1912, *Letters*, 7: 515n.; Jessup, *Root*, 243.

William Allen White later wrote that the Columbus speech "probably crippled [Roosevelt] more than any one thing that he did in his life" because he "was forced to a position much farther to the left than he would have taken naturally." *The Autobiography of William Allen White* (New York: The Macmillan Co., 1946), 456.

Association in particular. Early in the essay, Roosevelt portrayed Association members as honest men who had been deluded into opposing the recall, but on the final page, he censured them for flying "to the defense, not of justice, but of the betrayers of justice!"[26]

Roosevelt's position alienated even lawyers who considered themselves Republican insurgents.[27] In all, the number of influential lawyers who followed Roosevelt could be

---

26. Harbaugh, *Power and Responsibility*, 424; Theodore Roosevelt, "The Judges, the Lawyers and the People," *Outlook* 101 (August 31, 1912), 1003-07: "At least let any man who votes as the papers say the members of the Bar Association propose to vote cast off hypocrisy. Let it be understood distinctly that such a vote as I speak of will be a vote against the enactment of an eight-hour law for women, a vote against workmen's compensation laws, against prohibiting the labor of children, against laws for safety appliances, in short, against all legislation aimed to secure social and industrial justice."

27. Harbaugh, 423, 544. Judge Learned Hand, whose support of Roosevelt in 1912 later cost him a seat on the Supreme Court, first urged the former President not to advocate the recall of judicial decisions and then, when the die had been cast, convinced him to limit his proposal to constitutional decisions made by state courts. Roosevelt to Learned Hand, November 22, 1911, *Letters*, 7: 441.

Stephen Stagner, "The Recall of Judicial Decisions and the Due Process Debate," 24 *American Journal of Legal History* 257 @ 259 (1980), argues that the American Bar Association "took an extreme position in opposition to Roosevelt [and] did not speak for all attorneys." Stagner quotes seven lawyers who were to some degree sympathetic to the recall of judicial decisions. Only four of these could be considered influential in 1912: William Draper Lewis, Peter S. Grosscup, Harold Remmington, and Albert M. Kales. Stagner seems unaware of the research of Barbara Steidle, which documents the near unanimity of elite opinion with regard to judicial recall. Stagner also misunderstands the basis of the opposition, believing it to have been founded on "an archaic constitutional theory that saw property rights as absolute" (272).

numbered on the fingers of one hand. Among them were William Gaynor, mayor of New York; William Lynn Ransom, author of a book sympathetic to the recall of decisions; and William Draper Lewis, dean of the University of Pennsylvania law school and the only member of the American Bar Association leadership to wield his pen against the professional consensus.[28]

The ABA's Committee to Oppose Judicial Recall, which included a member from every state and territory, exhorted each bar association to make recall the subject of a regular or specially-called meeting that would take specific action against the proposal and influence public opinion by having their pronouncements reported in the press. Thirty state associations featured judicial recall at their 1912 sessions, and in twenty three of these meetings, only opposition to recall was voiced.[29]

Feelings ran high at the ABA convention of 1912. The meeting featured six speakers from across the political spectrum, and each, regardless of party or the stated topic of his speech, alluded to and condemned judicial recall. ABA

---

28. Steidle, 351-52. Roosevelt wrote an introduction for Ransom's book, *Majority Rule and the Judiciary* (New York: Scribner's, 1912). Ironically, Ransom was president of the ABA in 1935-36, when the Association was all but formally engaged in a fight against the New Deal. Elihu Root called Lewis a "crank professor" who should be collected by "a sheriff with a *writ de lunatico*." (Root to Taft, March 18, 1912, Taft Papers). Later, the two became friends, and Lewis persuaded Root to serve as titular head of the American Law Institute, of which Lewis became Secretary and *de facto* director.

29. 37 *ABA Rep* 575 (1912); Steidle, 354-68; Landon, 73. Of the remaining states, seven had either no bar association or no records, and three took up the issue later.

President S. S. Gregory and his successor, Frank Kellogg, were moderate progressives and sought to counter the growing conservative sentiment within the Association by explicitly supporting reform. In regard to judicial recall, however, they were adamant. Gregory announced his opposition to the proposal "in any form or under any conditions." Kellogg warned that judicial recall would destroy the "integrity of our system of government."[30] Conservative speakers denounced the recall at greater length and with grander enthusiasm. George Sutherland specifically condemned Roosevelt's recall of judicial decisions as "mischievous unwisdom...which in effect would...render a judicial decision by what practically amounts to a show of hands at the polls."[31]

By comparison with some of the speeches, the report of the Committee to Oppose the Judicial Recall was moderate in tone. The report supported measures that might ameliorate popular discontent with the courts and emphasized that removing judicial protection from the rich would remove the same protection from the poor. The Committee volunteered to help opponents of recall and noted that it had sent copies of anti-recall speeches to the entire electorate of Arizona.[32]

---

30. S. S. Gregory, "Address of the President," 37 *ABA Rep* 255 (1912); Frank B. Kellogg, "New Nationalism," 37 *ABA Rep* 341 @ 350 (1912).
31. George Sutherland, "The Courts and the Constitution," 37 *ABA Rep* 371 @ 379 (1912); Henry D. Estabrook, "The American Judicial System: The Judges," 37 *ABA Rep* 393 (1912); Joseph C. France, "The American Judicial System: The Lawyers," 37 *ABA Rep* 411 (1912).
32. "Report of the Committee to Oppose the Judicial Recall," 37 *ABA Rep* 574-89 (1912); 38 *ABA Rep* 579 @ 587 (1913). On November 5 Arizona adopted a constitutional amendment approving judicial recall by a vote of 16,272 to 3,705.

The pronouncements of the Association and its convention speakers were generally well received by the press. For instance, the *Independent* referred to Association members as "the choice of the legal profession, selected out of the select," and declared that their judgment on the recall question should be decisive: "That Mr. Roosevelt and his Progressive party should have against them the total weight of the American Bar Association is a fact of great importance."

The *Independent* correctly predicted that judicial recall would not be "strongly urged" during the remainder of the campaign.[33] Roosevelt continued to refer to the recall obliquely, and legal periodicals continued to publish negative articles on the subject; but the issue aroused little popular interest during the final months of the campaign. Even in Colorado, where the recall of judicial decisions was approved by a slim margin in November 1912, a majority of the voters ignored the question on their ballots.[34]

Nevertheless, the fervor with which the reform had been debated pushed interest in judicial recall past Roosevelt's defeat in the 1912 election. By September 1913, the recall had been adopted in five Western states—Oregon, California, Colorado, Arizona, and Nevada. The legislatures of Kansas and Minnesota had approved constitutional amendments that would have established judicial recall after popular ratification, and Arkansas voters had already ratified such an amendment, although the state

---

33. "A Select Jury," *Independent* 73 (September 5, 1912), 576-77; *New York Times*, September 2, 1912, 8.
34. Steidle, 373-74; Duane A. Smith, "Colorado and Judicial Recall," 7 *American Journal of Legal History* 198 @ 202 (1963).

supreme court promptly ruled that it had been improperly submitted. The ABA's Recall Committee acknowledged that judicial recall had "received surprisingly strong support" during the 1913 sessions of state legislatures. In North Dakota it had lost by only one vote. East of the Mississippi, considerable support for recall existed in Wisconsin, Illinois, Ohio, and even Massachusetts.[35]

The American Bar Association's campaign against judicial recall took a more openly anti-progressive stance beginning in 1912 when Frank Kellogg was succeeded as Recall Committee chairman by Rome G. Brown (1862-1926). In energy, diligence, and raw intelligence Kellogg and Brown were similar; in everything else, they were polar opposites. Whereas Kellogg excelled at political fence-straddling and diplomacy, Brown, a hardline conservative, seemed determined to insult everyone with whom he disagreed. Fifty years old in 1912, Brown had graduated *magna cum laude* from Harvard before moving from his native New England to Minneapolis. There he became an expert in riparian law and federal water power regulation. He enjoyed performing uncompensated duties for professional organizations and had already served as president of the Minnesota State Bar Association and as a member of both the ABA Executive Committee and the National Conference of Commissioners on Uniform State Law. A nominal Unitarian, Brown approached politics with a zeal usually

---

35. "Report of the Committee to Oppose the Judicial Recall," 38 *ABA Rep* 579 @ 581-83 (1913).

reserved for propagating religion. "Heresy" and "apostate" were choice epithets for judicial recall and its supporters.[36]

Under Brown the Recall Committee became an outlet for the growing conservative sentiment within the Association. As the *ABA Journal* editorialized some years later, the "work of the committee carried on under the chairmanship of Mr. Brown was in no sense dilettante or academic. It got right down to business." In the name of the committee, Brown promoted "special campaigns" against the recall in states that seemed especially likely to adopt the measure. In one year alone he saw to the distribution of over 350,000 anti-recall pamphlets—mostly reprints of speeches delivered by Association leaders—to newspapers, libraries, and public officials, and to every law school student in the country. (So much of this literature was mailed under the frank of sympathetic senators that progressives in Congress threatened an investigation, and Brown found it inadvisable to continue the practice.) Brown also arranged for judicial recall to be selected as a high school debate topic in the Northwest and then "furnished ammunition for the opposition"—the result being that the negative won more than ninety percent of the debates. Later, Brown sponsored contests among the high school and law school students of Minnesota for the best argument against the proposed recall amendment in that state

36. *Who Was Who*, I, 151; *Minneapolis Tribune*, May 23, 1926, 1. For more quasi-religious overtones in Brown's politics see, "The Dilemma of the Judicial Recall Advocate," a speech given to the Missouri State Bar Association on October 23, 1914 and included in the Taft Papers, Reel 143.

and had the winning essays published in Minnesota papers and in the national legal periodical *Green Bag*.[37]

Finally, Brown provided speakers for universities, law schools, bar associations, and business groups, especially in states where proponents of recall seemed vigorous. Brown did much of the speaking himself, delighting in his newfound celebrity and in the opportunity to flay progressives. If notable recall advocates were present, so much the better. Once Brown gloated to Taft about his "put-down" of a Colorado judge. On another occasion he exulted at the conversion of a prominent lawyer who had come to a state bar association meeting "determined to stand alone, if necessary, against [him] but who afterwards announced that he should henceforth preach against Judicial Recall as a socialist instrument of disruption." After speaking to the bar associations of Texas and Indiana in 1914, Brown bragged that the lawyers "liked the stuff that I gave them and the way in which I gave it. ... They will now go out and spread the gospel."[38]

At the 1914 meeting of the North Carolina Bar Association, Brown included a scathing denunciation of Chief Justice Walter Clark (1846-1924), a notable progressive, the only prominent judge of the period to have "the temerity to

---

37. "The Endless Battle for Constitutional Principle," 12 *ABAJ* 464 (1926); "Report of the Committee to Oppose the Judicial Recall," 38 *ABA Rep* 579 @ 580-81 (1913); Brown to Frederick Wadhams, July 23, 1914, Brown to Taft, December 17, 1913, October 12, 1914, Taft Papers; Rome Brown, 39 *ABA Rep* 38-39 (1914); H. S. Hoshour, "An Argument Against the Judicial Recall," 26 *Green Bag* 517 (1914).

38. Brown to Taft, February 26, 1914, July 18, 1914; Brown to Members of the American Bar Association Committee to Oppose the Judicial Recall, January 27, 1915, Taft Papers.

publicly attack the conservatism of his judicial brethren, denigrate the Constitution, and question the doctrine of judicial review."[39] Clark's attacks upon the Constitution, said Brown, had "never been surpassed in malignant vituperation by that of any socialist doctrinaire." The association sat stunned because the fiery Clark was there. Although Brown's address was omitted from the association's proceedings, Clark was furious that no resolution condemning the "imported Yankee" had been introduced during the meeting. Brown planned to publish his vituperative message in the Association *Report* but finally relented "as an act of courtesy" to the member of his committee from North Carolina. Still, Brown remained unrepentant. To a supporter of Clark's, Brown wrote that the Chief Justice could not be treated in a civil manner because he was like "a rabid animal running amuck. ... One cannot treat a man attempting to apply a firebrand to his house as he would treat a citizen who merely criticizes...the architect."[40]

---

39. Ross, *A Muted Fury*, 33. "Clark's antagonism toward the courts, especially the federal courts, reflected his background. As a scion of wealthy planters and a proud veteran of the Confederate army, Clark never wavered in his dedication to states' rights, and he feared that industrialism would corrupt the South....Throughout his public career, he was a sharp critic of the business interests that held sway in North Carolina. Although the tobacco and railroad interests actively opposed Clark's bids for the chief justiceship, he was regularly reelected by large margins." (33-34)

40. Aubrey Lee Brooks, *Walter Clark, Fighting Judge* (Chapel Hill: University of North Carolina Press, 1944), 192-93; William A. Guthrie to Clark, July 2, 1914; R. C. Lawrence to Clark, July 3, 1914; Clark to Frank S. Spruill, July 4, 1914; Clark to A. W. Graham, July 4, 1914, July 8, 1914, in Aubrey Lee Brooks and Hugh Talmage Lefler, eds., *The Papers of Walter Clark* (Chapel Hill: University of North Carolina Press, 1948); Tyrrell

Only a few years before, an Association member of Brown's temperament would not have been named chairman of an important committee. Now the most influential leaders of the Association, including Rawle and William Howard Taft, egged Brown on. A few months before Brown's attack on Clark, Taft had told Brown that the North Carolinian was an "old anarchistic crank." Three weeks after the speech, Taft encouraged Brown not to be "weary of well doing" and then urged Treasurer Frederick Wadhams to give Brown's committee an extra $500. "He has done more work than anybody connected with the Association," said Taft, "and he has done it well."[41] Brown craved a strong public commendation from Taft, but the former President was too shrewd for that.[42]

Williams to the Editor, *Nation* 99 (October 22, 1914), 497 and (November 19, 1914), 605; Brown to Tyrrell Williams, November 23, 1914, Brown to Taft, July 3, 1914, Taft Papers.

Clark suspected that local enemies had inspired Brown's attack and may have even supplied some of the more extravagant language. A friend hinted darkly that "Duke Water Power Company . . . had Brown carried down to North Carolina for the purpose of assailing you." C. C. Davis to Clark, July 9, 1914 in *Papers of Walter Clark*.

41. Taft to Brown, February 17, 1914, July 21, 1914; Taft to Wadhams, July 27, 1914; Taft to Horace Taft, March 21, 1915; cf. Rawle to Brown, June 15, 1921, Taft Papers; Rawle to W. Thomas Kemp, September 21, 1922, John W. Davis Papers, III, 14. By delightful coincidence, a few months after Taft had called Clark an "anarchistic crank," an ABA "process letter" in Taft's name was sent to the Chief Justice inviting him to become a member of the Judicial Section of the ABA. Clark thanked Taft for the invitation and joined. Clark to Taft, April 3, 1914, *The Papers of Walter Clark*, 242.

42. Brown to Taft, July 18, 1914, June 7, 1921, Taft Papers; Taft, "Address of the President," 39 *ABA Rep* 359 @ 380 (1914).

By 1915 Brown announced that "judicial recall had passed its climax." Kansas had adopted the recall in 1914, but Brown correctly predicted that it would be the last state to do so. Still, the chairman recommended eternal vigilance. "Keep your eyes open," he told the annual meeting of 1914. "[A]t every place where it shows any signs of life, be prepared to 'swat this bug.'" One measure of declining interest was the number of major addresses made to state bar associations on the subject: fifteen in 1913, seven (including four by Brown) in 1914, and five in 1915. By the summer of 1914, even Roosevelt had all but given up on judicial recall.[43]

The role played by Rome Brown and the American Bar Association in the demise of recall sentiment is uncertain but should not be underestimated. The activities of the Recall Committee at least accelerated trends already at work in the larger society. Progressives with political discernment realized there was little to be gained from advocating a measure that generated comparatively slight popular support, aroused violent and persistent antagonism from a powerful profession, and had virtually no practical effect once adopted. One of Brown's committeemen told him in 1915 that the only supporters of judicial recall in his state were one or two leaders of the Progressive Party, and "they

---

43. "Report of the Committee to Oppose Judicial Recall," 40 *ABA Rep* 518 @ 519 (1915); Rome Brown, 39 *ABA Rep* 40 (1914); Roosevelt to Hiram Johnson, July 30, 1914, *Letters*, 7: 787; Steidle, 377; Ross, *A Muted Fury*, 126-129.

are so mum about it that it would seem as if they had forgotten there was ever such an issue."[44]

In any case, lawyers hailed the Recall Committee's campaign as a victory for both the profession and the American Bar Association. In a banquet speech at the 1915 meeting, Senator J. Hamilton Lewis (1863-1939) of Illinois lauded his colleagues for having marshaled "the wisdom of conservatism...against the late crusade that, like hurled brands, went flaming through the nation—against all courts, all law and all justice." James Grafton Rogers, reviewing the first fifty years of the Association's history in 1928, declared the recall defeat one of the "great achievements" of the Association. Rome Brown, he said, had fought recall sentiment with the "whole strength of the American Bar Association" behind him, and he had "swept it away as a possibility in America."[45] Fortunately for the legal profession, most progressives were—according to a modern student of the episode—unwilling to step beyond rhetorical reminders to the judges not to thwart the popular will by nullifying progressive legislation.[46]

---

44. "Report of the Committee to Oppose Judicial Recall," 40 *ABA Rep* 518 @ 522-23 (1915); Botein, "'What We Shall Meet Afterwards in Heaven,'" 57. As *The World's Work* observed in 1912, "The power is in the people's hands, but they seem conservative in using it against the courts. They no doubt regard it as a gun behind the door." "The Recall of Judges in California," *The World's Work*, 23 (March 1912), 494; Ross, *A Muted Fury*, 128-29.

45. Hamilton Lewis, 1 *ABAJ* 556 (1915); Chief Justice Edward White, 39 *ABA Rep* 120 (1914); James Grafton Rogers, "Fifty Years of the American Bar Association," 53 *ABA Rep* 518 @ 525 (1928).

46. William G. Ross, *A Muted Fury: Populists, Progressives, and Labor Unions Confront the Courts, 1890-1937* (Princeton: Princeton University Press, 1994), 15-21: "The history of the attacks on the courts during the period helps to explain why attempts to curtail judicial power during

Victory in the recall controversy produced a psychological boost for the Association and stimulated membership growth. One of Taft's correspondents pledged support for the membership campaign because he was certain that "united professional action [was] needed to protect our courts from foolish attack." Gone was the earlier timidity of ABA members who feared any political activity would create only internal controversy. Defeat of judicial recall seemed to illustrate what lawyers might achieve through professional solidarity.[47]

To a vain and opinionated man like Brown, the recall victory seemed a prelude to some higher mission. The real enemy of the legal profession and of constitutional government, Brown believed, was not recall itself but the larger menace of socialism, of which recall was only one manifestation. As early as January 1914, Brown confided privately that Roosevelt's propaganda for judicial recall was "precisely a propaganda of socialism," and shortly thereafter he expressed the same sentiments in public. As interest in judicial recall declined, the stridency of Brown's rhetoric increased. In a 1917 speech Brown blasted judicial recall, the Adamson Act, the economic interpretation of the Constitution, attacks on judicial review, minimum wage laws, and the

---

every period of American history have failed, yet why those attempts have influenced judicial decision making and have had a salubrious impact upon the vitality of American democracy." (21)

47. Sidney T. Miller to Taft, January 28, 1914, Taft Papers; Max Radin, "The Achievements of the American Bar Association," 26 *ABAJ* 19 @ 24 (1940); Herbert Harley, "Organization of the Bar," *Annals* 52 (March, 1914), 17, 81.

government of North Dakota—all, he believed, to be hallmarks of socialism in America.[48]

That same year a Recall Committee member from North Dakota criticized Brown in a minority report, warning that Brown's attempt to play politics might backfire. Brown had heard that message before: that judicial recall was dead "unless the old time reactionaries" became "overconfident and invite[d] renewed disturbance." Undeterred, Brown succeeded in changing the name of his committee to the Committee to Oppose Judicial Recall and Allied Measures.[49]

Dissatisfaction with Brown and his politics continued to grow, both from within the Recall Committee and from the Association's Executive Committee, to whom Brown had become a potentially embarrassing freelancer. Bringing him to heel might have been more difficult had Brown not been in the habit of running up unauthorized expenses—mostly for the printing of his own speeches—and then blithely

---

48. Brown to Frank Cove, January 28, 1914; Brown to Winfield S. Hammond, September 25, 1914, Taft Papers; Brown, "The Dilemma of the Judicial Recall Advocate" (October 23, 1914), galley proofs in Taft Papers, Reel 143; Brown, "The Lawlessness of the Judicial Recall," [Annual Address, State Bar Association of South Dakota, January 14, 1915], in Taft Papers, Reel 148; Brown, "The Socialist Menace to Constitutional Government," 4 *ABAJ* 54 @ 71 (1918).

49. "Minority Report," 42 *ABA Rep* 444 (1917); "Report of the Committee to Oppose Judicial Recall," 40 *ABA Rep* 518 @ 523 (1915); Rome Brown to Frederick Wadhams, May 5, 1919, Taft Papers. By 1919 the National Nonpartisan League had taken control of the government of North Dakota with its basic grievance the alleged monopoly over the grain trade exercised by the Minneapolis Chamber of Commerce. Brown, of course, was a corporation lawyer from Minneapolis.

presenting the bills to the Executive Committee for repayment. In the spring of 1919, the committee refused to pay.[50]

Brown fumed and sputtered to Frederick Wadhams and the members of the Recall Committee. He boasted of his single-handed efforts against judicial recall that had "brought credit to the American Bar Association." He compared A. C. Townley of the Nonpartisan League to Lenin. He compared himself to Jesus Christ. When he tried to call a meeting of his committee at the annual meeting in Boston, three members appeared, two of whom opposed him. When he appealed personally to the Executive Committee, they stood firm against him.[51]

On the convention floor, Brown introduced a resolution that would have allowed his committee to "continue its campaign of education against the subversive doctrines of socialism." Believing that he had hundreds of friends and supporters at the convention, Brown was shocked when none came to his defense. Instead, his archenemy William Draper Lewis, a supporter of the recall of decisions, cleverly praised the committee's success in defeating the recall of judges but suggested that it was unwise to give committee members "*carte blanche* to fight anything and everything that in their opinion may be revolutionary." In the end, the

---

50. Hampton Carson to W. Thomas Kemp, June 28, 1921, Carson Papers; Brown to Frederick Wadhams, May 5, 1919; Brown to William A. Blount, July 17, 1919, Taft Papers; "Light from the Lawyers," *New Republic* 20 (September 17, 1919), 190, for an example of how the Association could be blamed for Brown's rhetoric.

51. Brown to Wadhams, May 5, 1919; Brown to Blount, July 17, 1919; Brown to George B. Young, August 1, 1919; Brown to Hampton Carson, December 5, 1919; Brown to Members of the Recall Committee, June 10, 1919, Taft Papers.

convention approved only the Committee's continuation with no further instructions.[52] The volatile Brown, "disgusted, mad, grieved [and] beaten," immediately resigned, both as the Chairman of the Recall Committee and as a member of the Association.[53]

Most of the leaders were glad to be done with Brown, but he had taught them an important lesson: that the name

---

52. Rome Brown, 44 *ABA Rep* 65-68 (1919); Brown to Carson, December 5, 1919, Taft Papers; 44 *ABA Rep* 68-70, 89 (1919). Although the Recall Committee had been specifically continued by the convention, it was dropped without explanation from the list of special committees.

53. Brown to Carson, December 5, 1919; Brown to George T. Page, September 4, 1919, Taft Papers; see Carson to W. Thomas Kemp, June 28, 1921, Carson Papers. A few other members left the Association with Brown, including one Henry S. Forester who had held a similar chairmanship in the New York State Bar Association. It was Forester's theory that recall was "really a Pan-German agitation carried on through pseudo-Swiss propagandists, the inevitable result of which would have been the disintegration of the United States so as to be over ripe for conquest by Pan Germany." Forester to Taft, June 11, 1921, Taft Papers.

Some months later Brown accused his enemies in the ABA of being "parlor Bolshevists" and of having been jealous of the "position of prominence" to which he had been raised by the recall struggle. Brown served for nearly two years as president and executive manager of the *Minneapolis Tribune*, (which allowed him the opportunity to write editorials), but in the fall of 1921 he was ousted in a "conspiracy [led by] a little Sheenie...so boastful and presumptuous that he is disgusting." Brown then seems to have suffered both a physical and mental breakdown. In 1922 he quietly rejoined the Association and seems to have made one final bid to regain the chairmanship of an ABA committee before dying in 1926 from complications of diabetes. Brown to Carson, December 5, 1919; Brown to Taft, November 19, 1920, September 24, 1921, October 3, 1921, Taft Papers; Francis Rawle to Thomas Kemp, September 1922, Davis Papers, III, 14

of the American Bar Association might be invoked with effect in support of a political cause if that cause could be plausibly related to the legal profession and was one on which lawyers had achieved a reasonable degree of unanimity. Even so, the next attempt to use this power was made not by the Association *per se* but by William Howard Taft and several other former presidents of the Association acting independently and without a professional consensus.

On January 28, 1916, President Woodrow Wilson nominated the progressive Louis D. Brandeis (1856-1941) to be an Associate Justice of the U. S. Supreme Court. Wilson had earlier considered nominating Brandeis as Attorney General, but conservative opposition had been strong, and Wilson had abandoned the idea. Now the President determined both to honor his economic adviser and portray himself as a true progressive. The Brandeis nomination precipitated a four-month long confirmation debate, ostensibly about the nominee's ethical qualifications for office but also about the future ideological composition of the Court.[54]

---

54. Melvin I. Urofsky, *Louis D. Brandeis and the Progressive Tradition* (Boston: Little, Brown and Company, 1981), 104-05; Arthur S. Link, *Wilson: Confusions and Crisis* (Princeton: Princeton University Press, 1964), 323-35; Lewis J. Paper, *Brandeis: An Intimate Biography of One of America's Truly Great Supreme Court Justices* (Secaucus, NJ: Citadel Press, 1983), 209-238; Leonard Baker, *Brandeis and Frankfurter: A Dual Biography* (New York: Harper & Row, 1984), 97-121. Brandeis had a tendency not to play the lawyer's game as the elite thought it should be played, and some of his conduct in regard to former clients would raise eyebrows even today. As friendly biographer Leonard Baker has written, "For many years Brandeis had pursued his causes relentlessly, and he was paying for it." (112).

Three weeks earlier, less than a week after the death of Justice J. R. Lamar, the ABA Executive Committee had met for its midwinter session and had approved a letter written by Alton B. Parker urging Wilson to name Taft to the Court. All twenty-nine members present signed the letter—fourteen Republicans, fourteen Democrats, and "one who had voted for Roosevelt in...1912."[55] As a man of political sophistication, Taft could hardly have been surprised at being passed over, but there is also no reason to doubt the sincerity of his declaration that the nomination of "Brandeis [was] one of the deepest wounds" he had ever received as "a lover of the Constitution and a believer in progressive conservatism." If any of Taft's opposition to Brandeis' nomination was actuated by anti-Semitism, that sort of prejudice remained below the threshold of his consciousness.[56]

As is typical for Supreme Court nominees, the confirmation hearings only indirectly addressed ideological

---

55. "Autobiographical Portraits," Box 16, Alton B. Parker Papers. Parker considered the letter so important, he had it photographed before ex-ABA president Edgar H. Farrar personally delivered it to Wilson.

56. Taft to Gus Karger, January 31, 1916, Taft Papers. Taft held no personal animosity toward Brandeis, and when they next chanced to meet on a Washington street in 1918, Taft went out of his way to be cordial. Brandeis to Alice Goldmark Brandeis, December 4, 1918, in Melvin I. Urofsky and David W. Levy, eds., *Letters of Louis D. Brandeis* (Albany: State University of New York Press, 1971-75), 4: 370. When Taft became Chief Justice, he and Brandeis got along well, though, of course, they continued to differ ideologically. Brandeis thought Taft had only a "first-rate second-rate mind," but Brandeis liked Taft because he was good-natured, had broad interests, and supervised the Court's business expeditiously. Paper, 299-301.

issues. Instead, Brandeis's detractors charged him with unethical behavior while his supporters accused critics of personal animus or the desire to even the score for some legal defeat suffered at the hands of their champion. In the end, despite a well-organized campaign led by Wall Street attorney Austen G. Fox (1849-1937), the worst that could be said of Brandeis's character was that he tended to play the game of law in a less gentlemanly and more self-righteous manner than was common among the elite. In the words of a Boston lawyer testifying before the Senate subcommittee, he "took a delight in smashing a bit the traditions of the Bar, which most of us revere."[57] Of course, ideologically the intuition of the elite was sure: just a few months later, Brandeis was to cast the deciding vote to uphold the Adamson Act.

As a final gesture of opposition, Taft urged publication of a statement written by Elihu Root and signed by several ex-presidents of the American Bar Association some weeks before. "I presume we cannot defeat the confirmation," Taft wrote to former Attorney General George Wickersham, "but I think we ought to go on record."[58] On March 14, Austen Fox read the statement to the Senate subcommittee: "The undersigned feel under the painful duty to say to you in their opinion, taking into view the reputation,

---

57. Urofsky, *Brandeis,* 111; Alpheus T. Mason, *Brandeis: A Free Man's Life* (New York: Viking Press, 1946), 489-90; Alexander M. Bickel and Benno C. Schmidt, Jr., *The Judiciary and Responsible Government, 1910-21* (New York: Macmillan Publishing Company, 1984), 382-84.

58. Taft to Wickersham, March 14, 1914; cf. Wickersham to Taft, February 1, 1916; Gus Karger to Taft, March 16, 1916; Taft to Wickersham, March 20 and March 27, Taft Papers.

character, and professional career of Mr. Louis D. Brandeis, he is not a fit person to be a member of the Supreme Court of the United States."

The letter was signed by Taft, Root, Simeon Baldwin, Francis Rawle, Joseph Choate, and Moorfield Storey. (Peter Meldrim sent a similar letter with slightly different wording.) The statement did not mention the ABA nor the office to which all the signers had been elected, but Fox encouraged his listeners to draw improper conclusions by noting that every signer had been president of the American Bar Association.[59]

The "painful duty" of the presidents was transmitted across the country by the Associated Press. An editorial in the *St. Louis Globe-Democrat* viewed the presidents' negative assessment of Brandeis as one that could not "be waived aside with an epithet. All [the signers] are great lawyers, who realize the significance of their act. . . . Any intimation that they are moved by racial prejudice is absurd.... Nor can the protest be ascribed to 'the interests.'"[60] Although the presidents' protest was imprudent, at least its signers were under no illusion that they could make it without personal cost. Signing the statement was neither a rash nor cowardly

59. Mason, *Brandeis,* 489; A. L. Todd, *Justice on Trial: The Case of Louis D. Brandeis* (New York: McGraw-Hill Book Company, 1964), 159. George Wickersham, who coordinated the effort to gather the presidents' signatures, asked Henry St. George Tucker to write a statement, but his effort appealed to neither Taft nor Baldwin. Draft statement, February 10, 1916, Tucker Papers.

60. Quoted in Todd, 160. The release of the protest was poorly timed. On March 15, General Pershing crossed the border of Mexico to begin his unsuccessful attempt to capture Pancho Villa, and this action captured the headlines the following day.

act. Brandeis remained untroubled by the letter and privately declared that if it were "properly used...[it] might be of great political importance."[61] At his suggestion, Walter Lippmann wrote a biting editorial in the *New Republic* pillorying Taft as "the last man qualified to express a judgment on Mr. Louis Brandeis." Other progressive publications attacked Root, Choate, and Meldrim.[62]

Some later historians were misled into believing that the American Bar Association itself had opposed the Brandeis nomination.[63] If contemporary progressives had responded with an attack on the Association, two significant facts about the episode almost certainly would have been revealed. First, Brandeis had been a member of the Association for more than two decades, had attended

---

61. Todd, 162-63; Louis Brandeis to Norman Hapgood, March 14, 1916, in Urofsky and Levy, eds., *Letters*, 4: 118-19.

62. *New Republic* 6 (March 18, 1916), 165; Burton J. Hendrick, "How Should a Lawyer Behave?" *World's Work* 33 (January, 1917), 328-335; Mason, *Brandeis*, 490; *New Republic* 6 (March 25, 1916), 202-04; L. A. Coolidge to Taft, March 16, 1916, Taft Papers.

63. "Before the hearings closed so triumphantly the American Bar Association launched an all-out attack." Mason, *Brandeis*, 489. "The American Bar Association, including seven former presidents of that organization...alleged that Brandeis was not fit to take a seat on the Supreme Court." J. Leonard Bates, *The United States, 1898-1928: Progressivism and a Society in Transition* (New York: McGraw-Hill Book Company, 1976), 147.

"That the opposition of the ABA to Brandeis did not come through 'channels,' but was articulated as the personal views of seven former presidents, should not be interpreted as something less than the accurate views of the then small membership of the ABA." Joel B. Grossman, *Lawyers and Judges: The ABA and the Politics of Judicial Selection* (New York: John Wiley and Sons, Inc., 1965), 55.

several meetings, and had served as a member of the Committee on Uniform Judicial Procedure.[64] Second, the seven ABA presidents who signed the protest were a minority of the seventeen living presidents, all of whose signatures had been sought by George Wickersham. Wickersham's lack of success in enlisting progressives such as Frank Kellogg and Stephen Gregory is hardly surprising, but it would be interesting to know why a superfluously wealthy traction magnate like Charles F. Libby refused to participate. Neither Alton Parker nor J. M. Dickinson signed the presidents' letter, although both had lobbied vigorously for Taft's nomination. Dickinson refused to lend his name because he believed that members might resent the appearance of the presidents acting "representatively" for the Association in a controversial matter.[65]

Some of them did. At least one Jewish member of the Association resigned, and Julius Henry Cohen (1873-1950), a noted writer on legal ethics, declared it "unfortunate" that the ex-presidents "gave the impression that what they were doing was official." Stephen Gregory and Roscoe Pound both testified before the Senate subcommittee in Brandeis's behalf, and Pound later helped Felix Frankfurter enlist seven Harvard Law School professors

---

64. Brandeis to John Hinkley, July 20, 1905, in Urofsky and Levy, eds., *Letters*, 1: 338-39. Brandeis's membership in the ABA stretched from 1893 to 1917.

65. Todd, 161. The living ex-presidents who did not protest Brandeis's nomination were Edmund Wetmore, Henry St. George Tucker, George R. Peck, Alton B. Parker, J. M. Dickinson, Frederick Lehmann, Charles Libby, Edgar H. Farrar, Stephen S. Gregory, and Frank Kellogg.

to sign a counter-petition testifying to Brandeis's legal ability and integrity.[66]

The Brandeis affair illustrates both change and continuity in the Association. On one hand, a majority of the ex-presidents chose the traditional posture of refusing to entangle the Association in partisan politics. On the other, some of the most influential of the ex-presidents, including charter members Simeon Baldwin and Francis Rawle, were willing to take the organization in the opposite direction.

Although the aftermath of World War I increased anti-progressive trends already manifest in the American Bar Association, the entrance of the United States into the war ushered in a brief but exhilarating interval of bar association unity, both internally and with the nation as a whole. Before American entrance into World War I, the ABA leadership had been no more bellicose than the leadership of the American Library Association. Taft told Whitelock in 1914 that he opposed Association consideration of a member's proposed rules of civilized warfare. "I think," said Taft, "the less we stick our nose into the contest the better. *Inter arma silent leges* [In time of war the laws are silent]."[67] Even in 1916, when a

---

66. *New York Times*, June 1, 1916, 9; Julius Henry Cohen to the *New York Times*, June 2, 1916, 10; Todd, 161; Grossman, *Lawyers and Judges*, 55; Urofsky, *Brandeis*, 115; Rebecca Roiphe, "A History of Professionalism: Julius Henry Cohen and the Professions as a Route to Citizenship," 40 *Fordham Urban Law Journal*, 33-74 (2012).

67. Taft to George Whitelock, October 6, 1914, Taft Papers; Arthur Young, *Books for Sammies: The American Library Association and World War I* (Pittsburgh: Beta Phi Mu, 1981). The ABA Executive Committee did endorse the raising of a fund for "European lawyers in distress," and though Taft was unenthusiastic, a group headed by Joseph Choate sent about

member proposed some anti-British resolutions to the annual meeting, there was no debate. The resolutions were simply shunted into the dead end of a committee. According to James Grafton Rogers, the "membership was really in active ferment by this time, and there was bitterness and some talk of resignations, but the official record reveals nothing."[68]

The fortieth anniversary meeting of the Association at Saratoga in September 1917, after the United States had declared war, was an entirely different matter, resembling less a professional convention than a cross between a camp meeting and the Fourth of July. At the opening session, Elihu Root presented a series of strongly worded resolutions that went beyond patriotic necessity. The *New York Times* reported that "[g]ray-haired men stood in their seats and shouted with the vigor of schoolboys." Root's resolutions condemned "all attempts in Congress and out of it to hinder and embarrass the government of the United States in carrying on the war with vigor and effectiveness." They flatly declared that even criticism made under "cover of pacifism or technicality" was "in spirit pro-German and in effect giving aid and comfort to the enemy." The assembly approved the resolutions unanimously by rising vote.[69]

The year's speeches mostly ran in the same vein. Former Supreme Court Justice and former Republican presidential candidate Charles Evans Hughes (1862-1948) delivered a brief for the constitutionality of measures being used

---

$13,000 to London for distribution to Belgian refugees. Rogers, *American Bar Leaders*, 201; Whitelock to Taft, January 28, 1915, Taft Papers.

68. 41 *ABA Rep* 34-35 (1916); Rogers, *American Bar Leaders*, 202.

69. *New York Times*, September 5, 1917, 5; *Washington Post*, September 5, 1917, 2; 42 *ABA Rep* 25-26, 98 (1917).

to prosecute the war: conscription, taxation, federal control of the militia, and the extraordinary powers of the President. When Hughes concluded his address with the words, "So the Constitution fights," the audience broke into "a wild burst of applause."[70]

Gaston de Leval, a Belgian attorney who had unsuccessfully tried to represent Edith Cavell before a German military court, spoke to the assembly on "Prussian Law as Applied to Belgium." De Leval was a personal friend of George Whitelock, and the Secretary had assured Taft that the Belgian would produce "the desired patriotic thrill." The address proved satisfactory along those lines, although Leval expressed a curious respect for the *Kriegsgerichtsrate* [judge advocate] who had accompanied German troops into his country and who, he said, had "a clear, judicial and fair mind."[71] Apparently the only good German was a German lawyer.

A greater patriotic thrill was generated by Robert McNutt McElroy (1872-1959), a jingoistic Princeton historian and an official of the National Security League, who was developing into a master of oratorical propaganda. McElroy began his speech temperately enough with a nod toward scholarship, but he soon paraded a catalog of German war crimes to illustrate the essential difference between the

70. Charles Evans Hughes, "War Powers Under the Constitution," 42 *ABA Rep* 232 (1917); *New York Times*, September 6, 1917, 1; William A. Hayes, 42 *ABA Rep* 84-85 (1917). Hughes's speech was printed by the *Times* nearly verbatim.

71. Gaston de Leval, "Prussian Law as Applied in Belgium," 42 *ABA Rep* 301 @ 316-17 (1917); Whitelock to Taft, June 4 and June 13, 1917, Taft Papers; *New York Times*, September 7, 1917, 5.

villianous enemy and the freedom-loving descendants of Simon de Montfort, William Pitt, and Abraham Lincoln.[72]

Although American Bar Association members shared the same patriotic motives for endorsing the war as other Americans, several other factors strengthened the Association's identification with the conflict. First, the war seemed to provide a way to demonstrate altruistic professionalism, especially after the recent sustained criticism of courts and lawyers. Future Illinois congressman Henry Riggs Rathbone (1870-1928), moving adoption of the Root resolutions,

---

72. George T. Blakey, *Historians on the Homefront: American Propagandists for the Great War* (Lexington: University Press of Kentucky, 1970), 30, 58-59; Robert D. Ward, "The Origin and Activities of the National Security League, 1914-1919," *Mississippi Valley Historical Review*, 47 (June, 1960), 51-65; John Carver Edwards, *Patriots in Pinstripe: Men of the National Security League* (Washington: University Press of America, 1982), 93-94, 100-02; Robert McNutt McElroy, "The Representative Idea and the War," 42 *ABA Rep* 249 @ 253 (1917). Joseph Choate, Elihu Root, and Alton Parker served as honorary officers of the organization, but there was otherwise no connection between the NSL and the ABA. McElroy assured the assembly that the racial ancestry of the Prussians should be no embarrassment to Anglo-Saxons because the former were "a mixture of many races, with more Slavonic than Teutonic blood."

After accepting an invitation to address the 1917 meeting, Senator Thomas W. Hardwick of Georgia opposed the Administration's foreign policy. On the evening before his speech, there was serious talk among ABA leaders of "disinviting" him. Eventually they contented themselves with an early presentation of the Root resolutions. Moorfield Storey gave Hardwick a one sentence introduction, and the senator expounded a states'-rights view of the Commerce Clause. Some leading members boycotted the session. Thomas W. Hardwick, "The Regulation of Commerce Between the State Under the Commerce Clause of the Constitution of the United States," 42 *ABA Rep* 215 (1917); *New York Times*, September 5, 1917, 5.

urged the association to demonstrate that "we are not mere money grabbers.... The medical profession, the businessmen are doing their share. Shall it be said of the legal profession that we did not play our part in the great cause of liberty and humanity?"[73]

A second reason for the ABA's enthusiastic endorsement of the war was the respect that the legal elite felt for England. For forty years, speeches at the annual meeting had included reverent allusions to "the mother country" and "good old England." Leaders of the British bar, including the Lord Chief Justice and the Lord Chancellor had addressed the assembly, emphasizing "the unseen crimson thread of kinship stretching from the mother Islands to your continent."[74] Snobbery too

---

73. Henry R. Rathbone, 42 *ABA Rep* 32 (1917). The version printed in the *Report* omits the reference to lawyers as "money grabbers."

74. C. C. Bonney, 7 *ABA Rep* 55 (1884); Henry C. Semple, 7 *ABA Rep* 63 (1884); Lord Russell of Killowen, Lord Chief Justice of England, "International Law and Arbitration," 19 *ABA Rep* 253 (1896); John Hinkley, "Reminiscences of the American Bar Association," 21 *ABAJ* 452 @ 458; *New York Times*, August 21, 1896, 1; Francis Rawle, "Address of the President," 26 *ABA Rep* 261 @ 263 (1903); James Bryce, "The Influence of National Character and Historical Environment on the Development of the Common Law," 31 *ABA Rep* 444 @ 461; Sir William R. Kennedy, "The State Punishment of Crime," 22 *ABA Rep* 359 @ 377 (1899); Richard Burton Haldane, "Higher Nationality," 38 *ABA Rep* 393 @ 413-15 (1913); Hampton Carson, 38 *ABA Rep* 16-17 (1913); Taft to Mabel Boardman, October 27, 1914, Taft Papers; Richard A. Cosgrove, *Our Lady the Common Law: An Anglo-American Legal Community, 1870-1930* (New York: New York University Press, 1987).

What was to become the 1924 Association trip to Great Britain had been discussed as early as 1913; Taft to Root, November 8, 1913, Root Papers; Taft to James M. Beck, November 11, 1913, Taft Papers.

It is comparatively easy to explain why lawyers looked to England during this period, more difficult to discern why accountants did the

was involved, as well as a barely concealed desire for respectability in English eyes; but neither diminished the perception of brotherhood nor its effect on foreign relations.

Finally, the ABA elite, like their progressive opponents outside the profession, believed the war to be pregnant with "social possibilities."[75] The dean of the Cleveland bar, Andrew Squire, welcomed the Association to his city in 1918 with the comforting thought that the war had forced the government to "override and sweep aside...statutes strangling cooperation...and regulating in the smallest detail many little things." Now, said Squire, the nation could use its resources efficiently.[76]

At a deeper, almost spiritual, level, some prominent conservatives maintained that the war would purge the United States of the materialism and socialism with which it had been blighted since the turn of the century. Former ABA president James M. Beck (1861-1936) became a tenacious conservative during the 1920s, in part because he believed that the Great War had been fought to preserve traditional values.[77] At the Association dinner of 1917 both

---

same thing. Paul J. Miranti, Jr., *Accountancy Comes of Age: The Development of a American Profession, 1886-1940* (Chapel Hill: University of North Carolina Press, 1990), 83-84.

75. The words are John Dewey's: see John Dewey, "The Social Possibilities of War," in Joseph Ratner, ed., *Characters and Events: Popular Essays in Social and Political Philosophy by John Dewey* (New York: Henry Holt, 1929), 2: 551-60; Allen F. Davis, "Welfare, Reform and World War I," *American Quarterly* 19 (Fall, 1967), 516-33.

76. Andrew Squire, 43 *ABA Rep* 24-25 (1918); Henry R. Rathbone, 42 *ABA Rep* 32 (1917).

77. Morton Keller, *In Defense of Yesterday: James M. Beck and the Politics of Conservatism, 1861-1936,* (New York: Coward-McCann, 1958), 12-13;

Elihu Root and New York corporation lawyer Job Hedges (1862-1925) emphasized the spiritual rejuvenation they assumed would accompany the war. Root pictured the United States before it entered the war as a nation "sleeping in wealth and ease and comfort." Since then, said Root, she had been "growing real instead of superficial.... We have grasped the opportunity for that sacrifice and suffering through which we shall find our souls again." Hedges denied that the United States had even had the moral courage to enter the war voluntarily: "God Almighty took America by the scruff of the neck and threw her in. Our soul was saved by an act of Providence." That remark was followed by five minutes of applause and cheering.[78]

But beyond the oratory, the ABA found it difficult to demonstrate the support of lawyers for the war effort. Senator Edgar T. Brackett (1852-1924), in welcoming the ABA to his hometown of Saratoga, openly voiced the sense of "uselessness" that lawyers felt in time of war. Fifteen years later James Grafton Rogers also noted the "odd sense of helplessness" that hung about the 1917 meeting. The Association passed some patriotic resolutions, invested its funds in Liberty Bonds, and urged local bar associations to aid conscription boards, to furnish patriotic speakers to government agencies, and to conserve the practice of lawyers in military service. It also appointed two special war

---

Walter George Smith, "Civil Liberty in America," 43 *ABA Rep* 209 @ 210-11 (1918).

78. *New York Times*, September 7, 1917, 5; "Speeches at the Annual Dinner," 3 *ABAJ* 655-66 (1917)

committees—though one of these exhibited little activity and the other none.[79]

Perhaps the most significant service rendered by the Association was in lending its name to the activities of John Lowell, Chairman of the ABA's War Service Committee. Lowell, an energetic and personable gentleman of means, volunteered his services to head a clearing house for lawyers required by the federal bureaucracy during the war. Under adverse physical conditions, he provided suitable men to the Shipping Board, the Housing Corporation, and the Department of Labor, as well as to semi-official bodies such as the Y.M.C.A. and the Committee on Training Camp Activities. The Bureau of War Risk Insurance alone obtained three thousand lawyers from Lowell. He also furnished Military Intelligence with men who spoke less familiar European languages.[80] Lawyers who worked for the government were, as a rule, reasonably compensated. Even when ABA members donated time to local draft boards, the government paid their expenses.[81]

The difficulty with the wartime alliance between the government and the legal profession was, of course, that it made defense of war critics by elite lawyers nearly impossible. The organized bar seemed oblivious to one of the lawyer's major

---

79. 42 *ABA Rep* 23 (1917); however, see S. S. Gregory, 42 *ABA Rep* 60 (1917); Rogers, *American Bar Leaders,* 202; 42 *ABA Rep* 29-31, 53-55 (1917).

80. Lawrence G. Brooks to the Editor of the *ABAJ,* January 4, 1923, 9 *ABAJ* 62 (1923); Lucien H. Alexander, "The Legal Profession and the War," 5 *ABAJ* 681 @ 686 (1919); John Lowell, "Report of the Special Committee for War Service of the American Bar Association," 5 *ABAJ* 178 (1919).

81. George Whitelock to Taft, October 6, 1917, Taft Papers.

responsibilities in wartime: to slow summary dispositions of justice. Progressives, who had bitterly criticized the courts a decade earlier, did no better. Before the war, ABA leaders had made no secret of their desire to restrict government regulation; during the war, there was little if any interest in investigating the limits of political dissent.[82]

Selective Service regulations declared that it was "inconsistent" for lawyers to act in "any other way than as disinterested and impartial assistants of the Selective Service System." Far from challenging this subservient role, elite lawyers abandoned professional shibboleths in order to demonstrate their patriotism.[83] The Illinois Bar Association declared that it was both unpatriotic and unprofessional for a member to represent a man seeking to avoid the draft. The president of the California Bar Association, warned his members to absorb the patriotic atmosphere of the country or "slip backward as a profession and [have] others ... take our places." Attorney General Thomas Gregory urged the ABA Executive Committee to "bring all [the] power and influence" of the American Bar Association to bear against that "greatest menace" to the nation—pacifists. ABA committeeman William A. Hayes asserted that it was to the credit of the bar that the few lawyers who opposed the war did so out of "ignorance or perversity."[84]

---

82. Ross, *A Muted Fury*, 166.

83. "Extracts from Selective Service Regulations," in Taft Papers, Reel 186; Auerbach, *Unequal Justice*, 102-06.

84. "Suggestions of Attorney General Gregory to Executive Committee in Relation to the Department of Justice, at Richmond, Va., April 16, 1918," in *Congressional Record*, 65 Cong., 2 sess., vol. 56, 6233-35; A. E. Bolton, "Individuality of Bench and Bar," *California Bar Association Proceedings*, 19 (1917), quoted in Auerbach, *Unequal Justice*, 105-06; William

Although Association leaders never questioned the validity of the war, by its end they doubted its value for accomplishing professional ends. At the meeting of 1918, president Walter George Smith noted with apprehension the sudden increase in federal regulation. Smith refused to criticize wartime emergency measures directly, but he expressed concern at "certain elements who are seizing the opportunity to force changes in our fundamental law." In 1919 there was open and strenuous criticism of the military justice system—which was, after all, a legal organization run by laymen.[85]

ABA leaders realized that despite good intentions and the trumpeting of membership chairman Lucien Hugh Alexander that lawyers had won the war, the organized bar had played "no great part in a crisis that really negatived most of the concepts and machinery with which the profession deals."[86] The trends the legal elite had feared before the war were only intensified by the conflict, and they became even more estranged from the American society they had hoped to direct.

A. Hayes, "The Purpose, History, and Present Program of the American Bar Association," *Reports of the State Bar Association of Wisconsin* 566 @ 581 (1918).

85. Walter George Smith, "Civil Liberty in America," 43 *ABA Rep* 209 @ 216 (1918); Thomas I. Parkinson, 43 *ABA Rep* 62 (1918); 44 *ABA Rep* 44-61, 70-84 (1919); *New York Times*, January 4, 1919, 11; March 16, 1919, III, 5; March 27, 1919, 1.

86. Rogers, *American Bar Leaders*, 202. Alexander's "proof" that lawyers had won the war was that President Wilson, Secretary of War Baker, Secretary of the Navy Daniels, and General Pershing were all lawyers. With similar logic he might have argued that Protestants had won the war.

Chapter 9

Anxious and Ineffectual

1918-1928

One might assume that elite lawyers would be reasonably satisfied with the political, economic, and cultural position of the United States during the decade between the Armistice and the Crash. Republicans had recaptured both houses of Congress in 1918 and the Presidency in 1920. In 1921 the ABA's most respected ex-president, William Howard Taft, became Chief Justice of the Supreme Court. The Twenties were the years of Harding and Coolidge, of Andrew Mellon and Bruce Barton, of Normalcy and the Fordney-McCumber Tariff (1922), a decade when the business of government was business. Superficially, the nation seemed to have returned to its conservative moorings after two decades of progressive experimentation.

Yet, as any number of historians have noted, the progressive movement survived in considerable vigor during the 1920s, even "broadening its horizons" in some areas.[1] Leaders

---

1. Arthur S. Link, "What Happened to the Progressive Movement in the 1920s?" *American Historical Review*, 64 (1959), 850; Clarke A. Chambers, *Seedtime of Reform: American Social Service and Social Action, 1918-1933* (Minneapolis: University of Minnesota Press, 1963); Paul W. Glad, "Progressives and the Business Culture of the 1920s," *Journal of American*

of the American Bar Association were cognizant of this continued strength and were troubled by it. To elite lawyers, America in the '20s was a nation out of joint, threatened by revolutionary socialism, the quickened pace of federal government control, and a growing disrespect for the Constitution, the judiciary, and the legal profession itself. Culturally, as author Bill Bryson has written, "among people of a conservative temperament, it was a time of despair."[2] One *Journal* editorial bemoaned "a generation which, to a rather alarming extent, has forgotten and ignored the good old-fashioned ideals of thrift, economy, conscientious performance of duty and thoroughgoing efficiency." Another of the same year advised that the great need of the nation was "better discipline in the home."[3]

At the 1921 convention, former ABA president and U.S. Solicitor-General James M. Beck—a Philadelphia corporation lawyer whose importance in Association affairs rose as his conservatism deepened—unloosed a torrent of melancholy reproach at contemporary culture in a speech entitled, "The Spirit of Lawlessness." Beck argued that revolt against authority was not only expressed in politics, but could be found in jazz—"a musical crime"—in the abandonment of beauty in the fine arts, in mendacious advertising, in the lack

History, 53 (1966), 75-89; James Weinstein, "Radicalism in the Midst of Normalcy," *Journal of American History*, 52 (1966), 773-790; Burl Noggle, "The Twenties: A New Historiographical Frontier," *Journal of American History*, 53 (1966), 311-312; Otis L. Graham, Jr., *The Great Campaigns: Reform and War in America, 1900-1928* (Englewood Cliffs, New Jersey: Prentice-Hall, Inc., 1971), 97-169.

2. Bill Bryson, *One Summer: America, 1927* (New York: Doubleday, 2013), 70.

3. "Thrift and the Law," 6 *ABAJ* 200 (1920); "Delinquent Children," 6 *ABAJ* 157 (1920); George W. Wickersham, "The Work of the National Crime Commission," 51 *ABA Rep* 233 @ 236 (1926).

of business integrity, and in the attempt to ignore "the fundamental difference of sex... ordained by God himself." In short, said Beck, the "very foundations of the great and primitive institutions of mankind—like the family, the church, and the state—have been shaken." Beck even had doubts about mechanization, that it might even have been better if the automobile had not been invented.[4]

A few decades earlier, ABA leaders had imagined evolutionary progress stretching into the indefinite future under the benign guidance of the legal profession; now they feared a regression beyond their control. Luther Z. Rosser (1857-1923), former counsel for the lynched Leo Frank, told the Association, "The tendency everywhere, in vegetable and animal life is to revert to original primitive types. In the absence of mental and moral training, the human biped steers constantly and inevitably backward to his cave ancestor." A Kansan, F. Dumont Smith (1861-1935), told his audience that though optimists viewed the United States as "the richest, the greatest, [and] the most powerful nation" in history, the nation had recently been afflicted with "fatty degeneration of the soul" and might, as had other great nations of the past, go "down to ruin and death."[5] James Beck believed that human beings were dancing on the edge of the "social abyss." Even

---

4. James M. Beck, "The Spirit of Lawlessness," 46 *ABA Rep* 167 @ 171 (1921); Beck, "The Future of Democratic Institutions," 51 *ABA Rep* 248 @ 260 (1926); Morton Keller, *In Defense of Yesterday: James M. Beck and the Politics of Conservatism, 1861-1936* (New York: Coward-McCann, Inc., 1958), 197; 152, 158.

5. Luther Z. Rosser (1857-1923), "The Illegal Enforcement of Criminal Law," 46 *ABA Rep* 266 (1921); F. Dumont Smith, "The Kansas Industrial Court," 47 *ABA Rep* 208 @ 218 (1922); George T. Page, "Civilization and Liberty," 6 *ABAJ* 47 @ 48 (1920).

the dancing, he thought, had "both in form and in accompanying music, lost its former grace and reverted to the primitive forms of uncivilized conditions."[6]

Even so, progressives of a mild and genial variety also spoke at Association meetings during the period, and they continued to say progressive sounding things. Furthermore, the conservative remedies that the Association conservatives proposed as remedies for the perceived maladies of the age proved dubious or at least impractical. With due allowance for the Association's vastly greater membership and financial resources in the 1920s, the last decade of the organization's first half century mirrored its first. In the 1880s, talk of reform had been attended by negligible action; during the 1920s, reactionary talk had hardly more effect.

The Association's response to the Red Scare of 1919-20 illustrated how temperately even the most jittery of conservative lawyers behaved during the postwar period. Certainly in 1919, President George True Page (1859-1941) demanded that the fires under the American melting pot be rekindled "until every man, whether born in this country or out of it, has either become thoroughly and wholly American...or is driven back to the country from which he came." And Massachusetts Secretary of State Albert P. Langtry (1860-1939) solemnly announced that ten per cent of the residents of Cleveland were Bolsheviks and that the I.W.W. had organized thousands of southern blacks "to kill all rich men."[7]

---

6. Beck, "The Spirit of Lawlessness," 46 *ABA Rep* 167 @ 176 (1921).

7. George T. Page, "Address of the President," 44 *ABA Rep* 151 @ 157-58, 161 (1919); Page, "Civilization and Liberty," 6 *ABAJ* 47 (1920); James Grafton Rogers, *American Bar Leaders* (Chicago: American Bar Association, 1932), 199. Page himself apparently had Polish forebears, whom he

Despite such inanity, Association leaders remained, as a group, more level headed than, say, contemporary Justice Department officials. Former Senator Albert Beveridge (1862-1927) strongly criticized deportations of aliens and warned that they were not only unfair but impolitic: radicals might use them to gain popular sympathy and the moral high ground.[8] Then too, during the summer of 1919, the Association called a halt to the red-baiting activities of Rome Brown. The only direct action taken by the ABA in response to the Red Scare was submission to the membership of a vague referendum calling for the use of necessary force "to maintain at all hazards the supremacy of the law and to suppress disorder and punish crime"—hardly an extreme proposition for an association of lawyers.[9] In any case, if ABA members had joined extremists in advocating summary action against radicals, that assent would have negated the ideals of their profession.

At the time, the ABA leadership was more concerned with extricating itself from the controversy surrounding United States entrance into the League of Nations. At the convention of 1918, three speakers endorsed a strong association of nations, and Associate Justice John H. Clarke

---

did not mention. *Boston Globe*, September 3, 1919, 4. The statements of Langtry, who was an editor by profession, were not published in the *ABA Report.*

8. Albert J. Beveridge, "The Assault upon American Fundamentals," 45 *ABA Rep* 188 @ 213-16 (1920): "One ignorant stump speaker of the 'stand-them-before-a-stone-wall-and-shoot-them-at-sunrise' type, creates more sympathy for so called 'radicalism' than a thousand street-corner orators." (215)

9. 6 *ABAJ* 3 (1920). Preliminary voting showed 4950 in favor and 58 against. To appreciate the ABA's moderation, see Robert K. Murray, *Red Scare: A Study in National Hysteria, 1919-20* (New York: McGraw-Hill, 1955).

dedicated his address to the proposition that it was the duty of the legal profession to help secure American membership in the League.[10]

By the following year, enthusiasm for the League had waned. David Jayne Hill (1850-1932), a diplomat and noted critic of Woodrow Wilson, was invited to deliver an attack on the Treaty of Versailles, and even Secretary of State Robert Lansing (1864-1928), who spoke the following day, agreed that Hill's "juristic approach" was the key to world peace. A special committee on the League divided three to two in *favor* of American membership in the League, but action on their report was delayed until 1920s, when the Executive Committee barred discussion on grounds that League membership "had become a political issue."[11]

One problem with the League of Nations was that it reminded elite lawyers of a legislature.[12] ABA leaders instead preferred the United States join the Permanent Court of

---

10. John H. Clarke, "A Call to Service: The Duty of the Bench and Bar to Aid in Securing a League of Nations to Enforce the Peace of the World," 43 *ABA Rep* 225 @ 233 (1918); Federico Cammero, "The Present Value of Comparative Jurisprudence," 43 *ABA Rep* 303 (1918).

11. George T. Page, "Address of the President," 44 *ABA Rep* 151 (1919); David Jayne Hill, "The Nations and the Law," 44 *ABA Rep* 171 (1919); Robert Lansing, "Some Legal Questions of the Peace Conference," 44 *ABA Rep* 238 (1919); Dexter Perkins, "David Jayne Hill," *DAB*, Supplement 1, 401-02; 6 *ABAJ* 190-99 (1920); *New York Times*, August 17, 1920, 3 and August 28, 1920, 6; Edgar A. Bancroft to the *ABAJ*, June 12, 1920, Taft Papers, Reel 219.

12. Walter S. Logan, 22 *ABA Rep* 7 (1899); Keller, *In Defense of Yesterday*, 53, 104; David J. Brewer, "A Better Education the Great Need of the Profession," 18 *ABA Rep* 441 @ 454, 456 (1895); "The Lawyer and the World Court," 12 *ABAJ* 100 (1926); Rokuichiro Masujima, "Address," 46 *ABA Rep* 245 @ 251 (1921).

International Justice. Elihu Root and James Brown Scott (1866-1943), chairman of the Committee on International Law, had helped frame the protocol under which the World Court began operation in 1922. By voice vote, the 1923 annual meeting endorsed U.S. membership in the Court, subject only to the reservations drawn up by Charles Evans Hughes. Only a few scattered noes were heard in the hall.[13]

Like other conservative Americans, ABA leaders were also shaken by the Russian Revolution. In 1921, James Beck pronounced the Bolsheviks "a possibly greater menace to western civilization than has occurred since Attila and his Huns stood on the banks of the Marne." A year before, President Hampton Carson called Bolshevism a dragon "with flaming eyes, poisonous fangs, flapping wings and cruel claws." The legal elite viewed revolutionary socialism as incompatible with the rule of law. Communism, they believed, was no wave of the future but a reversion to past ages of unreason when priests, not lawyers, held sway, its creed a "Great Idea" that had "been revealed to [communists] and to them alone...and that is nothing but pure theocracy."[14]

---

13. John D. Hicks, *Republican Ascendancy, 1921-1933* (New York: Harper & Row, 1960), 145-46; "Lawyers for the World Court," *New York Times*, September 3, 1923, 12; 48 *ABA Rep* 105 (1923); "The President's Proposal," 9 *ABAJ* 160 (1923). Although the United States did not join the Court until after World War II, in 1924, Manley O. Hudson, himself later a member of the Court, began publishing summaries of World Court opinions in the *ABA Journal*.

14. Beck, "The Spirit of Lawlessness," 46 *ABA Rep* 167 @ 173 (1921); Hampton Carson, "The Evolution of Representative Constitutional Government," 45 *ABA Rep* 151 @ 170 (1920); "Justice and Civilization," 7 *ABAJ* 234 (1921); David Jayne Hill, "The Nations and the Law," 44 *ABA Rep* 171 @ 174 (1919); Frank O. Lowden, "Fundamentals of

Fear of revolutionary socialism was so great that a few bar leaders even flirted with another "Great Idea": fascism. In "The Spirit of Lawlessness," James Beck expressed a rough respect for the *fascisti,* "a band of resolute men" who had preserved the Italian government from being overthrown by taking "law into their own hands, as did vigilance committees in western mining camps." When the Association made its official visit to Europe in 1924, a delegation of members headed by Supreme Court Justice Edward T. Sanford (1865-1930) paid a courtesy call on Mussolini and "expressed admiration for Italy's prosperity and progress."[15]

This tip of the hat towards fascism could be only a passing aberration. Fascism was predicated on totalitarian power exercised by a central government, the sort of power loathed by elite lawyers. While progressives mourned the dismantling of federal controls after World War I, conservatives disapproved of the extensive bureaucracy that remained. In 1922 President C. A. Severance warned his colleagues that governmental powers tended to expand after wars and that

---

Government," 8 *ABAJ* 475 @ 478 (1922); Viscount Cave, "The Future of International Law," 45 *ABA Rep* 181 @ 186 (1920); "Report of the Special Committee on American Citizenship," 49 *ABA Rep* 255 @ 257 (1924); Sir Auckland Geddes, "The Ancient Problem," 45 *ABA Rep* 171 @ 179 (1920).

15. Beck, "The Spirit of Lawlessness," 46 *ABA Rep* 167 @ 173 (1921); however, see "Report of the Committee on American Citizenship," 49 *ABA Rep* 255 @ 259 (1924); "American Lawyers See Mussolini," *New York Times,* August 14, 1924, 2. The Association was at this time investigating designs for an official seal. Someone, perhaps Frederick Wadhams, suggested the adoption of a device with fasces. Hampton Carson was frank in his disapproval, arguing that the fasces had "no proper association with the administration of justice in America." Carson to Wadhams, May 15, 1925, Carson Papers.

if lawyers did not check the federal bureaucracy, they were inviting disaster. More agitated still was Floyd E. Thompson (1887-1960), an Illinois Supreme Court judge and Chairman of the Section of Criminal Law. Thompson charged that the "brave heart of American business [was] being broken by government intermeddling." Americans needed to waken from their lethargy and defend their liberties "against this octopus of paternalism or it will suck the very life blood of the nation!"[16]

Though Thompson's tirade was probably the most agitated pronouncement on government expansion published by the American Bar Association during the Twenties, its sentiment was echoed in countless other addresses and reports during that decade.[17] The *Journal* did reprint one speech disparaging elite fears of paternalism, but its author, an obscure Iowa attorney, also denounced "Socialism, Communism, I. W. W.-ism, La Follette-ism or any other extreme radical proposal" and based his enthusiasm for increased governmental regulation on a conviction that a conservative judiciary would prevent federal encroachment on individual liberties.[18]

---

16. Cordenio A. Severance, "The Constitution and the Individual," 47 *ABA Rep* 163 @ 174, 176 (1922); Floyd E. Thompson, "Paternalism and Lawlessness," 48 *ABA Rep* 591 @ 593 (1923).
17. For instance, Frank O. Lowden, "Fundamentals of Government," 8 *ABAJ* 475 @ 476 (1922); R. E. L. Saner, "Governmental Review," 49 *ABA Rep* 127 @ 136 (1924); Chester I. Long, "The Advance of the American Bar," 51 *ABA Rep* 158 @ 174 (1926); Thomas James Norton, "National Encroachments and State Aggressions," 51 *ABA Rep* 309 (1926).
18. Dwight G. McCarty, "Protecting the Public: Encroachment of Social Legislation on Private Rights," 11 *ABAJ* 36 (1925); William Draper

Despite consistent opposition to the growth of the federal government, few convention speakers made specific suggestions about how it might be checked. Both ABA President Chester I. Long (1860-1934) and Columbia University President Nicholas Murray Butler (1862-1947)—the latter writing for the *Journal*—denounced federal grants-in-aid. Long called them "vicious in principle [and] destructive of local self-government" but urged only that such legislation "not be extended into other fields not now occupied."[19] The Child Labor Amendment sent to the states by Congress in June 1924 did come under fire from a few ABA leaders, but the Association itself took no position on the question until the amendment was revived during the New Deal. Then the ABA appointed a special committee to oppose it.[20]

In 1918, however, the leadership of the American Bar Association did make a serious effort to oppose national prohibition. As with ABA resistance to other progressive reforms, opposition to prohibition developed only after the first decade of the century. Earlier Association leaders had cautiously endorsed the temperance movement. In 1888, President George G. Wright predicted that, at the very least, the saloon

---

Lewis, "Adaptation of the Law to Changing Economic Conditions," 11 *ABAJ* 11 (1925).

19. Chester I. Long, "The Advance of the American Bar," 51 *ABA Rep* 158 @ 174 (1926); Nicholas Murray Butler, "The New American Revolution," 10 *ABAJ* 845 (1924).

20. Long, "The Advance of the American Bar," 173; Norton, "National Encroachments and State Aggressions," 310-312; Nicholas Murray Butler, "The New American Revolution," 849; Thomas W. Hardwick, "The Regulation of Commerce Between the States under the Commerce Clause of the Constitution of the United States," 42 *ABA Rep* 215 @ 224-25, 230-31 (1917); "The LaFollette Amendments," 8 *ABAJ* 418 (1922); 21 *ABAJ* 11 (1935).

was "doomed," and he warned his colleagues that in the matter of alcohol restrictions the people would have their way; "those opposed had as well get off the track or be run over and injured pecuniarily, politically and every way by the oncoming train freighted with...temperance determination."[21]

During the 1880s anti-liquor crusaders had concentrated on enacting state and local laws. Only after 1913 did the Anti-Saloon League and its allies try to amend the Constitution. At this point, elite lawyers began to join the opposition. They argued that sumptuary legislation should not be incorporated into the Constitution; that the "centralization" and "paternalism," inherent in Prohibition, would weaken both personal character and state sovereignty; and that government inability to enforce Prohibition would lessen respect for all laws. For instance, in his presidential address of 1917, George Sutherland (1862-1942) criticized what he viewed as an American "mania for regulating people" and charged that Prohibition would cause the loss of independence that had once allowed "the Anglo-Saxon to throw off the yoke of monarchical absolutism."[22] The legal elite also opposed Prohibition from motives less lofty. Most enjoyed their social glass (especially in convention assembled) and

---

21. George G. Wright, "Address of the President," 11 *ABA Rep* 169 @ 215 (1888); Cortlandt Parker, "Address of the President," 7 *ABA Rep* 147 @ 182 (1884); Alexander R. Lawton, "Address of the President," 6 *ABA Rep* 137 @ 170 (1883).

22. George Sutherland, "Private Rights and Government Control," 42 *ABA Rep* 197 @ 201-04 (1917); Elihu Root, "Address of the President: Public Service by the Bar," 41 *ABA Rep* 355 @ 370-71 (1916); F. Dumont Smith, *The Constitution: Its Story and Battles* (Los Angeles: Kerr-Jefferson Company, 1923), 393-94.

were not amused at middle class reformers trying to regulate elite behavior.[23]

In August 1918, nine months after Congress had approved the prohibition amendment and had sent it to the states, the ABA Committee on Jurisprudence and Law Reform submitted a resolution to the convention that would have put the Association in opposition to both the prohibition and women's suffrage amendments. The committee claimed to express no opinion as to the merits of either proposition but maintained that the amendments should be opposed because they made the national government "an instrument by which the people of some parts of the country may impose their ideas regarding the conduct of life upon the people of other sections." So convoluted was the language of the resolution that one member asked if he had understood it correctly. Once its thrust was clear, it encountered serious opposition. After a single speech from the floor favoring women's suffrage, the assembly voted to postpone the matter indefinitely by a vote of 123 to 87.[24]

Such a vote would have killed most other measures, but the leadership thought they might win a vote against prohibition alone. The next day, after the wording of the resolution had been tightened and the reference to women's suffrage dropped, the measure was reintroduced. Prohibition supporters vainly protested on parliamentary grounds. Not a single member of the Association leadership supported them.

---

23. The role of the wealthy in opposing, and then in helping to repeal, Prohibition was the subject of extensive comment in the Twenties and Thirties. Paul A. Carter, *Another Part of the Twenties* (New York: Columbia University Press, 1977), 88-99.

24. 43 *ABA Rep* 45-47, 65-67 (1918).

Everett Wheeler, George Sutherland, J. M. Dickinson, S. S. Gregory, Henry St. George Tucker, and Simeon Baldwin—all former presidents of the American Bar Association—opposed the Prohibition amendment. A letter from Elihu Root did the same. Henry St. George Tucker urged the rank-and-file not to ignore the advice of "the old landmarks...these old 'Fathers in Israel'...these men that we delight to honor and look up to." But, for once, a rump assembly did just that and voted the resolution down, 75 to 68.[25]

During the early years of national prohibition, the *Journal* exhorted Association members to support enforcement. So long as prohibition retained wide public support, ABA leaders had little alternative. Lawyers had sworn to support the Constitution; and the American Bar Association, committed to preserving the rule of law, could hardly recommend, or even officially wink at, its violation. U. S. Circuit Court Judge Kimbrough Stone (1875-1958) cautioned elite lawyers that respect for the law was "the keystone of our social arch. When it crumbles we will be buried in the collapsing masonry."[26] In 1921, Frederick Wadhams was horrified to discover that committee chairman Thomas Shelton (1870-1931), while planning a dinner in honor of a visiting British dignitary, had arranged for champagne and scotch to be sent to the venue via a foreign embassy. Wadhams warned Shelton he

---

25. 43 *ABA Rep* 97-113 (1918); also see various correspondents of Henry St. George Tucker, August 1918, Tucker Papers.

26. H. K. T., "Supporting the Constitution," 10 *ABAJ* 790-91 (1924); Kimbrough Stone, "Need to Enforce Respect for Law," 8 *ABAJ* 162-65 (1922); cf. Pierce Butler, "Some Opportunities and Duties of Lawyers," 48 *ABA Rep* 209 @ 222 (1923); Nicholas Murray Butler, "The New American Revolution," 10 *ABAJ* 845 @ 848 (1924).

was making a "great mistake," that the source of the alcohol "would surely leak out and subject the Association to very severe criticism."[27]

By 1926, however, the Association began to reflect the changing mood of the nation. The mayor of Chicago attacked prohibition laws at that year's convention, ostensibly in the interest of urban law enforcement.[28] In 1927, elite New York attorneys founded an anti-prohibition society incorporated as the Voluntary Committee of Lawyers, with Joseph Choate, Jr. (1876-1968), as chairman of the organization's executive committee, and Harrison Tweed (1885-1969) as treasurer. Anti-prohibition arguments made by these men were variations on the themes heard in 1918, and their lobbying efforts at the ABA conventions of 1929 and 1930 were so successful that the 1930 convention approved polling the membership on the issue. A remarkable three-fourths of the members participated, and the outcome of the referendum was a vote of 13,779 to 6,340 in favor of repeal. According to student of

---

27. Frederick Wadhams to Hampton Carson, July 11, 1921, Carson Papers. Shelton had already acquired the wine and whiskey before he received Wadhams's letter, but he managed to get rid of it before attracting attention.

28. William E. Dever (1862-1929), "The Problem of Law Enforcement in the Large Cities of the United States," 51 *ABA Rep* 221 (1926). Dever was followed on the program by George Wickersham, who mildly defended prohibition from Dever's assault. Ironically, Dever had reversed the lax enforcement policy of his predecessor, "Big Bill" Thompson, and had cracked down on bootleggers. The resulting destabilization of the industry resulted in a scramble for increased market share by the surviving entrepreneurs, resulting in about four hundred violent deaths and giving Chicago an international reputation for gangsterism. Samuel Walker, *Popular Justice: A History of American Criminal Justice* (New York: Oxford University Press, 1980), 181.

Prohibition David Kyvig, the two-to-one vote by the ABA "dealt national prohibition a severe blow."[29]

In 1922, the rise of international communism and the fear of expanding central government combined with the elite's longstanding distrust of the New Immigration to produce the most significant Association creation of the 1920s, the Committee on American Citizenship, created by the Executive Committee during its midwinter meeting of 1922.[30] Future ABA president Robert E. Lee Saner (1871-1938) became chairman, and committee members included the North Dakota supreme court judge Andrew A. Bruce (1866-1934) and former president Walter George Smith (1854-1924), both of whom had been outspoken in their criticism of postwar cultural trends.

Although in some respects a reincarnation of Rome Brown's Recall Committee, the Citizenship Committee was more fortunate in its first chairman, who possessed what James Grafton Rogers called "winning social qualities." Saner was a Mason, a Shriner, and a Methodist, and he had filled "nearly every subordinate post in the Association before coming to the presidency." Thousands of lawyers called him Bob. Saner used his influence, first as a member of the Executive Committee and then as president, to extract large appropriations for his Committee. In its second year, it received a larger appropriation than the Association had ever

---

29. David E. Kyvig, *Repealing National Prohibition* (Chicago: University of Chicago Press, 1979), 128-29; "A Referendum on Prohibition," 16 *ABAJ* 343 (1930); "Announcement of President Boston on Referendum," 16 *ABAJ* 756 (1930).

30. John Higham, *Strangers in the Land: Patterns of American Nativism, 1860-1925,* 2nd ed. (New York: Atheneum, 1973), 254-77, 300-24.

approved before. In 1924 its budget swelled to $11,500, or 30% of the appropriations for all twenty-eight ABA committees. Even when the reins of leadership fell to lesser lights, the Citizenship Committee was bolstered with hefty subsidies.[31]

In its first report, the Committee defined its mission as an attempt "to stem the tide of radical, and often treasonable, attack upon our Constitution, our laws, our courts, our lawmaking bodies, our executives and our flag, to arouse to action our dormant citizenship, to abolish ignorance, and crush falsehood, and to bring truth into the hearts of our citizenship."[32] To achieve this end, the Committee trusted to the theory that erroneous action could be checked by education—even though the ideas the Committee was attempting to teach were difficult to define and more mystical than rational.

In 1923 Saner told the National Education Association that there was "no room in the American conscience for the gospel of the socialistic agitator," that the schools "should no more consider graduating a student who lacks faith in our government than a school of theology should graduate a minister who lacks faith in God." Saner's Committee also published an affirmation of political faith called "Our Citizenship Creed" in which the confessor pledged to inform himself about the United States Constitution and swore to make patriotism "a constituent part of [his] religion" and the Constitution "as actual a part of [his] life and...religion as the Sermon on the Mount." The same quasi-religious aura was evident in the Committee's oft-stated major objective: "To re-

---

31. "Program for Promoting American Ideals," 8 *ABAJ* 585 (1922); Rogers, *American Bar Leaders*, 222-225; 49 *ABA Rep* 243 (1924); Landon, *The Honor and Dignity of the Profession*, 47, 60.
32. 47 *ABA Rep* 416 (1922).

establish the Constitution of the United States and the principles and ideals of our government in the minds and hearts of the people."[33]

Perhaps because the disparagement of the Constitution became more intellectually fashionable after the publication of Charles Beard's *Economic Interpretation of the Constitution of the United States* (1913), vague but pious references to the Constitution were introduced into more Association speeches and literature than in any previous era of the organization's history. In 1918 Hampton Carson said that in "so far as the thoughts of mortals can approach the Divine Mind, the architecture of our Constitution resembles that of the heavens." Thomas J. Norton (1863-1956), a Chicago railroad lawyer who had written a popular exposition of the document, declared it was "not of a past age but for all time....as unchangeable as are the principles of morals covered by the Ten Commandments." Ben W. Hooper (1870-1957), former governor of Tennessee and Chairman of the Railroad Labor Board, said there was "no problem of society or industry that [could not] be solved within the four corners of the Constitution," and he urged lawyers to "thank Almighty God for the inspiration that guided the genius which fashioned it." Even before the *ABA Journal* began publishing a series on "Decisive Battles of Constitutional Law" in 1923, a reader compliment-

33. Ross, *A Muted Fury*, 62; Saner, "The Schools Must Save America," *National Education Association Journal*, 12 (December, 1923), 395; Cordenio A. Severance, "The Constitution and Individualism," 47 *ABA Rep* 163 @ 188 (1922); 49 *ABA Rep* 271 (1924); 48 *ABA Rep* 442 (1923).

ed the editors for "hammer[ing] on the idea of Constitutional Government," especially by emphasizing its "sacredness."[34]

Thomas Norton declared that the legal profession must compel the teaching of the Constitution in grade schools so that every citizen would recognize a violation of the document on sight and thus dispel some of the ignorance "exhibited in legislative halls." The Citizenship Committee worked with other organizations, such as the American Legion, to secure passage of state laws that required the teaching of the Constitution in all schools and colleges that were supported by state funds. By 1928, thirty-seven states had adopted such laws.[35]

Nevertheless, teachers resisted adding another subject to their curriculum, or they taught the Constitution in such a mechanical way that it frustrated the committee's desire to win the hearts and minds of the children. Saner fancied that "any lawyer would be glad to 'brush up' on the Constitution and conduct a class for the teachers once or twice a week." But the Citizenship Committee discovered to its chagrin that only eight of the twenty-five leading law schools in the country required the study of Constitutional Law, and in two of these eight, the study was confined to its commercial aspects. In 1927 the Committee recommended that boards of

---

34. Hampton Carson, "Heralds of a World Democracy," 43 *ABA Rep* 241 @ 260 (1918); Andrew A. Bruce, 47 *ABA Rep* 68 (1922); Thomas James Norton, "National Encroachments and State Aggressions," 51 *ABA Rep* 309 @ 327 (1926); Norton, *The Constitution of the United States: Its Sources and Its Application* (Boston: Little, Brown & Company, 1922); Ben W. Hooper, "Labor, Railroads and the Public," 9 *ABAJ* 15 @ 18 (1923); S. E. N. Moore to the Editor, 6 *ABAJ* 124 (1920); Herman Belz, "The Constitution in the Gilded Age: The Beginnings of Constitutional Realism in American Scholarship," 13 *American Journal of Legal History* 110 (1969).
35. Norton, "National Encroachments," 327; 53 *ABA Rep* 327 (1928).

law examiners insist that candidates for admission to the bar show themselves "competent to 'support the Constitution' by expounding and teaching it."[36]

Still, Saner never thought an improved school curriculum alone could successfully combat "anti-American activities." Like Rome Brown, Saner enjoyed making public declamations, and he urged the Association to sponsor student oratorical contests in order to propagandize adults and "counteract Bolshevistic tendencies in this country." The Executive Committee balked at Saner's request for $10,000 to fund the contests and at first voted only one-tenth of that amount as the Committee's budget.[37]

Eventually the Association did make substantial financial contributions to, and supply literature for, a series of nationwide oratorical contests, although officially the competitions, featuring ten minute speeches on the Constitution by high school students, were sponsored by city newspapers. Judges for the contests of 1924 and 1925 included Chief Justice Taft and three of the four subsequent "Four Horsemen" of the Supreme Court. Large cash prizes ($3500 for first place) were awarded.

---

36. "Report of the Special Committee on American Citizenship," 49 *ABA Rep* 260, 263-64 (1924); *New York Times*, January 15, 1924, 30; "Teaching the Constitution in the Schools," 14 *ABAJ* 108 @ 109 (1928); George W. Ritter to John W. Davis, March 28, 1923, Davis Papers, III, 14; 49 *ABA Rep* 261 (1924); 52 *ABA Rep* 237-38 (1927). One law school professor who had correctly gaged the spirit of the age said, "I am not teaching my boys the Constitution. I am teaching them how to get into the Supreme Court and win their cases." (237)

37. Saner to Davis, May 1, 1922 and December 14, 1922; ? to Saner, February 13, 1923, Davis Papers, III, 14; 49 *ABA Rep* 266 (1924). John W. Davis, ABA president in 1922-23, suggested that Saner try to raise additional money from private sources.

Saner argued that if these competitions could be continued for a few years, the sentiment of the nation would be "revolutionized and the work of the Red and the Radical would no longer annoy us."[38] President Coolidge agreed, citing participation of nearly a million and half children in the contest as an important factor in the 1924 voters' rejection of La Follette's Progressives. A Chicago daily, less impressed, doubted the benefits of rewarding children for "pleasant vocalizing of borrowed truisms."[39]

In 1925, Josiah Marvel (1866-1930), Saner's successor as committee chairman, persuaded AT & T to broadcast a series of radio addresses on its network. Speakers included John W. Davis, Governor Albert Ritchie of Maryland, ABA President Charles Evans Hughes, and both a Methodist and an Episcopal bishop. The Committee insisted that radio addresses by "distinguished lawyers on the Constitution [had been] received with the greatest interest," although it apparently made no effort to discover who might have been listening. An attempt to produce a second series in 1926 failed for lack of prestigious volunteers to make the speeches.[40]

Another project of the Citizenship Committee was promoting patriotic holidays, not only Memorial Day and the Fourth of July but Patriot's Day (April 19), Thanksgiving, and

---

38. *New York Times*, June 7, 1924, 5; May 9, 1925, 1; R. E. L. Saner, 49 *ABA Rep* 88 (1924); "Report of the Special Committee on American Citizenship," 49 *ABA Rep* 255 @ 266 (1924).

39. *New York Times*, May 9, 1925, 1; "The Oratorical Contests," 11 *ABAJ* 309 (1925).

40. Josiah Marvel to Members of the American Bar Association, May 18, 1925, Carey Papers; 11 *ABAJ* 441 (1925); Report of the Standing Committee on American Citizenship," 50 *ABA Rep* 335 @ 336 (1925); 52 *ABA Rep* 235 @ 238 (1927); 53 *ABA Rep* 325 @ 326 (1928).

Constitution Week (September 16-22). The Committee urged lawyers to become "Minute Men of the Constitution" by serving as speakers on "all possible occasions." It provided suggestions for organizing celebrations, printed literature, and produced outlines of suggested speeches. The Committee went so far as to recommend biblical texts for clergymen that "would call attention to the blessings of our form of government."[41]

The suggested outline for the Patriot's Day celebration commenced with a recitation of Emerson's "Concord Hymn" and the Preamble to the "immortal" Constitution, but it quickly got down to business, attacking the Russian government and "anyone [who] tells you that we have outgrown the Constitution, that the rich are grinding down the poor, that this or that class do not enjoy equality of opportunity, [or] that other governments are better than ours." In a forward, the Committee cautioned sponsors that in "individual cases you may not deem it advisable to hand this outline to your prospective speaker; but we thought . . . it might save you the trouble of explaining the nature of the address desired."[42]

The Citizenship Committee also produced pamphlets and booklets such as "The Story of the Constitution," "The Declaration and the Constitution," and "The Real George Washington"—the latter described as an attempt to help the first President compete with the "leading actors of the movies [and] the notorious figures on the stage." By 1933, the

---

41. Saner to Carey, March 31, 1923, Carey Papers; "Report of the Special Committee on American Citizenship," 49 *ABA Rep* 255 @ 263, 265 (1924).
42. "Suggested Outline for Address on Patriots Day, April 19," in Carey Papers.

Committee had distributed over 150,000 copies of these three pamphlets alone.[43]

In 1923 *ABA Journal* supplemented the Committee's work by publishing what it called The "New Federalist" Series. These articles, written by elite lawyers and judges but "adapted to the fair intelligence of both native and foreign-born citizens," were distributed to newspapers and magazines simultaneously with their publication in the *Journal.* The Citizenship Committee claimed that the articles had been "widely republished throughout the United States" but provided no figures and never repeated the experiment.[44]

One avid enthusiast of literature distribution was the Kansas lawyer F. Dumont Smith (1861-1935), the third and most reactionary of the Citizenship Committee chairmen. His "Story of the Constitution" was blatantly racist, as was the book-length version, *The Constitution: Its Story and Battles* (1923)—probably the only American constitutional history ever written to devote an entire chapter to the exploits of the legendary Anglo-Saxons Hengist and Horsa. In the book, Smith condemned the Fourteenth, Fifteenth, Seventeenth, Eighteenth, and Nineteenth Amendments as "hasty [and] ill-considered." He called the "wholesale enfranchisement of a servile race...a ghastly mistake" and declared that many American women were as "backward, politically, as they were

---

43. "Revitalizing Our National Heroes," 12 *ABAJ* 33 (1926); "Report of the Committee on American Citizenship," 51 *ABA Rep* 361 (1926); Sunderland, 109.

44. The 'New Federalist' Series," 9 *ABAJ* 161 (1923); 9 *ABAJ* 142 (1923); "American Citizenship Movement" (printed announcement) in Carey Papers; "Report of the Special Committee on American Citizenship," 49 *ABA Rep* 255 @ 267 (1924).

in the Middle Ages." Representative institutions, he declared, had been developed by men who were "tall, large-boned, powerfully built, fair-haired, blue-eyed, and very light-skinned."[45] When, in 1926, the ABA Executive Committee was asked to provide a list of reference books for the newspapers' oratorical contest, Smith was appointed chairman of the special committee to draw it up. *The Constitution: Its Story and Battles* was cited as one of seven works considered "more or less indispensable for students of the Constitution."[46]

A few progressive ABA members at least indirectly opposed the Committee on American Citizenship. Robert L. Hale (1884-1969), a legal realist at Columbia Law School and a frequent contributor to the *Journal,* criticized the "pious and emotional and unthinking acceptance of 'fundamental principles'" as a "cheap substitute for...critical thinking." Roscoe Pound admonished the convention of 1924 that it was "not the business of the lawyer to fight an obstinate rear guard action in such a period of legal growth.... We shall attain nothing by vain attempts to convince laymen that all things legal are in

45. F[rederick] Dumont Smith, *The Constitution: Its Story and Battles* (Los Angeles: Kerr-Jefferson Company, 1923), 24-26, 387, 389, 308, 394, 20. Even the conservative Thomas J. Norton called Smith's writing "poetry not history."

46. "Report of the Committee on Reference Books on the Constitution," 13 *ABAJ* 166 (1927). The two other committee members were Edgar B. Tolman, editor of the *Journal,* and the great legal draftsman Ernst Freund.

Other "indispensable" books included John Fiske, *The Critical Period in American History*; Thomas J. Norton, *The Constitution of the United States*; James M. Beck, *The Constitution of the United States*; and Charles Warren, *Congress, the Constitution and the Supreme Court.*

substance perfect."[47] Otherwise, liberals within the Association remained quiescent, tending their own committee gardens, being fully aware that the Citizenship Committee retained considerable Association support.[48]

The real check on the activities of men like Bob Saner and Dumont Smith was exercised by the senior members of the Association leadership who were repelled by the exaggeration and boosterism—that is to say, bad taste—of the Americanization crusade. John W. Davis, for instance, confessed privately to Wadhams that one of Saner's schemes was "bizarre." And when Saner tried to coax a commendation of his Constitution Week celebration from Simeon Baldwin, the venerable founder replied tersely that the Citizenship Committee had used the term "re-establish the Constitution" to characterize its mission. "It implies," said Baldwin, "that a re-establishment is at present necessary, to which I could not agree."[49]

Without minimizing the significance of distributing "popular" literature and proselytizing the young, the Association's Americanism campaign appears to have been fairly innocuous considering alternative courses it might have taken. The Association might, for instance, have directed its attention to immigration restriction or lobbying state legislatures to raise bar admission standards. During the same

47. Robert L. Hale, "Some Challenges to Conventional Legal Views," 9 *ABAJ* 329 (1923); Roscoe Pound, "Some Parallels from Legal History," 49 *ABA Rep* 204 @ 223 (1924).

48. Rogers, *American Bar Leaders*, 224; Norbert Brockman, "The Politics of the American Bar Association," 79-80.

49. Davis to Wadhams, April 17, 1923, Davis Papers, III, 14; Baldwin to Saner [draft] on letter of Saner to Baldwin, May 23, 1923, Baldwin Papers.

period the American Medical Association shared the ABA's concern with the expanding federal government, but its resistance to compulsory health insurance and other "state medicine" was more narrowly focused than the ABA's Americanism campaign and therefore probably more effective in producing conservative results.[50]

One unusual beneficiary of the nativist trends within the American Bar Association was the legal aid movement, hitherto a stepchild of the profession. Legal aid societies had first been organized during the last quarter of the nineteenth century but had received little support from local bar associations. Largely dependent on charity, and unable to fashion a strong national network, individual agencies struggled to provide free legal services to the meritorious poor. During World War I, many lawyers who had worked for legal aid societies joined the army, and the poor encountered more legal problems than would have been the case in time of peace.[51]

At the conclusion of the war, public criticism of the legal profession, combined with nativist fears and the Red Scare, spurred lawyers to reconsider their responsibilities to the poor. Legal aid proponents, such as New York's Arthur von Briesen (1843-1920), had previously solicited funds from the

---

50. James G. Burrow, *AMA: Voice of American Medicine* (Baltimore: Johns Hopkins Press, 1963), 152-58. The AMA was, however, unsuccessful in preventing the passage of the Sheppard-Towner Act, which provided federal subsidies for maternity and infant medical care.

51. Auerbach, *Unequal Justice*, 53-59; "Report of the Committee on Legal Aid Work," 47 *ABA Rep* 404 (1922); Reginald Heber Smith, "The Bar Adopts Legal Aid," *Survey*, 47 (October 15, 1921), 81; Philip L. Merkel, "At the Crossroads of Reform: The First Fifty Years of American Legal Aid, 1876-1926," 27 *Houston Law Review* 1 (1990).

wealthy by emphasizing that justice for the underprivileged was "the best argument against the socialist who cries that the poor have no rights which the rich are bound to respect." By 1920s the ABA leadership was ready to adopt this argument and held a symposium on legal aid at its annual meeting. Every speaker agreed on the necessity for legal aid; they differed mainly over whether it should be financed by the government or by the private sector.[52]

Reginald Heber Smith, the nation's foremost expert on legal aid argued that lack of legal redress might lead to a "dangerous sense of injustice, bitterness, and unrest."[53] A Philadelphia lawyer told the story of an Italian immigrant for whom a misunderstanding with the local authorities had been cleared up by his city's legal aid society. That man, said the lawyer, "might have become one of those implacable of all the enemies to the Government, an Italian Red."[54] Charles Evans Hughes, who had recently defended the six Socialists expelled from the New York State Assembly, said that there was no more serious menace than discontent fostered by a belief that a poor man could not enforce his legal rights. "To spread that notion is to open a broad road to Bolshevism."[55] In 1921 the ABA appointed a permanent Committee on Legal Aid with

---

52. "Legal Aid for the Poor," *Annals*, 17 (January, 1901), 165-66; Merkel, 20-28.

53. Reginald Heber Smith, "The Relation between Legal Aid Work and the Administration of Justice," 45 *ABA Rep* 217 @ 220 (1920). Smith had recently published *Justice and the Poor* (1919), a study of legal aid work subsidized by the Carnegie Foundation.

54. Ernest L. Tustin, "The Relationship of Legal Aid to the Municipality," 45 *ABA Rep* 236 @ 242 (1920).

55. Charles E. Hughes, "Legal Aid Societies, Their Function and Necessity," 45 *ABA Rep* 227 @ 235 (1920).

Reginald Heber Smith as Chairman. Although, as usual, the ABA Committee "realized few tangible results," it did provide appropriate leadership until the legal aid bureaus werc strong enough to create their own national organization.[56]

By 1925 the focus of American Bar Association apprehension had shifted from perceived threats of immigrants and Bolsheviks. The Johnson-Reed Act of 1924, with its ethnically-based quota system, not only reduced the number of immigrants entering the United States, it also deflated the nativists. In 1925 the National Americanism Commission of the American Legion complained that Americans had "become apathetic to the monotonous appeal of the patriotic exhorter" and that the "utmost ingenuity" was now necessary to gain attention for its cause.[57]

At the same time, conservatives were heartened by the results of the 1924 election—not necessarily because Coolidge had been returned to office but because La Follette and the forces of "radicalism" had been so resoundingly defeated. That eloquent pessimist James M. Beck was momentarily confounded when he discovered that so many Americans "preferred the old order of things." In his Citizenship Committee report for 1926, Dumont Smith flatly declared that the "menace of Bolshevism [had] passed."[58]

---

56. 46 *ABA Rep* 159, 493 (1921); "Report of the Committee on Legal Aid Work," 47 *ABA Rep* 404 (1922); Reginald Heber Smith, "The Bar Adopts Legal Aid," *Survey*, 47 (October 15, 1921), 81; Smith, "The Interest of the American Bar Association in Legal Aid Work," *Annals* 205 (September, 1939), 108-113; Merkel, 40.

57. Higham, *Strangers in the Land*, 326.

58. Morton Keller, *In Defense of Yesterday*, 166; "Report of the Committee on American Citizenship," 51 *ABA Rep* 361 @ 364 (1926).

The legal elite now returned to other concerns, like its traditional solicitude for the prestige of the legal profession. The best that might be said for that prestige was that during the 1920s it declined more slowly than the prestige of the clergy. The decade had opened with jeers at the exaggerated alarms of Attorney General A. Mitchell Palmer. Then Palmer's successor was forced to resign in disgrace. While running for President in 1924, John W. Davis discovered that his Wall Street practice was more a handicap than an asset, and for similar professional achievement Charles Evans Hughes received some rough handling from progressive senators before his confirmation as Chief Justice in 1930. Nor is it probable that the standing of the legal profession was enhanced by the monkeyshines at Dayton, Tennessee, or by the Sacco-Vanzetti affair.[59]

The popular press also did nothing to increase respect for the legal profession. Yellow journalism was, of course, itself old news in the Twenties; it had grown up with the American Bar Association during the 1880s. Nevertheless, during the next four decades, the legal elite noted that journalists and editors were paying less-and-less homage to the collective wisdom of the bench and bar. In an address entitled "Has the Lawyer Lost Caste?" (1917), Thomas J. O'Donnell of Colora-

---

59. The ABA took no official position on the Scopes or Sacco-Vanzetti trials, but articles supporting the prosecution in Sacco-Vanzetti and the defense in Scopes were published in the *Journal*. William Renwick Riddell, "The Sacco-Vanzetti Case from a Canadian Viewpoint," 13 *ABAJ* 683 (1927); Blewett Lee, "Anti-Evolution Laws Unconstitutional," 11 *ABAJ* 417-21 (1925); Chester I. Long, "The Advance of the American Bar," 51 *ABA Rep* 158 @ 168 (1926).

do went so far as to call contemporary newspapers "lawless, licentious," "unbridled," and "criminal controlled."[60]

In a 1924 speech, future ABA president Guy A. Thompson (1875-1958) presented journalists with a list of requests. The press, Thompson said, should provide "fair and respectful criticism of the courts," that is, publish as few negative comments as possible, especially when discussing constitutional issues. The press should neither report trials in a sensational manner nor portray lawyers as charlatans. It should instead remind its readers that many of the problems with the judicial system were the fault of laymen, especially juries and political hacks. Editors should provide "stalwart and persistent defense against assaults from certain quarters now being made upon our system of government," and they should support the worthy goals of bar associations, helping them increase their memberships and sustaining their calls for higher educational standards for admission to the profession.[61]

Henry W. Taft (1859-1945), brother of the Chief Justice and president of the Association of the Bar of the City of New York, laid partial blame for the failure of technical law reform on the press. As a member of the ABA's Committee on Jurisprudence and Law Reform, he had presented draft bills to the

---

60. T. J. O'Donnell, "Has the Lawyer Lost Caste?" January 20, 1917, speech to the El Paso County Bar Association, in Wheeler Papers. As early as 1905, ABA charter member Alfred Hemenway had declared that "trial by newspaper [was] infinitely more harmful than government by injunction [and] as lawless as the shameful trials of witches in Massachusetts." Alfred Hemenway, "The American Lawyers," 28 *ABA Rep* 309 @ 400 (1905). Hemenway said that all the judges in the Salem witch trials were laymen.

61. Guy A. Thompson, "What the Lawyer Wishes from the Newspapers," 10 *ABAJ* 387 (1924). Thompson was elected president of the American Bar Association in 1931.

House and Senate Judiciary Committees, but, he said, "they attracted little attention from the press, favorable or adverse, and they have since appeared to be sleeping the sleep of death." To Taft, if the press contented itself "with being a mere reporter of news [about the legal profession] and an occasional commentator, frequently critical, it must bear a share of the responsibility for the continuance of present conditions."[62]

At an ABA-sponsored conference with journalists in 1924, New York City lawyer Wilson M. Powell (1872-1935) expressed irritation at such headlines as "Dog Outwits Judge to Decide Rightful Owner" and "Court Rules Lady Can Bob Her Hair." He suggested that newspapermen follow the legal elite and "become a select class operating under license of the state [with] grievance committees as a means for enforcing ethical standards."[63] More realistically, the *Journal* advised attorneys to answer press criticism of courts and lawyers "temperately, concisely and effectively" and warned them to be cautious when journalists were about so as to avoid misquotation.[64]

Press criticism directed at the judiciary most disturbed the legal elite, even though the press was often simply a messenger bearing bad news from legislators, radicals, labor unions, organized crime, and the Ku Klux Klan. Much of the dark mood of the Association in the 1920s may be attributed to the realization that attacks on the courts would continue indefi-

---

62. Henry W. Taft to the Editor, *New York Times*, July 16, 1924, 16. Taft frankly admitted that the bar had "ceased to be the most powerful group in the community," no longer wielding "the influence in public affairs attributed to it by Bryce...and...Tocqueville."

63. 10 *ABAJ* 819-20 (1924).

64. "Proper Defense of Court and Bar," 11 *ABAJ* 100 @ 101 (1925); "The Technique of Misquotation," 13 *ABAJ* 574 (1927).

nitely, that the anti-recall fight had been only a holding action in what a *Journal* editorial called "the Endless Battle for Constitutional Principle."[65]

Former president Walter George Smith blamed the increase in criticism of judges on foreign-born radicals who found "in the calm atmosphere of a court of justice influences deadly to the germs of revolution and disorder and therefore have directed their most desperate efforts to discredit the entire judicial system."[66] A related but more potent threat was the rise of labor union power and violence. Postwar strikes disturbed the legal elite—especially the Seattle general strike (1919), the Boston policemen's strike (1919), and the Herrin Massacre (1922) in Williamson County, Illinois.[67] Nor were their apprehensions diminished when AFL president Samuel Gompers (1850-1924) told the Lusk Committee, "God save us from the courts," or when a railroad labor leader presented with an injunction swore, "To hell with the order of the court." Moorfield Storey was loudly applauded at the 1919 meeting of the National Conference of Commissioners on Uniform State Law when he urged that body to make strikes a criminal offense.[68] Luther Z. Rosser noted that unlike a lynch mob, the labor mob did not "slink away in darkness or fear, but [dispersed] boldly, defiantly, boasting of its deeds"

---

65. 12 *ABAJ* 464 (1926).
66. Walter George Smith, "Civil Liberty in America," 43 *ABA Rep* 209 @ 224 (1918).
67. For instance, George T. Page, "Address of the President," 44 *ABA Rep* 151 @ 167 (1919); Page, "Civilization and Liberty," 6 *ABAJ* 50 (1920); F. Dumont Smith, "The Kansas Industrial Court," 47 *ABA Rep* 208 @ 217 (1922); Morton Keller, *In Defense of Yesterday*, 161-62.
68. Charles Thaddeus Terry, "Law and Order in Industrial Disputes," 9 *ABAJ* 115 (1923); *New York Times*, August 28, 1919, 2.

often surviving long enough "to vote and to exert its corrupting influence upon legislation and administration." Furthermore, said Ben W. Hooper, labor leaders were preaching "the pernicious doctrine that the courts are dominated by the rich and powerful" and thus were making a powerful "effort to poison the minds of millions of people against the courts."[69]

As a remedy against this erosion of faith in the judiciary, the ABA leadership recommended that labor disputes be submitted to courts for adjudication. One *Journal* editorial asked rhetorically if error were "not more likely to be avoided in the calm atmosphere of the temple of justice than in the passion and bitterness of industrial strife." The *Journal* argued further that lay arbitration would be ineffective both because it was "negotiation by advocates and partisans" and because it did "not command that prime essential—the confidence of the contending parties."[70]

Fear of societal disturbance and the perceived need to boost judicial prestige overcame the natural reluctance of Association conservatives to recommend a course of action that would involve increasing governmental power over economic affairs. By 1923 there was considerable sentiment within the ABA for the establishment of state industrial courts. Kansas had established such a court in 1920 and had given it the power to adjust wages and labor conditions in

---

69. Luther Z. Rosser, "The Illegal Enforcement of Criminal Law," 46 *ABA Rep* 266 @ 282-83 (1921); Ben W. Hooper, "Labor, Railroads and the Public," 9 *ABAJ* 15 (1923); John B. Winslow, 6 *ABAJ* 37 (1920).

70. "Industrial Warfare," 8 *ABAJ* 488 @ 489 (1922); "Industrial Warfare," 8 *ABAJ* 560 (1922); Hooper, "Labor, Railroads and the Public," 18; "Fundamental Trouble in Wage Dispute," 8 *ABAJ* 648 @ 649 (1922); "Justice or War," 7 *ABAJ* 168 (1921); "The President's Message," 7 *ABAJ* 660 (1921).

businesses that were "affected with a public interest." Although the Association itself never officially endorsed the idea, industrial courts were supported by the *ABA Journal*; the Committee on Commerce, Trade and Commercial Law; and the National Conference of Commissioners on Uniform State Laws.[71] Columbia Law professor and former Executive Committee member Charles Thaddeus Terry (1867-1923) made it the subject of a glowing speech to the Kansas Bar Association, which the *Journal* reprinted. Terry went so far as to say that he would have rather been the author of the Kansas Industrial Relations Act "than to have written the plays of Shakespeare or the works of Dante, or have discovered electricity."[72] The Supreme Court, less enamored, unanimously struck down the Kansas statute on the grounds that it interfered with freedom of contract under the Fourteenth Amendment.[73]

Another contemporaneous threat to the judicial system was the revived Ku Klux Klan. Even ABA leaders who were unimpeachable nativists flayed the Klan because it usurped the prerogatives of the law and of the courts. In 1923, former ABA president J. M. Dickinson paused long enough during

---

71. 49 *ABA Rep* 52-53, 279-280, 285-88 (1924); M. Louise Rutherford, *The Influence of the American Bar Association on Public Opinion and Legislation* (Philadelphia: privately printed, 1937), 306-07; W. E. Stanley, "The Kansas Industrial Court Act," 6 *ABAJ* 39 (1920); William L. Huggins, "A Few of the Fundamentals of the Kansas Industrial Court Act," 7 *ABAJ* 265 (1921); but also see, John S. Dean, "The Fundamental Unsoundness of the Kansas Industrial Court Law," 7 *ABAJ* 33 (1921).

72. Charles Thaddeus Terry, "Law and Order in Industrial Disputes," 9 *ABAJ* 115 @ 116 (1923).

73. *Wolff Packing Co. v. Court of Industrial Relations* 262 U. S. 522 (1923); *New York Times*, June 12, 1923, 1.

an attack on radicals and immigrants to condemn the Klan as "a vicious disease which will run its course and be a stench in the nostrils of all patriotic people." A *Journal* editorial of the same year referred to the Klan as "this species of midnight mummery" and declared that if Klan members believed "that a night-riding mob can administer justice in an organized community, then the long struggle of the race to give every man the benefit of counsel, a fair hearing, and the protection of orderly methods of testing evidence, has been for them without significance." At the annual meeting of 1923, Justice Pierce Butler warned that the Klan's dominance of "public affairs, public officers and courts by threats and intimidation" was "anarchistic and threaten[ed] society.[74]

While a number of influential ABA members served on urban crime commissions during the decade, the Association itself demonstrated comparatively little interest in what became a national political issue during the period. The ABA did establish a Section of Criminal Law in 1920s, but the Committee's recommendations dealt narrowly with procedural issues, such as the elimination of delays and technicalities in criminal trials. The few convention speeches that touched on the problem had a similar emphasis.[75]

---

74. Dickinson, "National Standards," 9 *ABAJ* 642 @ 645 (1923); "Ignorance of History is No Excuse," 9 *ABAJ* 33 (1923); Pierce Butler, "Some Opportunities and Duties of Lawyers," 48 *ABA Rep* 209 (1923); Henry D. Clayton, "Usurpation of Governmental Functions by Secret Societies," 8 *ABAJ* 626 (1922).

75. Samuel Walker, *Popular Justice: A History of American Criminal Justice* (New York: Oxford University Press, 1980), 161, 169-70; 45 *ABA Rep* 124 (1920); Rutherford, 181-82. From 1909 to 1920, the Association relied upon the American Institute of Criminal Law as a substitute for a Section of its own. The Institute, though legally independent, was associated with

Meanwhile, the *Journal* maintained an air of aggrieved disappointment that newspaper editors would blame courts and lawyers for the problem of crime. It devised a three-point, "workable program for more efficient criminal procedure" that included forcing the most egregious criminal lawyers out of the profession (driving "the false priests from the temple of justice"), restoring more courtroom power to the judiciary, and simplifying "indictments and the whole course of the pleading and procedure."[76]

Despite new threats to the authority of the courts, the legal elite clearly understood what it did not often verbalize: that the greatest challenge to the judiciary came from the legislatures. As had been true from the founding of the organization, the American Bar Association continued to denounce legislative attempts to weaken judicial power and prestige.[77]

During the 1920s, the elite often attacked senatorial progressives, such as Robert M. La Follette (1855-1925) and William E. Borah (1865-1940), who had urged that the "judicial oligarchy" be checked by constitutional amendment.

---

the ABA in much the same manner as the National Conference of Commissioners on Uniform State Laws (Sunderland, 121). Charles S. Whitman, "Unenforceable Law," 46 *ABA Rep* 260 @ 264 (1921); George E. Alter, "Securing a Model of Criminal Procedure," 49 *ABA Rep* 181 (1924); Chester I. Long, "The Advance of the American Bar," 51 *ABA Rep* 158 @ 160 (1926); Guy A. Thompson, "The Missouri Crime Survey," 51 *ABA Rep* 200 @ 219 (1926).

76. "Law Enforcement III: A Workable Program for Improvement," 9 *ABAJ* 784 @ 785 (1923); "Law Enforcement," 9 *ABAJ* 640 (1923); "Protecting the Public," 12 *ABAJ* 700 (1926); "The 'Threefold Necessity' in Effective Law Administration," 13 *ABAJ* 140 @ 141 (1927).

77. "Justice and Civilization," 7 *ABAJ* 234 (1921); "The Endless Battle for Constitutional Principle," 12 *ABAJ* 464 @ 465 (1926).

La Follette, the most venturesome of the progressives, proposed that no lower federal court be permitted to rule on the constitutionality of an act of Congress.[78] The Supreme Court would be allowed that power but only "subject to the right of Congress to nullify the Court's decision by reenacting the law." Borah advocated the more moderate remedy of requiring a majority of seven justices before congressional legislation could be invalidated.[79] Both proposals were repeatedly anathematized at annual ABA meetings and in the *Journal.* In his presidential address of 1923, John W. Davis declared that when these propositions were "reduced to their simplest terms," they stood "naked and undisguised as an attack upon our theory of government under a written constitution." Even William Draper Lewis described the progressive proposals as "the recent stupid attempts to modify the power of the Supreme Court."[80] Again, during this period, the Supreme Court enjoyed broad public support.[81]

---

78. Belle Case LaFollette and Fola LaFollette, *Robert M. LaFollette* (New York: The Macmillan Company, 1953), 2: 1055-57, 1128. La Follette first suggested a constitutional amendment in the summer of 1922 and later repeated the proposal during his Presidential campaign of 1924. He was most exercised over the 5–4 decision in *Hammer* v. *Dagenhart* (1918) that struck down congressional attempts to regulate child labor with the Commerce Clause.

79. LeRoy Ashby, *The Spearless Leader: Senator Borah and the Progressive Movement in the 1920's* (Urbana: University of Illinois Press, 1972), 32-33. Since even Chief Justice Taft regarded three of his brethren as "pretty radical," Borah was confident his plan could achieve the desired result without undermining the traditional separation of powers.

80. John W. Davis, "Present Day Problems," 8 *ABA Rep* 193 @ 206 (1923); "Four to Five Decisions," 9 *ABAJ* 232 (1923); Cordenio A. Severance, "The Proposal to Make Congress Supreme," 8 *ABAJ* 459 (1922); "Four to Five Decisions II.," 9 *ABAJ* 305 (1923); "Letters of

Virtually the only practical support American Bar Association could provide the courts was to lobby for increased judicial salaries during the inflationary postwar years. In 1918 the Executive Committee authorized its first referendum on the question of whether the salaries of federal judges ought to be increased. (The vote was 5750 to 975 in favor.) The Special Committee on Compensation then drafted a bill but, after consulting with members of Congress, declined to introduce it. Later committees did achieve some modest success in Congress, although much of their energy was expended compiling statistics about judicial salaries for the *Reports*.[82]

Another more subtle assault upon the power of the courts was the rising tide of statute law. Nearly everything about the

---

Interest to the Profession," 9 *ABAJ* 334-35 (1923); Thomas J. Norton, "The Supreme Court's Five to Four Decisions," 9 *ABAJ* 417 (1923); Norton, "What Damage Have Five to Four Decisions Done?" 9 *ABAJ* 721 (1923); Moorfield Storey, "The Bar and the U. S. Supreme Court," 9 *ABAJ* 431 (1923); Robert L. Hale, "Judicial Review Versus Doctrinaire Democracy," 10 *ABAJ* 882 (1924); "Preparing for the Supreme Court," 11 *ABAJ* 35 (1925); Chester I. Long, "The Advance of the American Bar," 51 *ABA Rep* 158 @ 167 (1926); William Draper Lewis, "Adaptation of the Law to Changing Economic Conditions," 11 *ABAJ* 11 @ 13 (1925).

81. Ross, *A Muted Fury*, 203, 317: "Critics of the La Follette proposal frequently pointed out that Congress and the state legislatures generally ranked low in public esteem and that the Supreme Court enjoyed broader popular respect, even though many of its individual decisions might be unpopular." (203)

82. Sunderland, 134-35; 43 *ABA Rep* 150-51 (1918); Levi Cooke, 45 *ABA Rep* 88 (1920); R. E. L. Saner, "Governmental Review," 49 *ABA Rep* 127 @ 146; Charles E. Hughes, "Liberty and Law," 50 *ABA Rep* 183 @ 197 (1925); "Counting the Cost," 11 *ABAJ* 652 (1925); *New York Times*, December 7, 1926, 2; 48 *ABA Rep* 467-72 (1923); 49 *ABA Rep* 318-24 (1924); 53 *ABA Rep* 492-94 (1928).

statue-making process ran counter to the instincts of the legal elite: laws were enacted in haste by laymen and members of the lower bar "to satisfy some momentary clamor"; they were promoted by "particular interests" and engendered class strife; they were paternalistic, encouraging the belief that "the state should protect everyone against all the trials and burdens of life." Statutes directly regulated the procedures and operations of the courts, indirectly pre-empted areas of the law that had once been fertile fields for judicial interpretation, and left in their wake confusion and uncertainty for which the entire legal profession was held accountable. President Chester Long suggested in 1926 that lawyers adopt the slogan "Slow down the Legislatures and Speed up the Courts."[83]

The growing volume of laws was an old complaint, but in the nineteenth century the legal elite could at least turn from the confusion of legislative enactments to contemplate the comparative orderliness of the judge-made common law. By the 1920s, such a vision was hard to conjure up. Conservatives were forced to agree with Benjamin Cardozo that there was no longer any "solid land of fixed and settled rules."[84] Even Elihu Root admitted in his presidential address of 1916 that the "vast and continually increasing mass of reported decisions which afford authorities on almost every side of

---

83. Charles Evans Hughes, "Liberty and Law," 50 *ABA Rep* 183 @ 185 (1925); George T. Page, "Address of the President," 44 *ABA Rep* 151 @ 155 (1919); Calvin Coolidge, "The Limitations of Law," 47 *ABA Rep* 270 @ 276 (1922); Pierce Butler, "Some Opportunities and Duties of Lawyers," 48 *ABA Rep* 209 @ 219 (1923); Edson R. Sunderland, "The Exercise of the Rule-Making Power," 51 *ABA Rep* 276 @ 279 (1926); Chester I. Long, "The Advance of the American Bar," 51 *ABA Rep* 158 @ 164 (1926).
84. Benjamin N. Cardozo, *The Nature of the Judicial Process* (New Haven: Yale University Press, 1921), 166.

almost every question admonish us that by the mere following of precedent we should soon have no system of law at all, but the rule of the Turkish cadi who is expected to do in each case what seems to him to be right."

The solution proposed by Root and other members of the legal elite was a "restatement" of the common law, an authoritative description of "generally recognized and accepted legal principles." Root was uncertain about who or what would undertake this task, and so the matter was held in abeyance during World War I.[85] In March 1922, shortly after Root and William Draper Lewis had contrived an endorsement of higher legal education standards at the ABA's Washington Conference, Lewis confided a plan for organizing a permanent body to undertake the drafting of restatements.[86]

Under the guidance of Root and Lewis, the American Law Institute (ALI) was established a few months later on

---

85. Elihu Root, "Address of the President: Public Service by the Bar," 41 *ABA Rep* 355 @ 364-66 (1916).

86. William Draper Lewis to Philip Jessup, August 30, 1937, in Jessup, *Elihu Root*, 2:470-71. One difficulty was that there already existed an organization with a similar purpose, the "American Academy of Jurisprudence," founded in 1914 by James D. Andrews. Andrews, Roscoe Pound's opponent in 1906, was the Chairman of the ABA Committee on Classification and Restatement of the Law. Furthermore, he had excellent window dressing for his Academy. William Howard Taft had been the nominal president until his resignation in April, and Roscoe Pound, Samuel Williston, and Root himself were members of the governing board. Andrews brought a resolution to the 1922 meeting that would have effectively involved the ABA in a promotional scheme to sell subscriptions for his unwritten restatements. The Executive Committee was adamant in its opposition and, after a rancorous debate, easily carried the day. 47 *ABA Rep* 82-94 (1922).

February 23, 1923. Of the 341 persons in attendance at the organizational meeting, only three were not members of the American Bar Association. Lewis became the first director, and Root, with the title of honorary president, provided the clout to obtain a $ 1.1 million endowment grant from the Carnegie Corporation.[87] Because the ultimate form of the proposed restatements remained ambiguous, the ALI was endorsed by virtually all the legal elite, practitioners and law professors, conservatives and progressives. Progressives imagined that the restatements would provide an opportunity to adapt "law to changing economic conditions."[88] Conservatives hoped that the restatements would restore nineteenth-century certainty to the common law and thus provide a bulwark for appellate judges engaged in contest with the legislatures. Progressives soon discovered that the restatements, even those drawn by liberal hands, quickly became conservative systematizations bereft "of any notion that rules had social or economic consequences."[89] Meanwhile, the

---

87. William Draper Lewis, "Plan to Establish American Law Institute," 9 *ABAJ* 77 (1923); Lewis, 48 *ABA Rep* 88-95 (1923); "The Improvement of the Law," 9 *ABAJ* 96 (1923); "The American Law Institute," 9 *ABAJ* 160 (1923); N.E.H. Hull, "Restatement and Reform: A New Perspective on the Origins of the American Law Institute," *Law and History Review*, 8 (Spring 1990), 55-96.

88. Lewis, "Adaptation of the Law to Changing Economic Conditions," 11 *ABAJ* 11 (1925).

89. Lawrence M. Friedman, *A History of American Law*, 676. Grant Gilmore says that Restatements "were the reaction of a conservative establishment, eager to preserve a threatened status quo," while N. E. H. Hull emphasizes that "the driving force behind the ALI's founding was a cadre of progressive law professors who set its original agenda." Both are correct. Gilmore, *The Ages of American Law*, 73; N. E. H. Hull, "Restatement and Reform," 86. See also G. Edward White, "The American Law

conservative Commissioners on Uniform State Laws were dismayed at the manner in which they believed their creations had been ignored or misconstrued by the state courts.[90]

The support of the American Bar Association for legal aid and for the American Law Institute demonstrates both the ideological ambivalence and the essential ineffectiveness of the Association during the 1920s. On those issues conservatives and progressives joined hands yet still achieved little. As for the Association's Americanism campaign, the ABA's hazy notion that domestic radicalism might be vanquished with homilies on the Constitution and the sponsorship of oratory contests for high school students seems more than quaint at a century's remove.

Indeed, the entire first half century of the Association's history makes insubstantial building material for anyone wanting to raise theoretical superstructures, whether hagiographic or demonizing. In theory, the turn-of-the-century American Bar Association ought to have exercised a force commensurate with the eminence of its leaders. Yet an examination of its pre-Depression history reveals an organization often cheerfully adrift, reacting to the larger society rather than commanding it, and often operating with such limited consensus that its sphere of influence hardly extended beyond its convention halls. One exception that proves the rule, the ABA's successful fight against judicial recall, was grounded on a near professional consensus that also took advantage of popular boredom with

---

Institute and the Triumph of Modernist Jurisprudence," *Law and History Review* 15: 1 (Spring 1997), 1-47.

90. "Report of the Committee on Uniformity of Judicial Decision in Cases Arising Under Uniform Laws," 1 *ABAJ* 24 (1915); Jacob Sicherman, "Construction of Clause in Uniform State Laws Providing for Uniformity of Interpretation," 2 *ABAJ* 60 (1916).

what was, in any case, an unfeasible notion. Even then the Association allowed its agenda to be executed by an extremist with his own fish to fry.

Simeon Baldwin died on January 10, 1927, seven months before the organization's 50th annual meeting. Just before leading the 1927 convention in a moment of silence for him, Francis Rawle, the last of the founders, successfully opposed passage of a constitutional amendment that would have restricted the secretary and treasurer to terms of three successive years. Rawle argued that such a measure would break the continuity of the Association, which he said, had been the basis of its success.[91]

Of course, Rawle meant a continuity of leadership. A largely social organization at its founding, the ABA had stumbled into an era of unmanaged expansion while still unintegrated with the state bar organizations and therefore was still heavily dependent on the character of its own leadership. Rank-and-file members had neither vote nor voice in ABA affairs unless they attended the business sessions at annual meetings; and at some conventions in the 1920s, those participants fell below one percent of membership. The inner circle continued to have its way. In honor of its 50th anniversary R.E.L. Saner suggested that the Association publish "a much needed complete and accurate history" of the organization. What it actually commissioned was James Grafton Rogers' biographical sketches of the first fifty

91. 52 *ABA Rep* 32, 40 (1927).

presidents, perhaps in the vague confidence that this opus was nearly the same thing.[92]

The history of the American Bar Association from 1878 to 1928 is important more as a mirror of American society than as a chronicle of organizational accomplishment. Members of the Association felt a need to magnify their professional status, "to parade before the public in an attitude of honor, self-improvement, and devotion to justice" but without exerting too much effort in the process.[93] To compensate for the relatively ineffectual wheel-spinning of much of the Association's organizational machinery, there remained to the "best men of the bar" the delights of the table, the sharing of professional gossip, and the hazy satisfaction of perhaps having done their part to promote the reputation and standing of the profession of law.

---

92. R. E. L. Saner, "Our Fiftieth Anniversary," 11 *ABAJ* 585 (1925); James Grafton Rogers, *American Bar Leaders: Biographies of the Presidents of the American Bar Association* (Chicago: American Bar Association, 1932), v.
93. Lawrence M. Friedman, "Law Reform in Historical Perspective," 13 *Saint Louis Law Journal* 351 @ 358 (1969).

Appendix

APPENDIX A

PRESIDENTS OF THE AMERICAN BARASSOCIATION, 1878-1928

1878-1879	James O. Broadhead	St. Louis, MO
1879-1880	Benjamin H. Bristow	New York, NY
1880-1881	Edward J. Phelps	Burlington, VT
1881-1882	Clarkson N. Potter	New York, NY
1882-1883	Alexander R. Lawton	Savannah, GA
1883-1884	Cortlandt Parker	Newark, NJ
1884-1885	John W. Stevenson	Covington, KY
1885-1886	William Alan Butler	New York, NY
1886-1887	Thomas J. Semmes	New Orleans, LA
1887-1888	George G. Wright	Des Moines, IA
1888-1889	David Dudley Field	New York, NY
1889-1890	Henry Hitchcock	St. Louis, MO
1890-1891	Simeon E. Baldwin	New Haven, CT
1891-1892	John F. Dillon	New York, NY
1892-1893	John Randolph Tucker	Lexington, VA
1893-1894	Thomas M. Cooley	Ann Arbor, MI
1894-1895	James C. Carter	New York, NY
1895-1896	Moorfield Storey	Boston, MA
1896-1897	James M. Woolworth	Omaha, NE
1897-1898	William Wirt Howe	New Orleans, LA
1898-1899	Joseph H. Choate	New York, NY
1899-1900	Charles F. Manderson	Omaha, NE

1900-1901	Edmund Wetmore	New York, NY
1901-1902	U. M. Rose	Little Rock, AR
1902-1903	Francis Rawle	Philadelphia, PA
1903-1904	James Hagerman	St. Louis, MO
1904-1905	Henry St. George Tucker	Lexington, VA
1905-1906	George R. Peck	Chicago, IL
1906-1907	Alton B. Parker	New York, NY
1907-1908	J. M. Dickinson	Chicago, IL
1908-1909	Frederick W. Lehmann	St. Louis, MO
1909-1910	Charles F. Libby	Portland, ME
1910-1911	Edgar H. Farrar	New Orleans, LA
1911-1912	Stephen S. Gregory	Chicago, IL
1912-1913	Frank B. Kellogg	St. Paul, MN
1913-1914	William H. Taft	Washington, DC
1914-1915	Peter W. Meldrim	Savannah, GA
1915-1916	Elihu Root	New York, NY
1916-1917	George Sutherland	Salt Lake City, UT
1917-1918	Walter George Smith	Philadelphia, PA
1918-1919	George T. Page	Peoria, IL
1919-1920	Hampton L. Carson	Philadelphia, PA
1920-1921	William A. Blount	Pensacola, FL
1921-1922	Cordenio A. Severance	St. Paul, MN
1922-1923	John W. Davis	New York, NY
1923-1924	R. E. L. Saner	Dallas, TX
1924-1925	Charles E. Hughes	New York, NY
1925-1926	Chester I. Long	Wichita, KS
1926-1927	Charles S. Whitman	New York, NY
1927-1928	Silas H. Strawn	Chicago, IL
1928-1929	Gurney E. Newlin	Los Angeles, CA

APPENDIX B

MEMBERS OF THE EXECUTIVE COMMITTEE, 1878-1928

1878-1887	Luke P. Poland	St. Johnsbury, VT
1878-1888	Simeon E. Baldwin	New Haven, CT
1878-1880	William A. Fisher	Baltimore, MD
1878-1893	Edward Otis Hinkley	Baltimore, MD
1878-1902	Francis Rawle	Philadelphia, PA
1880-1885	William Allen Butler	New York, NY
1885-1890	Charles C. Bonney	Chicago, IL
1887-1896	George A. Mercer	Savannah, GA
1888-1890	John Randolph Tucker	Lexington, VA
1890-1891	William P. Wells	Detroit, MI
1890-1899	Alfred H. Hemenway	Boston, MA
1891-1895	Bradley G. Schley	Milwaukee, WI
1893-1909	John Hinkley	Baltimore, MD
1895-1899	Charles Claflin Allen	St. Louis, MO
1896-1897	William Wirt Howe	New Orleans, LA
1897-1900	Charles Noble Gregory	Washington, DC
1899-1900	Edmund Wetmore	New York, NY
1899-1901	U. M. Rose	Little Rock, AR
1899-1902	William A. Ketcham	Indianapolis, IN
1899-1902	Henry St. George Tucker	Lexington, VA
1900-1903	Rodney A. Mercur	Towanda, PA
1900-1903	Charles F. Libby	Portland, ME
1901-1903	James Hagerman	St. Louis, MO
1902-1905	P. W. Meldrim	Savannah, GA
1902-1905	Platt Rogers	Denver, CO
1902-1926	Frederick E. Wadhams	Albany, NY
1903-1906	M. F. Dickinson	Boston, MA

1903-1906	Theodore S. Garnett	Norfolk, VA
1903-1906	William P. Breen	Fort Wayne, IN
1905-1908	Charles Monroe	Los Angeles, CA
1905-1908	Ralph W. Breckenridge	Omaha, NE
1906-1909	Charles F. Libby	Portland, ME
1906-1909	Walter George Smith	Philadelphia, PA
1906-1909	Rome G. Brown	Minneapolis, MN
1908-1911	William O. Hart	New Orleans, LA
1908-1911	Charles Henry Butler	Washington, DC
1909-1912	John Hinkley	Baltimore, MD
1909-1912	Ralph W. Breckenridge	Omaha, NE
1909-1912	Lynn Helm	Los Angeles, CA
1909-1920	George Whitelock	Baltimore, MD
1911-1914	Hollis R. Bailey	Boston, MA
1911-1914	Aldis B. Browne	Washington, DC
1912-1915	William H. Burges	El Paso, TX
1912-1915	John H. Voorhees	Sioux Falls, SD
1912-1915	William H. Staake	Philadelphia, PA
1913-1914	Albert W. Biggs	Memphis, TN
1913-1916	William C. Niblack	Chicago, IL
1914-1917	Selden P. Spencer	St. Louis, MO
1914-1917	William P. Bynum	Greensboro, NC
1914-1917	Chapin Brown	Washington, DC
1915-1918	Charles N. Potter	Cheyenne, WY
1915-1918	John Lowell	Boston, MA
1915-1918	Charles Blood Smith	Topeka, KS
1916-1919	Ashley Cockrill	Little Rock, AR
1916-1917	Walter George Smith	Philadelphia, PA
1917-1918	George T. Page	Peoria, IL
1917-1920	T. A. Hammond	Atlanta, GA
1917-1920	U. S. G. Cherry	Sioux Falls, SD
1917-1920	Charles Thaddeus Terry	New York, NY

1917-1920	Robert E. L. Saner	Dallas, TX
1918-1921	Edmund F. Trabue	Louisville, KY
1918-1921	Thomas H. Reynolds	Kansas City, MO
1918-1921	George B. Young	Montpelier, VT
1918-1921	Paul Howland	Cleveland, OH
1919-1922	Thomas C. McClellan	Birmingham, AL
1920-1923	Hugh H. Brown	San Francisco, CA
1920-1923	John B. Corliss	Detroit, MI
1920-1923	John T. Richards	Chicago, IL
1920-1923	W. O. Hart	New Orleans, LA
1920-1924	W. Thomas Kemp	Baltimore, MD
1921-1924	Thomas W. Blackburn	Omaha, NE
1921-1924	William Brosmith	Hartford, CT
1921-1924	S. E. Ellsworth	Jamestown, ND
1921-1924	Thomas W. Shelton	Norfolk, VA
1922-1925	A. T. Stovall	Okolona, MS
1923-1926	Gurney E. Newlin	Los Angeles, CA
1923-1926	Frederick A. Brown	Chicago, IL
1923-1926	Charles S. Whitman	New York, NY
1923-1925	Chester I. Long	Wichita, KS
1923-	Edgar B. Tolman	Chicago, IL
1924-1927	Jesse A. Miller	Des Moines, IA
1924-1927	William M. Hargest	Harrisburg, PA
1924-1927	Amasa C. Paul	Minneapolis, MN
1924-1927	William C. Kinkead	Cheyenne, WY
1924-1925	William C. Coleman	Baltimore, MD
1925-1926	Josiah Marvel	Wilmington, DE
1925-1928	Henry Upson Sims	Birmingham, AL
1925-	William P. MacCracken, Jr.	Chicago, IL
1926-	Edward A. Armstrong	Newark, NJ
1926-	James F. Ailshie	Coeur d'Alene, ID
1926-	J. Weston Allen	Boston, MA

1926-	Frank Pace	Little Rock, AR
1927-	John H. Voorhees	Sioux Falls, SD
1927-1928	Oscar C. Hull	Detroit, MI
1927-1928	James Grafton Rogers	Denver, CO
1927-	Charles A. Boston	New York, NY
1927-	Province M. Pogue	Cincinnati, OH
1927-	Ralph A. Van Orsdel	Omaha, NE
1928-	Thomas W. Davis	Wilmington, NC
1928-	Bruce W. Sanborn	St. Paul, MN
1928-	Guy A. Thompson	St. Louis, MO

APPENDIX C

DATES AND PLACES OF THE ANNUAL MEETINGS, 1878-1928

1878	Aug. 21, 22	Saratoga Springs
1879	Aug. 20, 21	Saratoga Springs
1880	Aug. 18, 19, 20	Saratoga Springs
1881	Aug. 17, 18, 19	Saratoga Springs
1882	Aug. 8, 9, 10, 11	Saratoga Springs
1883	Aug. 22, 23, 24	Saratoga Springs
1884	Aug. 20, 21, 22	Saratoga Springs
1885	Aug. 19, 20, 21	Saratoga Springs
1886	Aug. 18, 19, 20	Saratoga Springs
1887	Aug. 17, 18, 19	Saratoga Springs
1888	Aug. 15, 16, 17	Saratoga Springs
1889	Aug. 28, 29, 30	Chicago
1890	Aug. 20, 21, 22	Saratoga Springs
1891	Aug. 26, 27, 28	Boston
1892	Aug. 24, 25, 26	Saratoga Springs
1893	Aug. 30, 31, Sept. 1	Milwaukee
1894	Aug. 22, 23, 24	Saratoga Springs
1895	Aug. 27, 28, 29, 30	Detroit
1896	Aug. 19, 20, 21	Saratoga Springs
1897	Aug. 25, 26, 27	Cleveland
1898	Aug. 17, 18, 19	Saratoga Springs
1899	Aug. 28, 29, 30	Buffalo
1900	Aug. 29, 30, 31	Saratoga Springs
1901	Aug. 21, 22, 23	Denver
1902	Aug. 27, 28, 29	Saratoga Springs
1903	Aug. 26, 27, 28	Hot Springs, VA
1904	Sept. 26, 27, 28	St. Louis
1905	Aug. 23, 24, 25	Narragansett Pier, RI

1906	Aug. 29, 30, 31	St. Paul
1907	Aug. 26, 27, 28	Portland, ME
1908	Aug. 25, 26, 27, 28	Seattle
1909	Aug. 24, 25, 26, 27	Detroit
1910	Aug. 30, 31, Sept. 1	Chattanooga
1911	Aug. 29, 30, 31	Boston
1912	Aug. 27, 28, 29	Milwaukee
1913	Sept. 1, 2, 3	Montreal
1914	Oct. 20, 21, 22	Washington, DC
1915	Aug. 17, 18, 19	Salt Lake City
1916	Aug. 30, 31, Sept. 1	Chicago
1917	Sept. 4, 5, 6	Saratoga Springs
1918	Aug. 28, 29, 30	Cleveland
1919	Sept. 3, 4, 5	Boston
1920	Aug. 25, 26, 27	St. Louis
1921	Aug. 31, Sept. 1, 2	Cincinnati
1922	Aug. 9, 10, 11	San Francisco
1923	Aug. 29, 30, 31	Minneapolis
1924	July 8, 9, 10	Philadelphia
1925	Sept. 2, 3, 4	Detroit
1926	July 14, 15, 16	Denver
1927	Aug. 31, Sept. 1, 2	Buffalo
1928	July 25, 26, 27	Seattle

APPENDIX D

MEMBERSHIP AND ATTENDANCE AT THE ANNUAL MEETING, 1878-1928

	Membership	*Attendance*
1878	289	75
1879	524	no record
1880	552	97
1881	546	124
1882	571	107
1883	626	120
1884	671	108
1885	702	124
1886	740	137
1887	751	149
1888	752	121
1889	962	158
1890	943	132
1891	1,110	202
1892	1,062	143
1893	1,102	130
1894	1,144	140
1895	1,307	199
1896	1,393	276
1897	1,489	184
1898	1,496	227
1899	1,541	227
1900	1,540	230
1901	1,720	306
1902	1,718	230
1903	1,814	250

	Membership	*Attendance*
1904	2,000	451
1905	2,049	277
1906	2,606	369
1907	3,074	402
1908	3,585	312
1909	3,715	389
1910	3,690	324
1911	4,701	625
1912	5,584	558
1913	8,033	1,023
1914	9,855	1,184
1915	9,609	531
1916	10,636	943
1917	10,884	598
1918	10,995	604
1919	10,677	871
1920	11,941	727
1921	15,153	1,206
1922	17,426	1,447
1923	19,871	1,815
1924	22,024	956
1925	23,318	1,839
1926	24,883	2,116
1927	26,246	1,604
1928	26,595	2,033

Bibliography

Manuscript Collections

Lucien Hugh Alexander Papers, University of Michigan, Ann Arbor

Baldwin Family Papers, Yale University

Charles Henry Carey Papers, Oregon Historical Society, Portland

Margaret J. Carns Papers, Nebraska State Historical Society, Lincoln

Hampton L. Carson Papers, Pennsylvania Historical Society, Philadelphia

John W. Davis Papers, Yale University

Frederick William Lehmann Papers, Washington University Library, St. Louis

John Bassett Moore Papers, Library of Congress

Alton B. Parker Papers, Library of Congress

Roscoe Pound Papers, Harvard Law School Library

Elihu Root Papers, Library of Congress

Harlan Fiske Stone Papers, Library of Congress

George Sutherland Papers, Library of Congress

William Howard Taft Papers, Library of Congress

Everett P. Wheeler Papers, New York Public Library

Books, Articles, and Unpublished Manuscripts

Abel, Richard L. *American Lawyers.* New York: Oxford University Press, 1989.

Altman, James M. "Considering the A.B.A.'s 1908 Canons of Ethics." *Journal of the Professional Lawyer.*(2008), 235-343.

Auerbach, Jerold S. *Unequal Justice: Lawyers and Social Change in Modern America.* New York: Oxford University Press, 1976.

Baldwin, Simeon. "The Founding of the American Bar Association." *ABAJ* 3 (1917), 658-695.

Bannister, Robert C. *Social Darwinism: Science and Myth in Anglo-American Social Thought.* Philadelphia: Temple University Press, 1979.

Belknap, Michal R. *To Improve the Administration of Justice: A History of the American Judicature Society.* Washington: American Judicature Society, 1992.

Bloomfield, Maxwell H. *American Lawyers in a Changing Society, 1776-1876.* Cambridge: Harvard Press, 1976.

Boyd, Susan K. *The ABA's First Section: Assuring a Qualified Bar.* Chicago: American Bar Association, 1993.

Brockman, Norbert. "The History of the American Bar Association: A Bibliographic Essay." *American Journal of Legal History* 6 (1962), 269-285.

___ "Laissez-Faire Theory in the Early American Bar Association." *Notre Dame Lawyer* 39 (April 1964), 270-285.

___ "The National Bar Association, 1888-1893: The Failure of Early Bar Federation." *American Journal of Legal History* 10 (1966), 122-127.

___ "The Politics of the American Bar Association." PhD dissertation, The Catholic University of America, 1963.

Brown, Esther Lucile. *Lawyers and the Promotion of Justice.* New York: Russell Sage Foundation, 1938.

Bryce, James. *The American Commonwealth.* London: Macmillan and Co., 1888.

Burrow, James G. *AMA: Voice of American Medicine.* Baltimore: Johns Hopkins University Press, 1963.
___ *Organized Medicine in the Progressive Era: The Move Toward Monopoly.* Baltimore: Johns Hopkins University Press, 1977.

Calhoun, Daniel H. *Professional Lives in America: Structure and Aspiration, 1750-1850.* Cambridge, Mass.: Harvard University, 1965.

Calvert, Monte A. *The Mechanical Engineer in America, 1830-1910.* Baltimore: The Johns Hopkins Press, 1967.

Fine, Sidney. *Laissez-Faire and the General Welfare State: A Study of Conflict in American Thought, 1865-1901.* Ann Arbor: University of Michigan Press, 1956.

First, Harry. "Competition in the Legal Education Industry." *New York University Law Review* 53 (1978), 311-401.
___ "Competition in the Legal Education Industry (II): An Anti-Trust Analysis." *New York University Law Review* 54 (1979), 1074-1130.

Foster, James Carl. "Lawyers, Professionalization and Politics: Ideology and Organization in the American Bar, 1870-1920." PhD dissertation, University of Washington, 1976.

Friedman, Lawrence M. "Law Reform in Historical Perspective." *St. Louis University Law Journal* (1969), 351-372.
___ *A History of American Law.* New York: Simon and Schuster, 1973.

Furner, Mary O. *Crisis in Advocacy and Objectivity: The Professionalization of Social Science, 1865-1905.* Lexington: University Press of Kentucky, 1975.

Gawalt, Gerard w., ed. *The New High Priests: Lawyers in Post-Civil War America.* Westport, Conn.: Greenwood Press, 1984.

Gilmore, Grant. *The Ages of American Law.* New Haven: Yale University Press, 1977.

Goetsch, Charles C. *Essays on Simeon E. Baldwin.* Storrs, Conn.: The University of Connecticut School of Law Press, 1981.

Haber, Samuel. *The Quest for Authority and Honor in the American Professions, 1750-1900.* Chicago: University of Chicago Press, 1991.

Harbaugh, William H. *Lawyer's Lawyer: The Life of John W. Davis.* New York: Oxford University Press, 1973.

Hays, Samuel P. *The Response to Industrialism, 1885-1914.* Chicago: University of Chicago Press, 1957.

Hinkley, John. "Reminiscences of the American Bar Association." *ABAJ* 21 (1935), 452-458.

Hobson, Wayne Karl. *The American Legal Profession and the Organizational Society, 1890-1930.* New York: Garland Publishing, 1986.

Hofstadter, Richard. *The Age of Reform: From Bryan to F. D. R.* New York: Alfred A. Knopf, 1955.

Hull, N.E.H. "Restatement and Reform: A New Perspective on the Origins of the American Law Institute." *Law and History Review,* 8 (Spring 1990), 54-96.

Hurst, James Willard. *The Growth of American Law: The Lawmakers.* Boston: Little, Brown and Company, 1950.

Jackson, Frederick H. *Simeon Eben Baldwin.* New York: King's Crown Press, 1955.

Jessup, Philip C. *Elihu Root.* New York: Dodd, Mead and Company, 1937.

Johnson, William R. *Schooled Lawyers: A Study in the Clash of Professional Cultures.* New York: New York University Press, 1978.

Jones, Alan. "Thomas M. Cooley and 'Laissez-Faire Constitutionalism': A Reconsideration." *Journal of American History* 53 (March 1967), 751-771.

Katz, Joseph. "The Legal Profession, 1890-1915; The Lawyer's Role in Society: A Study in Attitudes." M.A. Thesis, Columbia University, 1954.

Keller, Morton. *Affairs of State: Public Life in Late Nineteenth Century America.* Cambridge: Harvard University Press, 1977.

___ *In Defense of Yesterday: James M. Beck and the Politics of Conservatism, 1861-1936.* New York: Coward-McCann, Inc., 1958.

___ *Regulating a New Economy: Public Policy and Economic Change in America, 1900-1933.* Cambridge: Harvard University Press, 1990.

Kennedy, David M. *Over Here: The First World War and American Society.* New York: Oxford University Press, 1980.

Kunitz, S. J. "Professionalism and Social Control in the Progressive Era: The Case of the Flexner Report." *Social Problems* 22 (October 1974), 16-27.

LaPiana, William P. *Logic and Experience: The Origin of Modern American Legal Education.* New York: Oxford University Press, 1994.

Larson, Magali Sarfatti. *The Rise of Professionalism: A Sociological Analysis.* Berkeley: University of California Press, 1977.

Martin, George. *Causes and Conflicts: The Centennial History of the Association of the Bar of the City of New York.* Boston: Houghton Mifflin Company, 1970.

Maru, Olavi. *Research on the Legal Profession: A Review of Work Done.* Chicago: American Bar Foundation, 1972.

May, Henry F. *The End of American Innocence: A Study of the First Years of Our Own Time, 1912-1917.* New York: Alfred A. Knopf, 1959.

McCurdy, Charles W. "Justice Field and the Jurisprudence of Government-Business Relations: Some Parameters of Laissez-Faire Constitutionalism." *Journal of American History* 61 (March 1975), 970-1005.

McFarland, Gerald W. "Partisan of Non-Partisanship: Dorman B. Eaton and the Genteel Reform Tradition." *Journal of American History* 54 (March 1968), 806-822.

Paul, Arnold M. *Conservative Crisis and the Rule of Law: Attitudes of Bar and Bench, 1887-1895.* Ithaca, New York: Cornell University Press, 1960.

Powell, Michael J. *From Patrician to Professional Elite: The Transformation of the New York City Bar Association.* New York: Russell Sage Foundation, 1988.

Prewitt, Audra L. "American Lawyers and Social Ferment: Prelude to Progressivism, 1870-1900." PhD dissertation, Northwestern University, 1973.

Radin, Max. "The Achievements of the American Bar Association: A Sixty Year Record." *ABAJ* 25 (1939), 903-910 ; *ABAJ* 25 (1939), 1007-1013 ; *ABAJ* 26 (1940), 19-26 ; *ABAJ* 26 (1940), 135-141 ; *ABAJ* 26 (1940), 227-234; *ABAJ* 26 (1940), 318-320, 358.

Rawle, Francis. "How the Association Was Organized." *ABAJ* 14 (1928), 375-377.

Reed, Alfred Zantzinger. *Training for the Public Profession of the Law.* New York: The Carnegie Foundation for the Advancement of Teaching, 1921.

Roalfe, William R. *John Henry Wigmore: Scholar and Reformer.* Evanston: Northwestern University Press, 1977.

Rogers, James Grafton. "The American Bar Association in Retrospect," 1: 166-190, in *Law: A Century of Progress.* New York: New York University Press, 1937.

___ *American Bar Leaders: Biographies of the Presidents of the American Bar Association, 1878-1928.* Chicago: American Bar Association, 1932.

___ "Fifty Years of the American Bar Association." *ABA Rep* 53 (1928), 518-531.

Ross, William G. *A Muted Fury: Populists, Progressives, and Labor Unions Confront the Courts, 1890-1937.* Princeton: Princeton University Press, 1994.

Rutherford, Mary Louise. *The Influence of the American Bar Association on Public Opinion and Legislation.* Philadelphia: privately printed, 1937.

Seymour, Whitney North. "The First Century of the American Bar Association." 64 *ABAJ* 1038-1050 (July 1978).

Schudson, Michael. "The Flexner Report and the Reed Report: Notes on the History of Professional Education in the United States." *Social Science Quarterly* 55 (1974), 347-361.

Sommers, Lawrence Edmund. "Lawyers and Progressive Reform: A Study of Attitudes and Activities in Illinois 1890 to 1920." PhD dissertation, Northwestern University, 1967.

Sproat, John G. *"The Best Men": Liberal Reformers in the Gilded Age.* New York: Oxford University Press, 1968.

Starr, Paul. *The Social Transformation of American Medicine.* New York: Basic Books, 1982.

Stevens, Robert. *Law School: Legal Education in America from the 1850s to the 1980s.* Chapel Hill: University of North Carolina Press, 1983.

Steidle, Barbara C. "Conservative Progressives: A Study of the Attitudes and Role of Bar and Bench, 1905-1912." PhD dissertation, Rutgers-The State University, 1969.

Stolz, Preble. "Training for the Public Profession of the Law (1921): A Contemporary Review," in *New Directions in Legal Education,* ed. Herbert Packer and Thomas Ehrlich. New York: McGraw Hill Book Company, 1973.

Sunderland, Edson R. *History of the American Bar Association and its Work.* Chicago: American Bar Association, 1953.

Twiss, Benjamin R. *Lawyers and the Constitution: How Laissez-Faire Came to the Supreme Court.* Princeton: Princeton University Press, 1942.

Wickser, Philip J. "Bar Associations." *Cornell Law Quarterly* 15 (1930), 390-419.

Wiecek, William M. *The Lost World of Classical Legal Thought: Law and Ideology in America, 1886-1937.* New York: Oxford University Press, 1998.

Wiebe, Robert H. *The Search for Order: 1877-1920.* New York: Hill and Wang, 1967.

Index

www.ingramcontent.com/pod-product-compliance
Lightning Source LLC
LaVergne TN
LVHW091523200926
848483LV00002B/294